PHOTO
SHOW

Translation from Italian by Ruth Taylor
Translation from French by David H. Wilson

First published in the United Kingdom in 2014 by
Thames & Hudson Ltd, 181A High Holborn, London WC1V 7QX

Original edition © 2014 Contrasto srl.
This edition © 2014 Thames & Hudson Ltd, London
Photographs copyright © 2014 the photographers
Text copyright © Contrasto

British Library Cataloguing-in-Publication Data
A catalogue record for this book is available from the British Library

ISBN 978-0-500-54442-6

Printed and bound in Italy

To find out about all our publications, please visit **www.thamesandhudson.com**. There
you can subscribe to our e-newsletter, browse or download our current
catalogue, and buy any titles that are in print.

PHOTO SHOW

Landmark exhibitions that defined the history of photography

Edited by Alessandra Mauro

With 125 illustrations, 75 in colour

Preface

Alessandra Mauro

This book is born out of experience. That experience is the complex, fascinating and, at times, undervalued task of designing and curating photography exhibitions so that they function like visual journeys.

After living this experience many times over the years, in different situations and different places, I felt I wanted to look more closely at what had been done in the past, in order to understand the common features and rationale that might have guided the task of curating photography exhibitions. Specifically I wanted to know whether photography followed its own path within prevailing exhibition practices - one dictated by its own dynamics and the medium's adaptable nature. In other words, I wanted to try to delineate a territory and trace its history, or at the very least its customs. This is how I arrived at an attempt to tell the story of the photography exhibition by looking at eleven examples, each of which in its own way constitutes a landmark.

Of course, the exhibitions highlighted here do not in any way form an exhaustive list, nor are they necessarily the most significant exhibitions in photographic history, but they do represent crucial turning points as far as the skill of filling a physical space with photographic images is concerned. All of them made images accessible for collective consumption and transformed the space in question into a special arena where photography might tell a story, support an argument or assert a particular vision. If it is true, as Manet once said, that preparing an exhibition is a question of securing allies for battle, photography has participated in many conflicts. Most were waged so that photography could assert its identity, reaffirm its presence and underline its important, even fundamental, role in the perception and representation of reality.

The eleven chapters that follow, therefore, are all accounts of battles waged by photography. Eight are devoted to events that soon became watersheds, presenting new ways to exhibit and perceive. One chapter is dedicated to four exhibitions staged by a single institution, the Museum of Modern Art in New York, which has long been viewed as a point of reference by the world of photography. The other two chapters are devoted not to single events, but to figures who brought about enormous changes in the realm of photography exhibitions: Alfred Steiglitz and his pioneering 291 gallery in New York, and Robert Delpire, who directed the Centre National de la Photographie in Paris, working with the direct backing by the French state and a specific remit to promote photography as an expression of contemporary life and cultural heritage to a wider public. All the events discussed in this book shared a common public vocation. Even where the exhibition space may appear to suggest the opposite (Steiglitz's 291 was a commercial gallery; the space that first housed *here is new york* was a private shop), the experience itself revealed the desire to enter into a dialogue with a potentially vast audience, be it citywide, countrywide or global.

The book's story is chronological, with occasional leaps forward of varying lengths. It begins in 1839 and concludes in 2001, stopping just a little short of the present so as to maintain a necessary distance and perhaps allow us to see, in the exhibitions dating from the beginning of the new millennium, the forms and practices that reflect the contemporary world of photography and its values. A conversation with Quentin Bajac, the current director of the Department of Photography at MoMA, serves as an introduction. He relates the book's themes to his own working practices, which on a daily basis involve confronting, evaluating and resolving issues surrounding the public experience of photography and the constantly changing definition of the roles of photographer, curator and audience. Ultimately, the book represents an attempt to discover new ideas about photography and new ways of communicating with the medium.

Any collective work will require plenty of acknowledgments. My thanks go to all those who believed in the project and in various ways helped to make it a reality.

My thanks, first of all, to Roberto Koch and the team at Contrasto. I am also grateful to the authors of the essays: Alessia Tagliaventi and Francesco Zanot, with whom I have shared many discussions about this book, as well as to Pierre-Louis Roubert, Gerry Badger, David Spencer and Michel Frizot. Thanks are due to Charles Traub, Quentin Bajac and Lélia Wanick Salgado for so kindly giving me their time. I am grateful to Stuart Smith and Justine Schuster for their graphic design work, which was far from straightforward.

Lastly, this book requires a discreet dedication: a dedication to a man who has used photography to communicate with the public through exhibitions large and small. His shows have provided the opportunity for encounters, debates and discussions, while at the same time remaining playful and celebratory, always managing to convey the sense of wonder, discovery and surprise that photography can provide. This book is dedicated to Robert Delpire.

Paul Nougé, *The Birth of the Object*,
from the series *Subversion of
Images*, 1929–30. © Cliché Doc AML/P.
Nougé/M. Trivier

Deviations from the Norm: Curating Photographs in the Internet Age

Interview with Quentin Bajac, chief curator of photography at the Museum of Modern Art, New York

Alessandra Mauro

AM: This book is not a theoretical work so much as the result of many years of working in photography. Like you, I'm also a curator. I've thought a great deal about the role and would like to ask you some questions.

You've worked for many great museums, and for a number of years you've been confronted with 'the space of choice', as Rosalind Krauss called it: the space of inclusion and exclusion. Selecting a work for a museum always involves making a judgment, and is therefore an aesthetic act, so how do you manage to work with the choices made by your predecessors, and how can you bring your own personal approach to bear?

QB: I'm not sure if I can answer your question. It's true that I work in an institution, MoMA, that is a major centre for photography and has long been considered its 'judgment seat', staging exhibitions that are much discussed and admired. I took over as curator of an institution already steeped in tradition and history, having benefited from four predecessors who all displayed photographs in different ways. Benjamin Newhall, the first, took a predominantly historical approach, showing photographs as if they were precious objects of some kind; Edward Steichen came from a different background and was interested in photography as a means of communication, a mass medium; John Szarkowski followed a more artistic bent (he favoured black-and-white prints, framed, with borders); and when Peter Galassi took over, I'd say he integrated photography and contemporary art, using works in a much bigger format. Each period had its own techniques and its own style of exhibiting the photographs.

I think my own generation has gone beyond the view of the photograph as just a print hung on a wall. After the 1980s and 1990s, when the predominant idea was that photographs were basically created to take their place on gallery and museum walls, nowadays we see photography as a language that can assume many forms. We have rediscovered the educational dimension of the 1920s and 1930s, when photography had begun to experiment and was also, if not fully, then at least very broadly engaged in a dialogue or relationship with the art world in general.

There is no doubt that exhibitions today display a far wider range of form and content: we no longer have just photographs on walls, but also slide shows, films, books, illustrated magazines, all of which recognize - and also force the viewer to recognize - the different ways in which artists and photographers express their creativity. I think it is especially important that museums should not prescribe norms. In my opinion, they should go with the evolutionary flow of practice, which today is towards ever increasing diversification and also - even if photographers are still a little reticent about it - a greater degree of immateriality.

AM: You have worked for some very important museums whose photographic holdings have always been considered in the context of their other collections. Can a space that has been designed to display paintings be used just as precisely and effectively for photographs?

QB: It's true: the institutions where I've worked- the Musée d'Orsay, the Centre Pompidou and MoMA - have departments of photography, and as a result there's a kind of dialogue with other disciplines - painting, sculpture, the decorative arts, and so on. That really suits me. I love that sort of comprehensive dialogue between the arts. And those institutions organize frequent exhibitions. That's where we see the link between exhibition and permanent collection.

There are two different aspects here. First, I don't think curators prepare exhibitions in the same way they display collections. In my view, visitors don't look at things in the same way, with the same degree of attention. Anyone who comes to see a specific exhibition will focus more intently than someone who spends half a day at the museum looking at paintings and sculptures and just wanders into a room full of photographs. You can't expect people to view a collection in the same way they view a particular exhibition. It's more a matter of picking and choosing. An exhibition needs a more structured plan, otherwise the visitor's attention is likely to stray.

Having said that, we do generally try to establish a degree of homogeneity between exhibition and collection - partly because exhibitions very often give us the chance to enhance our collections - and nowadays the distinction between the two is becoming increasingly blurred. This is also because spaces that used to be reserved for collections now house exhibitions that are based on those collections. If we consider MoMA, the presentation of the museum's photographic holdings has evolved enormously - and not before time. Forty years ago, when Szarkowski opened rooms dedicated exclusively to photography, his idea was to present a historical panorama, from the earliest days through to the present, because at that time no other museum had done such a thing. But today lots of other institutions offer the same kind of panorama. In my opinion, the public has probably had enough of these chronological presentations, all of which tend to follow the major technical developments - starting with the daguerreotype, moving on to paper, the snapshot, colour images in the 20th century, and so on. I think that approach has run its course. We now prefer to interweave chronology and subject matter, with a view to presenting collections that are more expressive.

AM: Within a museum's historical collection, it's obvious what does and doesn't belong to the sphere of photography. But for a contemporary exhibition, where would you draw the line between what should and should not fall under your remit? How do you define the border between the contemporary art department and your own? Are there any precise rules?

QB: I don't think there are any precise rules. I believe that - fortunately - there are still photographers who only take photographs, and artists who stick to a single medium of expression, and often do so very well. But there are also many artists - often from a younger generation - who move from one genre to another, alternating between photography, installation, video art, etc.

For me, we shouldn't think in terms of departments or administrative frameworks. If a curator has a concept, he or she must try to put together the best possible exhibition for illustrating that idea. If it means including images or works that are not purely photographic or come from a different department, it really doesn't matter. At the Centre Pompidou, as well as at MoMA, you'll find photography represented in all the collections - obviously in the photography department, but also in paintings and sculpture, which in the past has collected photographs (often on canvas) and continues to do so from time to time. And of course the architecture department has a very impressive collection of photographs, which initially were documentary but whose status has altered over the years. The same applies to design, and obviously the film department, too. At MoMA there are 4 million photographs: stills, some of Dziga Vertov's photograms, lots of valuable items. Sometimes the Department of New Media purchases photographs of performances and so on. In major multidisciplinary institutions, photography has expanded way beyond the walls of the photography department. I don't mind that at all, because it creates a dialogue, interaction. Photography makes it possible to bring departments together, to establish a link between different art forms, a common bond between the disciplines. You can find this everywhere, on a variety of levels.

AM: A degree of academic preparation goes into the 'correct' presentation of historical exhibitions. But how far should this exactitude go? Should we aim to reproduce past methods of displaying the works? Is there any point in that?

QB: I think that, for certain works, it's interesting to consider how they were exhibited at the time. Sometimes it can also be interesting to show that an image was not displayed on a wall, but may have existed in a number of different forms. This also applies to some of our contemporary artists and photographers. James Welling told me recently that, when he organized the layout of his retrospective at the Hammer Museum in Los Angeles, he went to a great deal of trouble to reconstruct the way his photographs had originally been displayed. However, that said, you sometimes need to be wary of what I would call the 'period room' - an attempt to reconstruct the past, which will not always mean much to the visitor. All the same, this question follows on from what we were saying earlier: it's important for the visitor to be aware that, even if museums do like to put prints on walls in an all-purpose frame, that may not be the way they were first seen or experienced. For instance, they may first have appeared in magazines or books.

A few years ago I saw a large installation at Tate Modern in which pages from *USSR in Construction* [a Soviet propaganda journal] were displayed, showing how photos taken by El Lissitzky and others were disseminated - not just as images, but also within the context of the page, supported by the graphic design. It looked as if the pictures had been taken for that purpose - to be incorporated within a page, a catalogue, a book, and not exhibited in isolation, cut off by a frame. A photo taken by El Lissitzky for *USSR in Construction* does not have the same value or meaning as one stuck in a frame on a museum wall, where it loses its whole political dimension as a piece of propaganda. That's why I think that, although it's important to show the beauty of the print or the object, we must also demonstrate how photography takes many forms and has many distribution channels.

From a historical viewpoint, there's certainly more interest today not merely in the image, but also in its context and its method of distribution (this book is a fine example). Photographs as integral parts of magazines, exhibitions and books have become new subjects for study, and I think this clearly demonstrates the fact that images take on different meanings according to the context in which they are shown.

AM: So perhaps we can say that historical accuracy depends on what we want to express?

QB: Yes, I think so. Exhibitions also need the input of an architect or set designer. We need to have the right kind of space for an exhibition, a place where we can show how these are not just images, but also objects. We need to emphasize their materiality and the different forms they can take. A show can be very cinematic (it's a montage of images, rather like a book) and yet also the opposite of cinema, since it's the spectator who moves, whereas the images remain stationary. In a sense, it is the visitors who make the exhibition, by creating their own itinerary. We may try to guide them, to map out a route, to tell a story, but the fact is that any curator who spends a quarter of an hour at an exhibition will see that visitors use the space differently, in ways that the curator has never even thought of. They may reverse the order, linger here, pass by there.

AM: Sometimes all it needs is for the visitor to meet a friend and start talking, and they'll retrace their footsteps or lose their way completely.

QB: That's right. You might say it's the same with books. There's no standard way to read. We all know how our attention can fluctuate, and with illustrated books we often skim anyway. All the same, the fact that physical bodies can pass through a space automatically, without really thinking, means that each visit provides a different perspective. Many artists throughout history have exploited this fact.

The great luxury of the exhibition as opposed to the printed page is the vast number of ways in which you can mount the images, providing any number of different perspectives and approaches that sometimes we ourselves may never have considered. We've all had the experience of discovering new perspectives – some close up, some from further away – and there can be no doubt that a visit to an exhibition affords this variety. Sometimes it's rather like Le Corbusier's 'promenade architecturale': a path one follows through a building or through a garden, allowing the constant discovery of different viewpoints.

AM: Many writers and curators talk of exhibition space in terms of narrative space. In *Cautionary Tales*, András Szántó says that every exhibition tells a story, and he draws a parallel between the good curator and the good storyteller. The good curator needs to have a grasp of the rhetoric of discourse, so that he can use it to compose a complex narrative with moments of tension, relaxation, and so on.

QB: In a way this is true, and in antiquity Latin orators used to imagine a mental walk through a particular space to help them memorize their speeches. But having said that, I must admit that

I'm a little uncomfortable when people talk of narrative. I don't think it's always a question of storytelling, but more like speech, which is different. The nuances are more philosophical; it's not like simply making. Even if there is a narrative, I think that sometimes it should seem a bit jerky, unstructured, more of a montage of contrasts than a linear development. We don't always tell a story, and sometimes it's a good thing to shock the viewer out of his or her lethargy!

AM: When you design an exhibition, is it a good idea to play with the different elements of photography, its different 'souls' - its multiplicity and uniqueness, as Christopher Phillips wrote in 'The Judgment Seat of Photography'?

QB: The difficulty, especially when you're organizing a thematic exhibition, is to support your concept without forgetting that your photographers have a thousand and one voices - without constricting or instrumentalizing the images too much. That was the criticism levelled at Steichen's *The Family of Man*, in which everything was subservient to the overall theme and the aim of the curator. The individual voices and names were ultimately forgotten.

It's important always to try to express an idea or tell a story, while at the same time bearing in mind that, within this montage, there will sometimes be dissonant, opposing voices that of course should not be forgotten. By all means pursue the idea, but allow each photographer to preserve his or her individuality - those specific features that are his or hers alone. Let the images speak for themselves. And I think we also need to accept that images often depict things that differ from what we want them to depict at one particular moment, for one particular exhibition, on one wall, in one space. Images always go beyond the bounds of your concept: they elude you, and it seems to me very important that we should not try to hold them back.

There is a world of difference between organizing a historical exhibition - when all the artists are dead - and working with living photographers. Of course I much prefer to have a discussion, an exchange of ideas. In certain respects you have to take a back seat when you're working with a photographer, though of course it depends on how sensitive you both are - and it's essential that the artist should be interested in the space that will house the exhibition. And so each exhibition becomes a dialogue in which you try to find common ground between two visions, the artist's and the curator's. Sometimes the dialogue goes smoothly, but sometimes there's a conflict between two different readings of the work - though I would argue that the two views are not equally valid, because of course the artist has to take precedence. However, I think the artist must also accept that, at a particular moment, the work is out of his hands, and whoever is looking at it - be it a historian, a curator or a visitor - will have their own opinion that may transcend or even contradict that of the photographer.

AM: For a photographer, an image is often first and foremost an emotional object. That is its prime significance, even before he or she realizes that it might be an important document that should be preserved and hung in a museum.

QB: Yes, and the curator often has a more detached view of the work, which may well lead to disagreement. Not to mention the fact that artists very frequently prefer to exhibit their more recent works. Sometimes the historical perspective proposed by a museum or other institution is not so interesting, or even irksome, for them.

AM: In a recent interview published by the magazine *Aperture*, you said you had worked in other artistic disciplines. What were your experiences, and how do you think photography can best collaborate with other forms of artistic expression?

> **QB:** I'm interested in links between photography and other arts. For example, when we were preparing the exhibition *La Subversion des images: Surréalisme, photographie, film* for the Centre Pompidou, initially we thought we would focus on photography. Later, however, we realized that it was not so easy nowadays to isolate photography or to ignore the fact that, even early on, many photographers were influenced by the cinema and moved between the two media. Some directors even printed photograms directly from the films they had made. It's what we were talking about a moment ago - photography as a link between disciplines. It's very hard to isolate it because, although it obviously has certain specific qualities, at the same time it's ubiquitous in many different contexts. By using the exhibition space to juxtapose photographs with other disciplines - paintings, sculptures, and so on - we can demonstrate more clearly that it is not only an image, but also an object. We can draw a visitor's attention to the photograph's materiality, its physical dimensions, and to the fact that institutions do not collect just 'images', but prints and photographs reproduced in books and magazines.

AM: In the *Aperture* interview, you also said that a museum of photography should serve to illuminate the history of art and the history of culture.

> **QB:** Photography can't be reduced to an artistic practice. It's something that feeds on a variety of practices, from the commonplace to the esoteric. There's amateur photography, scientific, technical and commercial photography - and there have always been bridges between them. The great multidisciplinary institutions have a place for all of these types of photography, whether they're artistic, practical or commonplace. Of course, it's sometimes difficult to distinguish between them, so anyone who is interested in the history of the medium must combine the two views of photograph as object and photograph as artistic expression. Shifts between the vernacular and the artistic are inherent in its history: you can't pin it down as a single practice. You must always consider it in a wider context: the photograph as a cultural object.

AM: What comes next? Do you think the internet could be next?

> **QB:** It's possible. We're having to think about it, especially now that there's a new generation querying the materiality of the photographic image. A lot of photographers now are emphasizing materiality and insisting on making prints. I wonder if, to a certain degree, this reveals a fear of a general movement towards immateriality. If you compare the situation now with that of a hundred years ago, isn't this a new form of Pictorialism? The Pictorialists took a defensive stance against the advance of Kodak, and in order to distance themselves focused on the materiality of the image, producing platinum prints, prints in gum bichromate and works that resembled drawings or engravings. The current interest in the physical image is perhaps a form of reaction.

> With this in mind, museums must foster the artistic practices of those who can develop such an approach. Personally, however, I believe that the future of photography, whether we like it or not, will favour immateriality, despite the reluctance of photographers, artists and the market to embrace this trend. It will come, and we shall have to devise new exhibition practices.

I have no doubt that the future lies in the digital museum - by which I don't mean just a website, but a way of hosting projects created specifically for this kind of space rather than the physical space of a museum. For example, it could mean images appearing on screens instead of being printed on paper. This does not mean that we should stop exhibiting photographs as objects, however. To an extent, museums and the art market have not yet become fully aware of, let alone embraced, this paperless form of photography, unlike the public at large. Digitization is a way to make this work more collective: it's a way images can be exchanged, but its rules or guiding principles haven't been invented yet. At the moment (and I am speaking about institutions in general here, not MoMA), artists, galleries and the market all seem to be lagging behind.

AM: If the work of a museum curator means having to make choices, doesn't a website - with its potential for endless inclusiveness - present a contradiction? The relationship between images and space is important. Think of all the images uploaded to the Erik Kessels online exhibition in a single day. That exhibition is based on the fact that the space allows - and indeed compels us - to see the same images in different ways. But supposing that space becomes the web itself?

QB: Yes, you can imagine a virtual museum that commissions works to be viewed online, that collects them, and that can put virtual collections on the internet - not a physical building, but still a place for selection, collection and legitimization of images and artistic practices. I can imagine a future in which technology provides an extension to, and complements, the physical museum - a truly digital museum.

AM: In the same article, you talk of new fields of photography that have not yet become a subject of study - stock photos, for instance. In such cases, what do you think should be the focal interest of a curator who is not also a sociologist ?

QB: In the case of all those images that are not 'artistic' - you mentioned stock photography, but there are many other examples - what generally interests the curator or historian is any deviation from the norm. For instance, if you look at daguerreotype portraits taken between 1840 and 1850, the fact is that most of them are deadly dull, devoid of originality. But then suddenly you may come across something different - a person who moved, perhaps. This aberration is what attracts historians, aesthetes and curators. On the other hand, sociologists won't be very interested. Their focus, I think, will be much closer to the norm. The deviation may be technical or some other curious element. But it might also be an original viewpoint - that is to say, not just an accident. The most common and obvious practices are often overlooked precisely because they are too self-evident and too important to be treated collectively - and that may also result in their being neglected. All of these things need to be taken into consideration. A museum of the future will welcome all images that, in their own way, differ from the aesthetic norm and have caught the eye. Whatever happens, museums will respond to the needs of the moment.

AM: When museums do begin to tackle these different fields, they will have to devise new ways of displaying them. You won't be able to hang them on walls in identical white frames.

QB: Definitely not. We'll have to invent new ways of showing them.

Louis Daguerre, *View of the Pont Neuf*, **1836–39, daguerreotype.**
© Musée des Arts et Métiers-Cnam, Paris/photo P. Faligot

First Visions: The Invention of Photography

Paul-Louis Roubert

In the history of photography 1839 is generally regarded as Year One, for this was when the first stable photographic process was revealed to the public: the daguerreotype, invented by the Parisian stage designer Louis-Jacques-Mandé Daguerre.[1] Although the process was the fruit of many years' hard labour, its inventor made use of great deal of earlier research, particularly studies carried out after 1816 by Joseph Nicéphore Niépce, with whom Daguerre worked in 1829. Despite this early, 'prehistoric' period, covering the years from 1816 to 1839, modern historians unequivocally pinpoint the birth of photography as the moment when a practicable technique was first made freely available.

However, the revelation of the daguerreotype in 1839 signified more than just a new technique; as it happens - at least as far as the general public was concerned - the process remained purely theoretical for a number of years. The truly radical change came about not through the practice of photography so much as through the profusion of pictures that now found their way into the public domain. Before 1839 very few people had had any direct contact with the research carried out by Niépce or Daguerre, and so very few even knew of the existence of this new kind of image. It was a jealously guarded secret. Although Niépce saw his first positive results in the early 1820s, and Daguerre was in possession of a stable process from 1837 onwards, only a small number of artists, journalists, scientists and members of Louis-Philippe's court had actually handled daguerreotypes or any other form of photographic image before January 1839. After that date, however - owing to a number of factors that led up to the unveiling of the daguerreotype in August that year - a series of images began to appear. They had varying degrees of public exposure, and were made public to support the claim of several figures to be the inventor of the new medium. What emerged during the course of 1839 was the first instalment - relayed to us by first-hand witnesses - in a parallel history of photographic images and of the public's first true experience of them.

Invisible images

On 12 January 1839 Delphine de Girardin, using the pen name Charles de Launay, published the following account in *La Presse*:

> A lot of attention is also being paid to M. Daguerre's invention, and nothing is more enjoyable than the description of this wonder, as delivered in all seriousness by our salon experts. M. Daguerre need not lose any sleep, for his secret is safe. No one would dream of betraying it, and when people speak of it, they have only one thing in mind, which is to make the most of the few scientific terms they have somehow managed to keep in their heads ... What delight! What pretentious rubbish! It's enough to drive a madman crazy: until now, this is what we have understood: the invention is a means of fixing the image, and so by reflection of obtaining a faithful portrait of the Pont des Arts, for example ... This invention is truly admirable, but we understand absolutely nothing about it - the explanations were all too much for us.[2]

Following the great revelation of 7 January, the whole of Paris was interested only in Louis Daguerre and his daguerreotype, the invention of which had been announced by François Arago at a meeting of the Académie des Sciences. On this occasion, the permanent secretary of the Académie merely described the main characteristics of Daguerre's invention: 'M. Daguerre has invented special screens on which the optical image [from a camera obscura] leaves a perfect imprint; screens on which everything contained in the image is reproduced in the most minute detail, and with extraordinary precision and finesse. In truth, it is no exaggeration to say that the inventor has discovered the means of *fixing images*.'[3] Although the basic principle had been announced, neither Daguerre nor Arago revealed the method by which the images were made. There was not a single detail about the support used, its photosensitivity or the method required to produce the images. Even more strikingly, not a single picture had been displayed - not even to the members of the Académie des Sciences. The press published numerous attempts to explain the wonder, but these resulted only in confusion. The general lack of comprehension was rendered absolute by the fact that nobody was allowed to see it. The editor of the scientific weekly *L'Écho du monde savant* complained about this state of affairs in his account of the

Latticed Window
(with the Camera Obscura)
August 1835

When first made, the squares of glass about 200 in number could be counted, with help of a lens.

meeting at the Académie: 'The reports we are given about these pictures and their perfection arouse a fervent desire to actually see them and form an impression. Unfortunately, not a single one was shown at the Académie, and the only people who can form a judgment are those who have actually been to the home of M. Daguère [*sic*].'[4]

Although it would have been easy to show some actual examples, and thus demonstrate the benefits of the new invention more clearly, it would seem that the inventor himself did not yet feel ready to expose it to the public gaze. By now he had known about the daguerreotype method for almost two years, but during this time had continued to search for private ways of publishing and exploiting his discovery. Torn between his desire to make commercial use of it and his fear of seeing his secret becoming common property, Daguerre was faced with a paradox that he sought to resolve in his own way.[5] At the very end of 1838 he distributed a prospectus praising the qualities of his invention, in the hope of attracting investors who might back the commercial exploitation of the daguerreotype under his direction. The document was in the form of a rather confusing text, set in two columns, that mingled historical and biographical details with aesthetic descriptions and examples of possible applications. However, sensing that he could not rely on the text alone to make his point, he clearly decided that it would be better to show some images to the public. At the end of the prospectus he announced: 'On 15 January 1839, an exhibition consisting of some forty prints, confirming the results of the daguerreotype, will open at the same time as a subscription, the conditions of which will be announced at that time.' If Daguerre had not met François Arago a few days after publishing this document, the birth of photography might well have been celebrated through an exhibition.

Why, under these circumstances, did Daguerre not display some of his photographic images during his announcement of 7 January? The reason was that, between the printing of the prospectus and his address to the Académie, a new solution had presented itself. François Arago, who, in addition to his position as permanent secretary to the Académie des Sciences, was a member of parliament for the Eastern Pyrenees, suggested to the inventor

William Henry Fox Talbot, *Latticed window in the south gallery of Lacock Abbey, Wiltshire*, photogenic drawing negative, 1835. © National Media Museum/ Science & Society Picture Library

that a law might be passed which, in exchange for a life annuity, would permit the French State to acquire ownership of the invention, so that it could enter the public domain. The famous meeting on 7 January thus became a means of communication but not revelation, its main aims being to affirm Daguerre's rights as the inventor of photography, to authenticate his claim through Arago's support, and to launch the legal process that would lead to the 'Daguerre law'. From that moment on, photography was inextricably linked in the public mind to the name Daguerre - a perception that was widely reinforced by numerous articles in the press that discussed and evaluated the invention. There was no need to put any prints on display and thus risk having the secret formula stolen or putting ideas in the heads of potential competitors.

A scene in a library

That, however, is precisely what happened. On the other side of the Channel, a brilliant English physicist named William Henry Fox Talbot, then 38 years old and living in Lacock, about 100 miles (160 km) west of London, was impressed by the news from Paris, which he read about in the press early in January 1839.[6] Without knowing any details of Daguerre's formula, and in particular the nature of the metallic support used in the daguerreotype, Talbot immediately linked the news to the research that he himself had been carrying out since 1834 in an attempt to record the image produced by a camera obscura. The images he had obtained, which he called 'photogenic drawings',[7] used paper as their support. Not knowing that Daguerre had had a contractual association with Niépce in 1829, Talbot thought he would be able to claim antecedence for his own process. He wrote to Arago in Paris at the end of January to tell him that he intended to put in an official claim to that effect and to make a presentation to the Royal Society in London on 31 January. But he did not mention the fact that a few days earlier, on 25 January, he had organized the first presentation of his process at the Royal Institution - the British equivalent of the French Académie des Sciences. Talbot had taken advantage of the very popular lecture course that Michael Faraday gave there every Friday. The plan was for Faraday to announce the invention of photography on 25 January to an audience of more than 300 people. Talbot had also asked Faraday to organize an exhibition of his process in the library, as was often done at that time. This duly came to pass, as the *Literary Gazette* reported: 'At the conclusion of the lecture, Mr. Faraday directed attention to drawings in the library, sent there by H. F. Talbot, F.R.S. [Fellow of the Royal Society], and by him named "Photogenic Drawings." They were of the same character as those of M. Daguerre. The two processes, he observed, of M. Daguerre and of Mr. Talbot, effecting the same objects, may be different or may be the same.'[8] Thus, without Talbot himself saying a word, the audience was able to admire some of his earliest photogenic drawings, dating from 1834-35: photograms of botanical specimens, negatives based on engravings, negatives produced in a camera obscura representing pieces of architecture or sculpture, and a few micrographic negatives. There were also two or three very

William Henry Fox Talbot, *Bryonia dioica – The English Wild Vine*, photogenic drawing, c. 1835.
© National Media Museum/ Science & Society Picture Library

pale positives, based on negatives, that reproduced engravings.[9] This was the first public photographic exhibition, which the photographer Vernon Heath was to recall fondly more than thirty years later:

> On the 25th January, 1839, I had the privilege to be present in this theatre, and hear, to my intense surprise and gratification, Mr. Faraday announce the two discoveries - the daguerreotype and Mr. Fox Talbot's invention, then named 'photogenic drawing'. Mr. Faraday invited his audience to inspect the specimens displayed in the library of this institution, and I, being one of those who did so, was from that moment in heart and spirit a disciple of the new science - Photography.[10]

As well as being the very first photographic exhibition, this was a strategic move.[11] It was not possible for Talbot to deliver a second lecture after Faraday's, so he kept his technical explanations for his address to the Royal Society on 31 January.[12] Under the benign supervision of

Faraday and the Royal Institution, the first exhibition of 'photogenic drawings' was there-fore clearly a pre-emptive strike against any accusation of plagiarism that might be made against him. The *Literary Gazette* noted that 'The principal object of the exhibition of the photogenic drawings, on this occasion, was meant (as was understood) to establish a date, in order that should M. Daguerre's discovery be made public previously to the reading, before the Royal Society, of Mr. Talbot's paper detailing his process, no charge of imitation could be brought against Mr. Talbot, in case of identity of process.'[13] In the absence of any precise information about the daguerreotype, this exhibition - which allowed 300 people to see the results of a complex technique combining photograms, images from a camera obscura, negatives and positives - had just one purpose: to provide evidence of Talbot's results before any exhibition of the daguerreotype or other such inventions took place.[14]

The first exhibition had few repercussions, but it gave Talbot the lead, and he was now able to push ahead in public. Meanwhile in Paris, Daguerre was dependent on Arago, and had to wait for both the academic and the legal processes to run their course. There were two phases: first, the Académie des Sciences had to pass scientific judgment on the daguerreo-type, and then, following the Académie's evaluation, the national legislative machinery had to prepare, and secure a vote for, the 'Daguerre law'. Talbot's sudden arrival on the scene while these steps were under way proved to be critical, providing Arago and Daguerre with a powerful rival, and thus lending credibility to the daguerreotype and proving that the inven-tion of photography was the now the focus of scientific competition on an international scale.[15] This rivalry preoccupied the press for several weeks, until eyewitnesses were able to confirm the differences between the two processes. And so it transpired that the main impact of the first photographic exhibition was indeed journalistic.

All the articles in the French press following the 7 January meeting mentioned that Arago would be approaching the government with a view to the public purchase of the invention. Following this announcement, the press waited until May before returning to the subject of the daguerreotype. It was then that a public declaration put an end to Talbot's claims and launched the legislative process. That month, Arago invited a delegation of British scientists to Paris so that they could see the results of the daguerreotype process for themselves and thus compare them with the images Talbot had produced on paper. They were the physicists James Forbes and John Robison, the astronomer Thomas MacDougall Brisbane, the engineer James Watt junior, the geologist Robert Murchison, the explorer Joseph Barclay Pentland and the astronomer John Herschel. Arago's announcement of this news to the Académie des Sciences on 27 May 1839 was also the moment when he could declare that public ownership of Daguerre's invention was imminent.[16] This piece of news was mainly ignored by the press, however, who were far more interested in what the reporters of *Le National* described as the 'national French baptism' of Daguerre's invention.[17] Herschel, who was one of Talbot's first supporters and had helped him with his research - and was thus one of the very few people qualified to compare the British and French inventions - had no hesitation in iden-tifying their main differences and came down heavily in favour of the latter. The magazine

L'Artiste, which published a short piece on the subject the day before the Académie meeting, quoted Herschel as follows: 'In comparison with these daguerreotype masterpieces, Mr Talbot produces nothing but mist! There is as much difference between the two products as between the moon and the sun.'[18] As someone closely connected with Talbot's research, Herschel was accorded the rare privilege of an invitation to Daguerre's studio. Daguerre was still very suspicious, and wary of offering any kind of demonstration until the legislative process had run its course. But Herschel's reaction was characteristic, because it focused on the visual experience of photography, as he wrote to Talbot after the Paris trip: 'It is hardly saying too much to call them miraculous. Certainly they surpass anything I could have conceived as within the bounds of reasonable expectation ... In short if you have a few days at your disposition I cannot command you better than to Come & See. Excuse this ebullition.'[19]

And so in May 1839, although recognizing the common ground between the two inventions as well as the different supports they used, the press began to draw attention to one essential distinction: 'It is no longer a question of priority ... but one of originality, and this does not concern similarities or comparisons, no matter how distant, to Mr Talbot's process. The daguerreotype is French in every aspect, and this is indisputable.'[20] This affirmation of the uniqueness and nationality of Daguerre's invention opened the door to the process of national recognition, which reached its desired end in July, paving the way for the emergence of the photograph as we know it today.

The invisible exhibition

However, a third, more private claimant would also open up new avenues for photography. A week before John Herschel's verdict was presented to the Académie des Sciences, a young official from the Ministry of Finance named Hippolyte Bayard went to see François Arago. There can be no doubt that the emergence of this new competitor, modest though he was, spurred Arago into accelerating matters. Hippolyte Bayard, born 20 January 1801, was nothing like as well known or as technically proficient as Daguerre or Talbot. Employed at the Ministry of Finance since 1825, he also had many friends in the artistic and theatrical circles of bohemian Paris. Impressed by the announcement of the invention of photography

William Henry Fox Talbot,
Astrantia major – The Melancholy Gentleman,
photogenic drawing, 1838.
© Royal Photographic Society/ National Media Museum/Science & Society Picture Library

in January 1839, he began his own first attempts on the 20th of the same month. Using paper as a support, he mounted his results in an album, and by following his notes we can reconstruct the development of his work. Despite his lack of scientific training and skill, Bayard rapidly produced some negative images on paper that he showed to the physicist César Desprets on 5 February. On 20 March he claimed that he obtained 'images directly within the camera obscura'. This new process on paper, the 'direct positive',[21] was different from Daguerre's images, which were on metal, and from Talbot's, which, although on paper, were negative images that had to then be turned into positives. Encouraged by his results, Bayard showed his pictures to some friends, and on 13 May met the chemist Jean-Baptiste Biot, a close colleague of Arago's in photographic matters, as well as someone who had talked to Talbot. Finally, on 20 May, Bayard met Arago himself.

However, Arago did not regard Bayard's process as an alternative. On the contrary, Arago was completely focused on Daguerre's method and on Talbot's rival claims, and had no desire to increase the competition, even though Bayard's work was genuinely different from the British process. On the other hand - as Herschel's reaction clearly demonstrated - the daguerreotype had already set the photographic standard for its earliest viewers: the

Louis Daguerre, *The Louvre from the Left Bank of the Seine*, 1839, daguerreotype.
© Musée des Arts et Métiers-Cnam, Paris/photo P. Faligot

alternative solutions that now began to appear could only seem second best by comparison with the fascinating precision and minute detail that gave the daguerreotype its power. Talbot had now been eliminated from the contest, thanks to Herschel's judgment and also to the proof that the association between Niépce and Daguerre went back as far as 1829. So it was that, at the end of May, Bayard found himself in sole competition with Daguerre and compelled to pursue his own case. Daguerre, on the other hand, followed the institutional path laid down for him by Arago: on 14 June 1839, Tannegui Duchâtel, Minister of the Interior, received the inventor together with Isidore Niépce (who since the death of his father, Nicéphore, in 1833 had represented the family's interests) in negotiating a preliminary agreement. The following day the proposed law was read out in parliament. *L'exposé des motifs et projet de loi*, presented by Tannegui Duchâtel to the Chambre de Députés on 15 June 1839, was the first official step in the legislative process. On 17 June, Daguerre was named an officer of the Legion of Honour. The following day, a committee chaired by Arago was appointed by the Chambre de Députés to examine the invention. This committee reported back to parliament on 3 July. The vote on the 'Daguerre law' was due to take place on 9 July, so for two days several daguerreotypes were put on display in the chamber. The newspaper *Le Capitole* published a report on 8 July:

> This morning M. Daguerre exhibited several daguerreotype products in the Chambre de Députés; on show were three Parisian streets, the interior of M. Daguerre's studio, and a group of busts from the Musée des Antiques. We admired the exquisite precision of the many details that filled the pictures of the Parisian streets, notably the view of the Pont Marie. The tiniest irregularities in the ground or the buildings, the goods piled up on the bank of the river, the most delicate objects, the little pebbles under the water by the riverside, and the different degrees of transparency in the water - all this is reproduced with astonishing exactitude; but the astonishment is doubled when we look through a magnifying glass and discover, particularly among the leaves of the trees, a profusion of details so fine that they would not be seen even by the keenest naked eye. In the picture of the interior of M. Daguerre's studio, all the folds in the curtain and the effects of light and shade that they produce are captured with marvellous accuracy. The head of Homer, which is the centrepiece of the picture depicting several antique subjects, has retained all the beauty of its character; not one of the qualities we find in the sculpture has been lost in this reproduction, despite the considerable difference in size ... The pictures exhibited in the chamber are all nine or ten inches high and six or seven inches wide ... Quite a large number of deputies assembled in the chamber this morning in order to see this unusual exhibition, with M. Daguerre himself doing the honours.[22]

It should be noted that, even in these circumstances, Daguerre put very few of his pictures on display. In January 1839, a journalist from *Le Constitutionnel* counted about twenty pictures in Daguerre's studio,[23] and on 15 January he himself proposed to exhibit about forty, yet at the beginning of July only half a dozen were to be seen. The reason was that on 8 March Daguerre's studio went up in flames. There can be little doubt that these few examples were all that remained at his disposal. Nonetheless, they served their principal purpose, as *Le*

Moniteur Universel related: 'The legal proposal to grant an annuity to Messrs Daguerre and Niépce junior for their fine invention was the order of the day, and so several pictures made by Daguerrotype [*sic*] were exhibited in a room in the Palais de la Chambre. The deputies continuously lined up in the room to admire the results of this marvellous process. Among the pictures one can see a head of the Olympian Jupiter, a view of the Tuileries, a view of Notre-Dame and several interiors, of which the effect, truthfulness and sheer perfection surpass anything one might imagine. The conclusions reached by the report [Arago's] could not be based on a more powerful argument.'[24]

By 9 July, the day of the vote, news of the exhibition had spread via the press, and the deputies were joined by a number of additional visitors: 'During the counting [of the vote] many deputies and quite a large number of curious outsiders entered the room used for the budget committee; on display there were several specimens of the daguerreotype, the verdict on which was to be announced in the chamber a few minutes later. In the middle of a group was M. Arago, explaining the technical side and *modus operandi* of this wonderful invention.'[25] The law was passed by the chamber without debate, and it was the same in the upper house, the Chambre des Pairs, where the vote had been scheduled for 1 August. The *Journal des Débats* reported: 'Before the session, in the presence of several peers, M. Daguerre demonstrated his invention, although a packed agenda did not allow for a ruling today. The apparatus was displayed in a reading room, looking out onto Rue Vaugirard and Rue Tournon. In less than ten minutes, thanks to the bright sunlight, a facsimile of the

Louis Daguerre, *Interior of a Cabinet of Curiosities*, 1839.
© Collection Société Française de Photographie (SFP), Paris

monuments was reproduced with perfect accuracy. Initially the picture had a purplish-blue tinge, but this subsequently disappeared. The other six pictures that had been shown to the Chambre des Députés were exhibited in the same room. During their moments of relaxation between votes, the peers never stopped going over to see them.'[26]

In the end, the same six daguerreotypes, displayed in both chambers, were enough to gain the support of the nation - despite the fact that it had been necessary to place strict limitations on the images' visibility. In striking contrast to Talbot - who had staged his exhibition on 25 January in a similar setting, in so far as it, too, was institutional - Daguerre did not in effect present himself as an 'artist' but as an entrepreneur promoting his own invention. The idea of showing his work in a national institution was simply a means of persuading the people's representatives rather than the people themselves. This restriction, however, served to feed the expectations of a public who had been denied a sight of the pictures for seven months and who scarcely understood what all the fuss was about. The frustration was exacerbated when, following the revelation of the hitherto secret process at a meeting of the Académie des Sciences on 19 August 1839, the press realized that, in practice, the daguerreotype - initially heralded as being accessible to all - turned out to be particularly difficult to master, once more making the promised wonders inaccessible to all but a tiny number of adepts: 'So long as the daguerreotype remained a secret, people called it a miracle ... It was much too beautiful, and it was made much too easy for the purchaser, for anyone not to see very clearly that the inventor was dying to get rid of his invention. To this end, he spared nothing in his efforts to arouse everybody's curiosity. He promised the earth ... Once M. Daguerre had pocketed his immortality, his inventor's glory and his gentleman's annuity, he let the truth be known ... by giving away his store of pipedreams that nobody understood, apart from M. Arago, whom we cannot understand anyway.'[27]

Photographic charity

It was in this context that Hippolyte Bayard and his pictures entered into the public gaze. Not having the means to compete with the institutional power wielded by Arago, who had elevated the daguerreotype to a status of legitimacy and public funding, Bayard employed an artistic strategy. A tragic event that took place at the beginning of 1839 had given him an opportunity. On 11 January, at 5.55 am local time, a particularly violent earthquake rocked the island of Martinique, a French colony and major supplier of sugar. Half of the town of Fort Royal (now Fort de France) was destroyed, and there were more than 300 deaths, with almost as many people injured. There was an emotional response in Paris, and early in March a central committee was set up to coordinate aid to the stricken island. The committee, chaired by the Minister for the Navy and the Colonies, was responsible for centralizing the donations that came from all over France, from different dioceses as well as from private institutions and individuals. There were also concerts, theatre productions, song recitals, dances and other spectacles organized in an almost feverish outburst of charitable goodwill.

'As soon as Paris learned of this sad news, the elegant city began to dance - that is its style. It really is. A ball was held in aid of the Martinique victims. That is how the Parisian millionaire gives alms ... That is the logic of the rich: somewhere there is great misery that demands relief, so let us start by wasting our money more than usual; the surplus will go into the collection box ... Martinique has been destroyed, so let us put on our finery for the ball. Since production has dropped, let us overdo our consumption,' surmised one columnist in *Le Constitutionnel*.[28] As part of this explosion of artistic generosity, an exhibition was announced displaying ancient and modern works of art, with the proceeds going directly to the subscription committee. At the end of the exhibition there would be an auction serving the same purpose. Initially scheduled for 24 June, the exhibition was postponed until 1 July. *Le Moniteur Universel* reported how:

> Some of our most distinguished artists have come up with the noble idea of holding an exhibition of paintings, drawings and sculptures in aid of the victims of the earthquake in Martinique. This thought will become reality, and from 1 July the exhibition will be open to the public in the beautiful room that the auctioneers have had built for the sale of pictures, at 16 Rue des Jeûneurs. Several works of great merit are being presented free of charge in aid of this charity. Many distinguished art lovers who wish to take part will provide connoisseurs with the opportunity to see once more works that an admiring public has certainly not forgotten but of which it has long since been deprived ... At the end of the exhibition, the gifts kindly donated by the artists will be auctioned in aid of the victims of the Martinique earthquake. The exhibition will last from three weeks to a month. The price of entry each day will be one franc per person. Those art lovers who would like to have a more leisurely viewing can make a reservation for the Friday of each week, when the entrance fee will be three francs.[29]

The setting for this exhibition was not without significance. The auction rooms at 16 Rue des Jeûneurs were a relatively new business set up by two former auctioneers. These two secessionists created an establishment not far from the Bourse that aimed to be radically different from traditional auction rooms: one reporter described how 'The branch in the Rue des Jeûneurs had a special and very marked aristocratic cachet. Everything there was more beautiful, more lavish, more massive than in normal auction rooms. It was to this branch that valuable paintings, elegant furniture and high-class items made their way. The reason was very simple. The rooms had been built and laid out expressly for the purpose of containing and showing off the best-quality items. Art lovers, dealers and viewers could wander round in comfort. You were no longer in an ordinary auction room, but in a bazaar - almost a museum.'[30] Less vulgar than the establishment in the Place de la Bourse, 'which was scarcely suitable for quiet, contemplative lovers of paintings, drawings and engravings, etc.', the rooms in the Rue des Jeûneurs benefited from their location in a 'tolerable' neighbourhood and 'were extremely well suited to the sort of sales that require space, good lighting, calm, and something approaching comfort'.[31]

Once the exhibition finally opened, on 14 July, the setting proved ideal for the contemplation of the works that had been offered, as is evident from the enthusiasm of the critic

Jules Janin: 'The location of this exhibition is well chosen … You enter through a gallery that is already filled with fine canvases. Then it is up to you to decide what you would like to go and admire amid this admirable confusion of all the periods, all the schools and all the masters.'[32] In the event, the show primarily featured historical works lent by great collectors such as Comte Olympe Aguado and the banker Édouard Delessert all mingled together: Géricault, Zurbarán, Canaletto, Claude, Poussin, Rembrandt, Rubens, Titian, Tintoretto, Girodet and Horace Vernet.[33] In addition, however, were the pieces donated by living artists such as Tony Johannot, Ernest Meissonier and Hippolyte Sebron. Janin concluded: 'All in all, it is a very unusual collection of fine things that you will see together only this once, and which for the most part you will never see again if you miss this wonderful opportunity to go and look at them.'[34]

Amid this eclectic gathering of arts and styles was no. 206 in the catalogue, the one and only item in the section headed *Curiosité*: 'M. BAYARD … 206 - Specimens of photogenic drawings, created *on paper* with the aid of the camera obscura by a new process different from that of M. Daguerre.'[35] We can safely say that Bayard's presence in these rooms had

Sales room at an auction house on the Rue des Jeûneurs, from Edmond Texier, *Tableau de Paris*, 2 vols., Paris: Paulin et Chevalier, 1853. © Bibliothèque Nationale de France, Paris.

all the signs of opportunism. Following Arago's rejection, the exhibition offered Bayard an alternative way of gaining publicity, although not of furthering his research. Of course, the Rue des Jeûneurs was not a state institution, but having his work displayed in such a context gave him not only a platform, but also the potential benefits of an audience of connoisseurs and journalists who specialized in aesthetic matters, all boosted by interest in the drama of Martinique and the revelation of the daguerreotype process.

How had Bayard able to get secure this opportunity? It is possible that one of his artist friends, who included Amaury Duval, a pupil of the painter Ingres, told him about the planned exhibition. Another possibility is that, as an official at the Ministry of Finance, he might have got wind of it through the subscription committee set up by the Ministry of the Navy and Colonies. Whatever the reason, it would seem that Bayard knew about the event well in advance. A cartoon preserved at the Société Française de Photographie, probably exhibited in 1913 during the photographer's first retrospective, explicitly states that thirty positives Bayard exhibited in the summer of 1839 had been made during May. Bayard

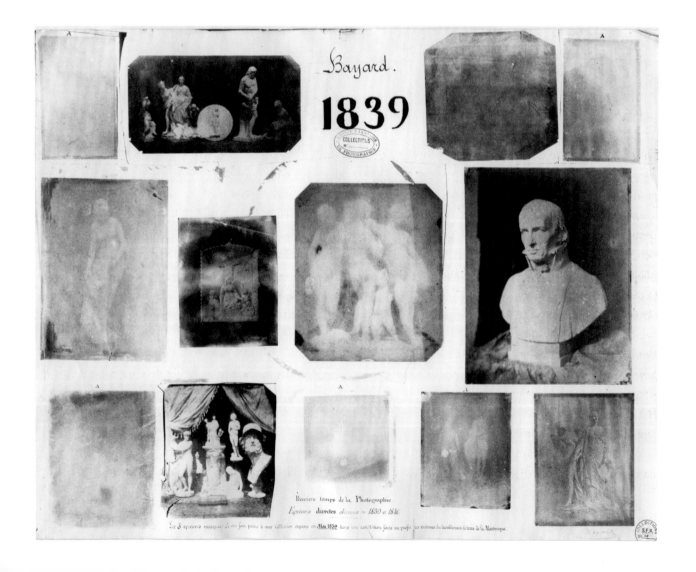

must, therefore, have prepared for the show at the time of his unfortunate meeting with Arago, his thirty positives thus constituting the first truly public exhibition in the history of photography.[36] When the exhibition on the Rue des Jeûneurs opened on 14 July, both Talbot and Daguerre had already presented their findings, but only within a restricted context. Bayard was able to display his images for a month and a half, until the end of August, and benefited from several articles about his work. It was obvious that, lacking any frame of reference, the writers could not describe his work in much detail and found it difficult to establish the differences between his invention and Daguerre's. Nonetheless, the catalogue notes carefully distinguished between them:

> In order that nothing curious should be left out of this collection, on display within a large frame are several specimens of photogenic or photographic drawings made on paper and obtained with the aid of the camera obscura, using a process different from that of M. Daguère [sic]. These specimens augur well: although they do not reproduce the colour of the object and still leave something to be desired as regards perspective, we can at least feel that the refractive process invented by M. Bayard must be capable of rapid improvement, and one is already astonished by the precision of the reduced forms in chiaroscuro of the objects transferred here onto paper.[37]

Théophile Thoré, the official art critic for *Le Constitutionnel*, declared that, of the whole event, it was Bayard's display 'that aroused the most lively interest', but unfortunately he pronounced himself unqualified 'to judge the intrinsic merits of M. Bayard's process and to compare it with that of M. Daguerre'.[38] Now the situation was reversed: in the case of Daguerre's and Talbot's experiments, the public had found itself facing a welter of description but no images; with Bayard's work, on the other hand, the images were exhibited publicly but there was an almost total absence of descriptions. This allowed some critics to dismiss immediately any pretensions photography might have to being art: 'The results obtained by M. Bayard are exquisitely fine, with a harmony and a gentleness of light that painting will certainly never attain. There is nothing more charming than these small figures bathed in elusive halftones, as in the chiaroscuro of nature. In this respect, art will have to resign itself to being inferior to reality … But no matter how perfect the images in which man's genius plays only an indirect part - as with the inventions of M. Daguerre and M. Bayard - in which nature gazes at its own reflection, so to speak, these images can never replace true art, or true invention.'[39]

The newspaper articles informed readers that 'the inventor of the photogenic drawing on paper … is a young employee at the Ministry of Finance', and that 'during the short

Hippolyte Bayard, *Allegory of Fame*, direct positive, 1839. © Collection Société Française de Photographie (SFP), Paris

The work of Hippolyte Bayard, who died in 1887, was rediscovered by the historian Georges Potonniée, who held an exhibition of Bayard's photographs in 1913. This exhibition included the board shown opposite, featuring a selection of photographs taken by Bayard in the summer of 1839 (above and overleaf). These images were stabilized but not fixed by Bayard, and have lost much of their contrast over time. Nevertheless, they offer invaluable visual evidence of the earliest photographs to be exhibited to the public.

moments that his occupation allows, he has devoted himself for three months to the research whose results amaze even those people who have admired M. Daguerre's pictures'.[40] The exhibition, therefore, seems to have fulfilled Bayard's main purpose: it allowed him to participate in the debate by exposing his work to the public gaze. Historians never tire of recounting Bayard's triumphant launch, citing press articles to prove how his process was completely original even at the risk of somewhat over-embellishing the legend.[41] We should not overestimate the impact this exhibition had at the time but, equally, the tale is worth telling: the lone Bayard, neglected by the public authorities, forced to seek refuge in an 'obscure' exhibition of no great significance. To have shown thirty pictures for a space of six weeks and found his name associated with those who laid claim to the invention of photography (news of the event reached Talbot, too[42]) would certainly have made Bayard feel that the whole enterprise had been extremely worthwhile. Indeed, so worthwhile did it prove that his name appeared in the catalogues for the Exposition des Produits de l'Industrie Française of 1844 and 1849, the Great Exhibition of 1851 in London, and the Paris Exposition Universelle of 1855. In 1854 he helped found the Société Française de Photographie, which staged the first in a long series of exhibitions devoted specifically to photography.

To the list of exhibitions held in 1839 we might also add the demonstration Talbot gave to a meeting of the British Association for the Advancement of Science in Birmingham at the end of August. It should be noted that after 19 August, when the secret of the daguerreotype was revealed, the situation changed: the story now became a matter of images displayed in urban spaces, as photography rapidly lost its scarcity value and joined the ranks of the commonplace. Exhibitions became a challenge from the moment photography's practitioners decided to use them as a means of legitimizing the medium's artistic potential rather than demonstrating its industrial applications. And yet, if there is one exhibition that history should commemorate from all those held in 1839, it is Bayard's, because it represented the first attempt by an artist to exhibit photography within a pictorial space. What is most significant here is not whether Bayard's exhibition took place a few days before or after Daguerre's presentation to the Chambre des Députés, but the mindset of a man who, from the medium's very earliest days, chose to make his mark as a photographer rather than as the inventor of photography. It was Bayard who, through a process of disclosure, invented the idea of the photographic exhibition.[43]

Hippolyte Bayard, *Sculpture group*, direct positive, 1839.
© Collection Société Française de Photographie (SFP), Paris

Hippolyte Bayard, *Self-portrait*, direct positive, 1839.
© Collection Société Française de Photographie (SFP), Paris

NOTES

1   'Daguerreotype' was the name Daguerre gave to the support he used for recording views taken with the camera obscura. This support was a silver-coated copper plate, made photosensitive by exposure to iodine fumes. It was placed in the bottom of the specially designed camera, so that within a few minutes an invisible image would form. This was then revealed by exposing it to heated mercury vapour. The metal plate was thus a unique item and did not allow any form of reproduction.

2   Vicomte Charles de Launay, 'Feuilleton de la Presse. Courrier de Paris', *La Presse*, 12 January 1839, p. 2.

3   *Comptes rendus hebdomadaires des séances de l'Académie des sciences*, vol. 8 (1839), p. 4.

4   *L'Écho du monde savant*, no. 402 (9 January 1839), p. 17.

5   See François Brunet, *La Naissance de l'idée de photographie* (Paris: PUF, 2000).

6   The first article in English on this subject appears to be that published in the *Literary Gazette* on 12 January 1839.

7   The term 'photogenic drawing' describes the results obtained by Talbot from 1835 onwards. The process consisted in using silver nitrate to make a sheet of paper photosensitive. Talbot then placed plant specimens or pieces of lace on the paper, exposing them to sunlight. The result was that the object left a negative image of itself on the support - a 'photogram'. From this negative, one could produce a positive by reversing the process with a new photosensitive sheet of paper. This process of 'direct darkening' - that is to say, without any development - required a very long exposure time. Talbot used the same support in the camera obscura. The technique is not the same as the calotype process, which required a development stage, on which Talbot took out a patent in 1841.

8   'Royal Institution', *Literary Gazette; and Journal of the Belles Lettres, Arts, Sciences &c.*, no. 1150 (2 February 1839), p. 75.

9   'The Specimens of this art which I exhibited at the Royal Institution, though consisting only of what I happened to have with me in Town, are yet sufficient to give a general idea of it, and to shew the wide range of its applicability. Among them were pictures of flowers and leaves; a pattern of lace; figures taken from painted glass; a view of Venice copied from an engraving; some images formed by the Solar Microscope, viz. a slice of wood very highly magnified, exhibiting the pores of two kinds, one set much smaller than the other, and more numerous. Another Microscopic sketch, exhibiting the reticulations on the wings of an insect. Finally: various pictures, representing the architecture of my house in the country; all these made with the Camera Obscura in the summer of 1835. And this I believe to be the first instance on record, of a house having painted its own portrait': W. H. F. Talbot, 'Photogenic Drawing. To the Editor of the Literary Gazette', *Literary Gazette; and Journal of the Belles Lettres, Arts, Sciences, &c.*, no. 1150 (2 February 1839), p. 74.

10 Vernon Heath, 'On the Autotype and other Photographic Processes and Discoveries', in *Notices of the Proceedings at the meetings of the members of the Royal Institution of Great Britain*, vol. 7 (1873-75), p. 220.

11 Talbot's letter to the *Literary Gazette* underlines the speed with which he had acted: 'Under these circumstances, by the advice of my scientific friends, I immediately collected together such specimens of my process as I had with me in town, and exhibited them to public view at a meeting of the Royal Institution'; Talbot, 'Photogenic Drawing', p. 73.

12 W. H. F. Talbot, *Some Account of the Art of Photogenic Drawing, or the Process by which Natural Objects may be made to delineate themselves without the aid of the artist's pencil*, treatise read before the Royal Society, 31 January 1839 (London: R & J. Taylor, 1839).

13 'Royal Institution', p. 75.

14 'As the process of M. Daguerre is at present a profound secret, even at Paris, it is evident that no one could imitate him here, or exhibit pictures formed in the same way, or depending on the same optical principles, who was not already fully acquainted with a secret, not, indeed, the *same*, but similar or tantamount to his': Talbot, 'Photogenic Drawing', p. 73.

15 On this subject, see André Gunthert, 'La réception française de l'oeuvre de W. H. F. Talbot', *History of Photography*, vol. 26, no. 2 (summer 2002), pp. 119-23.

16 'Procédé photogénique de M. Daguerre', *Comptes rendus hebdomadaires des séances de l'Académie des sciences*, session of 27 May 1839, vol. 8, no. 21, p. 838.

17 D. and J. G., 'Académie des sciences. Séance du 27 mai', *Le National*, 29 May 1839, p. 1.

18 *L'Artiste*, 26 May 1839.

19 Letter from John Herschel to W. H. F. Talbot, 9 May 1839. See *The Correspondence of William Henry Fox Talbot*, http://foxtalbot.dmu. ac.uk, document no. 3875. Accessed 15 April 2014.

20 D. and J. G., 'Académie des sciences', p. 1.

21 Bayard had initially obtained negative images on paper, as Talbot had done, but he changed his method in March. After sensitizing a sheet of paper with silver chloride, he exposed it to the light until it was fully darkened. Next, the sheet was dipped in a solution of potassium iodide and put into a dark room. Those parts of the sheet that were subsequently exposed to light lit up, thereby recording the image directly projected as a positive. Like the daguerreotype, the image was unique, not having been produced from a negative.

22 'Intérieur, Paris, 7 juillet', *Le Capitole*, 8 July 1839, p. 3.

23 'It is only since a few months ago, during the fine days of last summer, that M. Daguerre's invention has been perfected in his hands. Furthermore, he still has only 20-24 pictures that he regards as perfect enough to put before the critics, or rather before the

admiring and astonished eyes of connoisseurs': Isid. B., 'Invention de M. Daguerre ou Daguerrotype [*sic*]', *Le Constitutionnel*, 29 January 1839, p. 3.

24 'Intérieur. 7 juillet', *Le Moniteur Universel*, 8 July 1839.

25 *Journal des Débats*, 10 July 1839, p. 3.

26 'Chambre des Paris. Séance du 1er août', *Journal des Débats*, 2 August 1839, p. 3.

27 'Les professeurs en daguerréotype [*sic*]', *Le Figaro*, 22 September 1839, p. 1.

28 T. [Théophile Thoré], 'Exposition au profit des victimes du tremblement de terre de la Martinique', *Le Constitutionnel*, 3 August 1839, p. 1.

29 'Exposition de tableaux et objets d'art au profit des victimes du tremblement de terre de la Martinique', *Le Moniteur Universel*, 27 June 1839, p. 1104.

30 Charles Ballard, 'L'hôtel des ventes', in Paul de Kock, *La grande ville, nouveau tableau parisien*, vol. 5, 1842, p. 291.

31 *Bulletin des Arts*, vol. 6 (1845-46), p. 235.

32 Jules Janin, 'Exposition de peinture et de sculpture', *L'Artiste*, 2nd series, vol. 3, no. 12 (21 July 1839), p. 195.

33 See *Exposition au profit des victimes du tremblement de terre de la Martinique, rue des Jeûneurs, 16, hôtel de MM. les Commissaires Priseurs, salle n. 1* (Paris: Imprimerie et lithographie de Maulde et Renou, 1839).

34 Janin, 'Exposition de peinture', p. 197.

35 *Exposition au profit des victimes*, p. 31.

36 The figure of thirty items is first mentioned in the report of the Académie des Beaux-Arts, edited by Désiré Raoul-Rochette, in October 1839, at the time when Bayard was seeking its support. See 'Rapport sur les dessins produits par la procédé photogénique d'Hippolyte Bayard, 31 octobre 1839', *Procès-verbaux de l'Académie des beaux-arts*, vol. 6 (1835-39) (Paris: École nationale des Chartes, 2003), pp. 517-22. Elsewhere, in an article in the *Journal des Débats* dated 26 August 1839, we read that Bayard had been working on the process for three months, i.e. since March.

37 'Beaux-arts. Exposition au profit des victimes du tremblement de terre de la Martinique', *Le Moniteur Universel*, 22 July 1839, p. 1480.

38 T. [Théophile Thoré], 'Exposition au profit des victimes du tremblement de terre', p. 2.

39 Ibid.

40 *Journal des Débats*, 26 August 1839, p. 4.

41 Accounts of Bayard's exhibition in the Rue des Jeûneurs appeared in the newspaper *La Lumière* (2 September 1854, p. 140, written by Ernest Lacan), in the *Bulletin de la Société française de photographie* (1856, p. 44, written by Eugène Durieu), in 1860, and then on the publication of his obituary in 1887. All these accounts were summarized and published in Georges Potonniée, *Histoire de la découverte de la photographie* (Paris: Montel, 1925), p. 208.

42 Talbot was informed of the Bayard exhibition by an Italian botanist, Michele Tenore, on 30 September 1839: 'Very recently we read in the Paris newspapers that a Mr Bayard, at the Martiniquan exhibition, had put in photogenic drawings on paper, obtained by a different process than that of Daguerre, that everyone had admired.' See *The Correspondence of William Henry Fox Talbot*, http://foxtalbot.dmu. ac.uk, document no. 3941. Accessed 15 April 2014.

43 On this subject, see the *Catalogue of the Illustrations of Manufactures, Inventions and Models, Philosophical Instruments, etc., Contained in the Second Exhibition of the British Association for the Advancement of Science* (Birmingham: Wrightson and Webb, 1839). I am grateful to Professor Larry J. Schaaf for the information and reference.

**Crystal Palace, built to house
London's Great Exhibition of 1851,
lithograph.** © Science Photo
Library/Contrasto

2

'The Most Remarkable Discovery of Modern Times': Three Photographic Exhibitions in 1850s London

Gerry Badger

Photography was invented, more or less simultaneously, in two countries: Britain and France.[1] This simple fact had much significance, symbolically and practically, for both the future development of the medium and the cultural relationship between the two powers. At the time of the introduction of William Henry Fox Talbot's calotype method of 'photogenic drawing' (in 1841) and the announcement of Louis-Jacques-Mandé Daguerre's daguerreotype (in 1839), Britain and France were the two most powerful countries in the world. They were both at the forefront of technological invention, and both possessed vast empires reaching to the farthest regions of the globe, which were exploited ruthlessly for their material and cultural wealth.

Just over two decades before photography's invention, Britain and France had been engaged in an all-out war for global influence. Napoleon's defeat at Waterloo in 1815 at the hands of Britain and her European allies had ended France's bid to dominate Europe, leaving Britain the richest and most powerful nation in the world, and ushering in the Pax Britannica, a period of relative stability that lasted for over half a century.

By 1840, therefore, when photography first began to appear, the two empires were at peace with each other. Yet a sense of rivalry prevailed - a rivalry that lasted until the First World War, and of which certain vestiges remain even today. In every area of national life - from economic, diplomatic and military enterprise to engineering, scientific invention, shipping, railways and cultural life, Britain and France strove to outdo each other. If France built a grand new engineering structure, Britain had to build a bigger one. If Britain developed a nationwide railway system, France had to develop a more extensive network.

This endemic rivalry is apparent in two phenomena that emerged and coalesced at the beginning of the 1850s: the grand, 'universal' cultural and trade exhibition, which increased in popularity in the latter half of the 19th century, and exhibitions of the fledgling art of photography - a technique that would have a profound effect upon the way the world perceived itself.

The Great Exhibition of 1851 (or, to give it its full title, 'The Great Exhibition of the Works of Industry of All Nations') - the first 'World's Fair' - sparked off a series of trade exhibitions that celebrated the technological achievements of the 19th century and became such a feature of that modernizing era. Located in Hyde Park, London, the 1851 exhibition was a reaction to the smaller Exposition des Produits de l'Industrie Française of 1844, held in a temporary structure on the Champs-Élysées in Paris - an event that spawned a number of European imitations and was itself repeated in 1849. But none was as grand as the Great Exhibition, which inspired imitations by the other industrial nations, in particular France.

The Hyde Park extravaganza was promoted and organized by Queen Victoria's consort, Prince Albert, and a specially created Royal Commission. Although an international enterprise nominally involving 'All Nations', it was basically designed to prove that Great Britain and her empire 'held the lead in almost every field where strength, durability, utility and quality were concerned, whether in iron and steel, machinery or textiles'.[2] At a time when British industrial might was approaching its zenith, the Great Exhibition also sought to prove that technology held the key to the future and would be the best way of solving the world's problems.

The main attraction for the public who flocked to Hyde Park to see the show after it opened on 1 May 1851 was the exhibition building itself: an enormous structure that almost eclipsed the wonders displayed inside and certainly proved British technological achievement. The so-called 'Crystal Palace' proved to be the enterprise's lasting symbol, just as other engineering marvels, such as Gustave Eiffel's Parisian tower of 1889, defined later universal exhibitions.

By reason of its lightness and its modular construction, the Crystal Palace, designed by Joseph Paxton, heralded the modernist period in architecture. Paxton drew upon his experience as a garden designer and architect to the 6th Duke of Devonshire at Chatsworth, Derbyshire, where his most notable construction achievement was the Great Conservatory. The Crystal Palace was a glasshouse on a scale never seen before. It was technologically innovative, using plate glass on a prefabricated cast-iron framework based on a module of 7.3 m (23 ft 11 in.). The building used 300,000 sheets of glass in what at the time was the largest size ever made, 130 × 25.4 cm (4 ft 3 in. × 10 in.).

The structure was 563 m (1,847 ft) in length by 139 m (456 ft) in width, reaching a height of 41 m (134 ft) in the central transept. The building was so large that mature elm trees standing in the Park could be incorporated within the interior. In all, it provided some 92,000 square metres (nearly 1 million square feet) of exhibition space. Because it used prefabrication techniques, this enormous structure was erected with extraordinary speed, about 5,000 workers ensuring that it was ready for use in only five months.

Once complete, the Crystal Palace was not only unique - a cathedral in glass - but also provided an unrivalled space for exhibits, since it was essentially a self-supporting shell standing on slim iron columns, with no internal structural walls whatsoever. So novel was the building that, in effect, it became the main exhibit.

If the aim of the Great Exhibition was to prove to the world the superiority of British technology, the decision to include photography was a natural one. Indeed, the previously mentioned Exposition des Produits de l'Industrie Française of 1844 had included around a thousand examples of the art of the daguerreotype. But in 1850 the development of British photography had not proceeded quite according to plan. That was because, in essence, there was no grand design for British photography - at least not in the way that the photographic medium was both perceived and supported in France.

In his 1990 survey of photographic history, *Photography Until Now*, John Szarkowski made a shrewd observation about the differences between British and French culture that had a profound effect upon the medium's initial reception in each country. The French, noted Szarkowski, had a more collective sense of national identity than the English. That is to say, the French looked to their government to actively promote the idea of their *patrimoine*, or cultural achievements, whereas the English looked to their local squire and, beyond him, to the monarch. Having suffered a series of violent revolutions, the French were more inclined - at least on a symbolic level - to be inclusive. As Szarkowski writes: 'Those who were not eager for a return to fratricidal violence tended to favor projects that

Benjamin Brecknell Turner, *Crystal Palace transept, Hyde Park, London*, c. 1852, albumen print from calotype negative. © Victoria and Albert Museum, London

promised to celebrate national rather than parochial achievements in the hope that these would nourish a sense of shared identity.'[3]

Interior of Crystal Palace during the Great Exhibition of 1851.

The notion, if not the actuality, of the French Revolution - the concepts of *liberté*, *égalité* and *fraternité* that together became the country's national motto - was a powerful factor in fostering the attitude of both the government and its citizens. This pertains even today: French citizenship comes with a series of rights, but also duties and responsibilities, both of which are taught in school. Perhaps supporting Szarkowski's point is the fact that Britons today are still not citizens of their country but, rather, subjects of the monarch.

Shortly after the invention of the daguerreotype was announced in 1839, the French government bought the rights to the process and magnanimously gave them 'free to the world'. Daguerre himself was not quite so magnanimous towards the English, having taken out a patent a few days before in England and Wales (but not in the rest of the British Isles). Although it was taken up eagerly in Europe and America, therefore, arguments concerning the commercial licences attached to its use in England meant that the daguerreotype did not evolve as quickly there as it did elsewhere.

The development of photography in Great Britain (or, rather, England) in the 1840s was hampered by several factors. First, the fact that would-be daguerreotypists required a licence ensured that fewer good daguerreotypes were in existence in England than in either France or the United States, which took enthusiastically to the process. Second, Talbot, who felt he had expended a great deal of capital in developing the calotype, took out a number of patents requiring calotypists to purchase a licence to use his system. He became quite litigious in guarding this patent (which did not endear him to many), with the result that English photography in the decade leading up to the Great Exhibition could almost be considered as Talbot and his small circle of friends versus everyone else.

In Talbot's defence, he had been all but ignored by the British government, whereas Daguerre received both French government support and public recognition. Nevertheless, Talbot still managed to make what was undoubtedly the most important contribution to 1840s photography: the mass production of photographic prints for publication, where they could compete with lithographs and engravings as a source of visual knowledge. With Talbot's financial support, his former valet, Nicolaas Henneman, opened the so-called Reading Establishment printing works late in 1843; and in June 1844 the first fascicle of *The Pencil of Nature* was available to subscribers. *The Pencil of Nature*, rather like one of today's 'zines', was illustrated with six pasted-in calotypes and a text (a bold and prescient text) that extolled the virtues of photography and its potential as both an art and a science. In 1845 the first photographic travel book, *Sun Pictures in Scotland*, was published by subscription, illustrated with twenty-three photographic prints.[4] And then, in possibly the most ambitious venture of all, some 6,000 prints were produced for inserting into a volume of the *Art-Union* magazine in June 1846.

These were great advances, yet even here there was a degree of failure for Talbot. His calotypes were prone to fading, often within a very short space of time, and often to the derision of his enemies. This was especially true of the prints given away in the *Art-Union*, causing some observers to compare the rapid deterioration of the calotype to an auction - going, going, gone. Even *The Pencil of Nature*, a huge step in the development of the medium, was discontinued after twenty-four prints in six fascicles had been published.

Such was the state of English photography just before the Great Exhibition. It was not quite as advanced as in France, despite Talbot's monumental achievement. In Scotland, however, owing to the influence of Talbot's friend Sir David Brewster, there was an enthusiastic group of calotype aficionados based at St Andrew's University and in Edinburgh. Among them was the painter David Octavius Hill, who, together with one of the St Andrew's calotypists, Robert Adamson, produced several thousand calotypes of an extremely high quality from July 1843 to January 1848 (when Adamson died). The oeuvre of Hill and Adamson can be considered one of the first large, cohesive bodies of work in the history of photography, and one might have thought it was destined for the highest measure of approbation when shown at the Great Exhibition. The same goes for the work of Henry Fox Talbot, as both an inventor and producer of photographs. But it was not to be. Talbot, the creator of what might called the 'English' method of photography - the process that became the basis for all photographs taken before the advent of digital technology - did not show at the Great Exhibition.

The Great Exhibition has been described as the first great international exhibition of photography. Such an interpretation would imply a cohesive, coordinated attempt to present the new visual medium and to survey its achievements. That, however, was not quite what happened. Indeed, to use a vulgar English expression, it was much more of a 'bugger's muddle'.

There was no photography section in the exhibition because of the way it was structured and the complicated system of classification by which exhibits were accepted for inclusion. Thirty classes of exhibits were grouped under four broad headings: 'Raw Materials', 'Machinery', 'Manufactures' and 'Fine Arts'. British exhibits were required to adhere to this classification, but those from the British empire and elsewhere were shown according to country. So many exhibits that might have benefited from being grouped together, such the photographic works, were scattered throughout the displays.

With regard to the fine arts, the exhibition's industrial character was of paramount importance in deciding what was included. Sculpture was allowed, but not painting. Engraving, a mechanical process, was acceptable, as was photography - the 'half art, half science'. But photography was divided into different categories. Photographic images demonstrating a process, such as daguerreotypes or calotypes, came under Class XXX, 'Fine Art', while cameras, together with examples of their practical application, came under Class X, 'Philosophical Instruments and Processes Depending Upon Their Use'.

A further problem for English photography was the method of selection that had been decided upon for the exhibition. Selection was undertaken by local committees composed of local dignitaries and businessmen, making the acceptance of anything submitted without clear commercial associations - amateur photography, for example - somewhat difficult and unpredictable. Relatively unknown and unpractised photographers were accepted while prominent figures were not. Talbot, the leading figure in British photography, even believed that he was ineligible, stating (in a typical show of upper-class Victorian snobbery) that the exhibition was a showcase for 'manufacturers or shopkeepers' rather than gentlemen like himself.[5]

So the best of British photography was not only under-represented, but also rather lost in the grand spectacle. Some 700 photographs were shown overall, but a print measuring 26×18 cm ($10\frac{1}{4} \times 7$ in.) could hardly compete with a steam engine, a Jacquard loom or a reaping machine - and certainly not the fabled Koh-i-Noor diamond, one of the exhibition's talking points. As the photographic historian Roger Taylor has somewhat dryly noted, 'most visitors headed straight for the diamond rather than the Daguerreotypes'.[6]

Of the twenty-two photography exhibitors from Britain, only the names of Hill, Adamson and Hugh Owen are generally known today from among the calotypists, while the

daguerreotypists John Jabez Edwin Mayall, Richard Beard and Antoine Claudet are familiar to photo-historians. The French, however, fielded a strong team and had the advantage of exhibiting together. Hippolyte Bayard, Louis-Désiré Blanquart-Evrard, Frédéric Flachéron, Henri Le Secq and Gustave Le Gray could hold their own among any company of early photographers. Their calotypes were particularly strong, since they took advantage of the substantial technical improvements Blanquart-Evrard and Le Gray had made to Talbot's method. However, the surprise in the proceedings for both nations was the inclusion of American daguerreotypists. Figures such as Mathew Brady (who would become famous in the 1860s with his images of the American Civil War), John Adams Whipple and Jesse H. Whitehurst - who showed twelve views of Niagara Falls - impressed the members of the jury handing out the medals.

When it came to the awards, photography was judged as a whole. A total of fourteen medals were awarded (four at the highest level), together with seven honourable mentions.

William Henry Fox Talbot,
The Haystack, c. 1842, talbotype.
© National Media Museum/
Science & Society Picture Library

Only five medals were given to the British, and Hill and Adamson received only an honourable mention. The published memorial volume of the exhibition (which in fact stretched to four volumes), the *Reports by the Juries*,[7] was unstinting in its praise of the American daguerreotypes, favouring them over the French because of their adherence to what we would now term 'straight' photographic values, and claiming that the works, 'with few exceptions, reject all accessories, [and] present a faithful transcript of the subject'.[8] As for the French calotypists, their work was 'unrivalled': 'France has concentrated all her energies in the further development of those of Talbot and his school.'[9]

The Great Exhibition closed in October 1851 after an extremely successful six months. The enterprise made a profit of £186,000, or some £13.86 million ($23 million) as of 2014. But those concerned with the status of British photography were left somewhat chastened - especially Henry Fox Talbot, who felt he was given little or no credit for his invention and wrote bitterly that 'The French have shown a fixed determination to claim for themselves the invention of photography on paper, although purely of English origin from first to last.'[10]

Another disappointment for the inventor of the calotype was the decision to illustrate the *Reports by the Juries* with photographs. Talbot's protégé, Nicolaas Henneman, was passed over for the job of making the pictures and producing the prints in favour of the amateur calotypist Hugh Owen and the Frenchman Claude-Marie Ferrier, who used the albumen-on-glass process. Even worse from Talbot's point of view was the fact that most of the prints used in the volumes were printed in Versailles, under the supervision of Robert Jefferson Bingham. Notwithstanding Talbot's own *The Pencil of Nature*, the *Reports by the Juries* was in effect the most ambitious use of photography to date, so it was another slap in the face for photography's inventor. Over 200,000 photographic prints had to be produced for the volume from a total of 155 negatives.

As for the art of photography itself in the context of the Great Exhibition, let the *Reports by the Juries* have the last word. The book talked about 'the most remarkable discovery of modern times - the art of photography', and claimed that 'never before was there so rich a collection of photographic pictures brought together, the products of England, France, Austria, and America'.[11]

The Great Exhibition had one abiding lesson for British photography: that it was not as good as those involved in it had fondly imagined. At the very least, the exhibition did not include the best of British photography (Hill and Adamson notwithstanding), nor did it display the photographic arts to their best advantage.

This, however, was the Victorian age, when Britons felt they could do anything, so the lesson was quickly absorbed, and steps were taken to put right this anomaly in the natural order of things. In the same year as the Great Exhibition, in fact, another significant step forward in photographic technique had been taken in Britain, by Frederick Scott Archer. His collodion-on-glass method allowed for the light-sensitive chemicals necessary for photography to be supported by glass rather than paper. It was the process that prefigured modern photographic emulsions and, as Mark Haworth-Booth has noted, was a technique 'that combined many of the best features of the Daguerreotype and calotype. Archer's collodion-on-glass negative combined the coveted clarity of the French process with the ready repeatability of the English one.'[12]

On 1 April 1852 an article appeared in the *Art-Journal Advertiser* calling for the establishment of a 'Photographical Society' devoted to the furtherance of the art and science of photography. The great and good of British photography got busy, but it was felt that the barriers imposed by Talbot's licences would hinder the development not only of a society, but also of the medium generally - especially since Talbot believed that Scott Archer's collodion-on-glass system should be subject to licensing restrictions. Accordingly, representations were made, and negotiations took place, until Talbot finally conceded defeat. In a published letter, dated 30 July 1852, he wrote that, except in the matter of portraiture for commercial gain, 'I present my invention to the country.'[13]

Plans for the formation of a society grew apace, and on 22 December 1852, in the Great Room of the Society of Arts in London, came the inauguration of the first exhibition anywhere dedicated solely to the art and science of photography. Organized primarily by Joseph Cundall, Philip Delamotte and Roger Fenton, three of the society's prime movers, *Recent Specimens of Photography* was such a public success that it was extended for several weeks. It also did much to restore English photography's self-esteem. *The Times* trumpeted that, in the matter of the photographic art, 'there is no doubt that England will resume the pre-eminence which she ought never to have lost'.[14]

At that inaugural gathering Roger Fenton, a rapidly rising name in English photography, presented a paper entitled 'On the Situation and Future Prospects for the Art of Photography'. In his address, he summarized the events leading to the society's formation and identified the main question exercising its members, namely: Is photography an art? This was far from resolved, as the *Recent Specimens* exhibition revealed. The event was a big step forward, displaying photographic prints in frames, hung from floor to ceiling, like the annual Royal Academy salon. Photography was shown as an end in itself, but, as Francesco Zanot has noted, 'without excluding the possibility of its being a useful support to the sciences and other arts'.[15]

Of the 76 photographers, who together showed some 800 images, most were British. And it was an exhibition solely of photographic prints. Owing to potential commercial applications, and perhaps because the event was intended to showcase British photography, daguerreotypes were not included. This was the first and only time that a photographic exhibition in England was dominated by perhaps the most beautiful of early processes, the calotype. And for the first time the cream of English photography was represented. Showing their work were such figures as Philip Delamotte, Roger Fenton, John Stewart and Benjamin Brecknell Turner. From the Great Exhibition, Samuel Buckle and Robert Bingham exhibited prints, and there were even two lady amateur photographers, Lady Augusta Nevill and her sister, Lady Isobel Nevill. The highlight of the exhibition was probably a group of images by William Henry Fox Talbot, acknowledged at last as the fountainhead of British photography. Talbot showed six of his best pictures, including *The Stable Door* and *The Haystack* (p. 43) from *The Pencil of Nature*.

There was also a small but strong French contingent, reflecting the recent Great Exhibition: Le Gray, Du Camp, Le Secq and - an entry that delighted visitors - images by the Carlist pretender to the Spanish throne, Don Juan, Count of Montizón. The count, who lived in London, showed a number of prints of animals and birds he had photographed at the Zoological Gardens in Regent's Park.

The exhibition's success gave British photography the boost it needed, and the impetus was carried forward by two significant, connected events. First, on 20 January 1853, in a meeting chaired by Sir Charles Eastlake at the Society of Arts, the Photographic Society was inaugurated, with Roger Fenton as its first secretary. Second, the exhibition's popularity prompted the establishment of a touring version that travelled all over Britain and as far north as Aberdeen until at least 1855, in several guises.[16] The first touring exhibition included a selection of eight-three pictures from *Recent Specimens of Photography* and travelled for one year, although the pride of Britain, her railway system, caused a few problems. The journeys resulted in missing pictures, broken frames and smashed glass, but the travelling exhibition was such a success that a second show toured between April and November 1854, with one edition covering the south of Britain and another covering the north. There was even a third version, also in two editions, which toured in 1855. These touring exhibitions were perhaps even more important for the acceptance and appreciation of photography than the original Society of Arts exhibition. For, as Roger Taylor has rightly noted, 'it is easy to forget that, even as late as 1853-54, few people in Britain had seen a photograph'.[17]

As well as the Photographic Society and the Society of Arts, a third factor was at work in the London photographic scene of the 1850s. Most of the substantial Great Exhibition profits were channelled into improving education for the arts and sciences in Britain. Henry Cole - a friend of Queen Victoria's consort, Albert, a Royal Commissioner and a prime mover behind the Great Exhibition - was instrumental in encouraging the prince to envisage the creation of a whole new cultural quarter in London, in the area known as South Kensington. Accordingly, some 35 hectares (86 acres) of land just south of Hyde Park was purchased, to be developed as the centre for a number of educational and cultural institutions.

In 1852 Cole was appointed to the post of General Supervisor of the Board of Trade's new Department of Practical Arts, becoming the cultural tsar of his day. And in May of that year, under his directorship, a museum was founded. Known initially as the Museum of Manufactures, it opened at Marlborough House, transferring to Somerset House four months later. The name, with its reference to British manufacturing, reflected Cole's vision for the institution. Like the Great Exhibition, in which Cole had played such an important part, the museum would concentrate largely on science and the applied arts, with an emphasis upon practical applications and the continuing success of the British manufacturing industry.

Gustave Le Gray, *The Great Wave,*
***Sète*, 1856.** © Victoria and Albert
Museum, London

The so-called 'fine arts' would be left to the National Gallery in Trafalgar Square and, to a lesser extent, the British Museum in Bloomsbury.

Photography fitted Cole's brief precisely. He took a keen interest in the medium, appreciating its potential to function as both science and art. He had played a leading role in the photographic documentation of the Great Exhibition's displays, ensuring that they were properly printed in the *Reports by the Juries*, and was thus undoubtedly involved in the machinations that resulted in Nicolaas Henneman having his contract to print the volumes rescinded.

Photography became an important part of the Cole museum and its educating mission from the very beginning. In 1856 Cole appointed the photographer Charles Thurston Thompson, who had assisted Robert J. Bingham in producing the *Juries* prints, to the post of the museum's Superintendent of Photography. The museum began to collect photography officially in 1856, even if in February 1855 its first circulating exhibition had included photographs. The notion of the circulating exhibition was an important part of the pedagogical imperative Cole had established for the institution, taking art to the masses and raising the general standard of education in Britain. This first show travelled to Birmingham, and consisted of 430 objects and 'specimens', plus 150 framed prints, drawings and photographs.

In January 1856 Cole, together with Thompson, visited the *Exhibition of Photographs and Daguerreotypes*, the third show organized by the Photographic Society of London, which was held in the gallery of the Society of Painters in Water Colours, Pall Mall. The exhibition included a number of photographs by Thompson himself, but their visit was notable for the fact that Cole bought some of the first art photographs for the museum's collection – photographs made either as ends in themselves or to compete with the genre of painting.

Oscar Gustav Rejlander, *The Two Ways of Life*, 1857. Combination print constructed from more than 30 negatives. © Victoria and Albert Museum, London

The year 1856 was a highly significant one for Cole. It was then that his fledgling museum was granted land and buildings on the site where it still stands, now renamed as the Victoria and Albert Museum.[18] It opened its doors as the South Kensington Museum on 22 June 1857. Queen Victoria, accompanied by Prince Albert, inaugurated the new venture. Among its attractions - a novelty that has since become the norm - the building boasted a refreshment room, the first ever museum restaurant.

Having appointed a Superintendent of Photographs and begun a photography collection, the next step for Cole was to organize an exhibition of photography. The South Kensington Museum did so in 1858, by hosting simultaneously the annual exhibitions of both the Photographic Society and the Société Française de Photographie in an impressive display of photographic *entente cordiale*. The works were hung in the famous refreshment room, and Queen Victoria herself attended a private viewing. Thompson was on hand to make a photograph of the show, depicting the room and some of the 750 works displayed in typical 19th-century art salon style.

Most of the best English photographers of the 1850s were represented, both calotypists and those photographing with collodion on glass. Prominent among the exhibitors were Roger Fenton, Benjamin Brecknell Turner, Francis Bedford, Robert Howlett, Charles Dodgson (Lewis Carroll), William Lake Price, Oscar Gustav Rejlander and Henry Taylor. Some of Talbot's circle from the 1840s also exhibited, such as John Dillwyn Llewelyn and Horatio Ross. There were images taken in the colonies: photographs of India by Dr John Murray, and of Egypt by Francis Frith. And, of course, there was a strong French and European contingent. The Alinari brothers from Italy exhibited a splendid view of the waterfalls at Terni in Umbria, a favourite subject for both painters and early photographers. Among the French, who contributed 150 photographs, Gustave Le Gray, Édouard-Denis Baldus, Charles Nègre and Nadar deserve mention. Nègre showed a group of magnificent photogravures of Chartres Cathedral. Gravure - a so-called photomechanical process, in which the image was reproduced in ink rather than by chemical means - would have important implications for the future publication of photography. In all, the South Kensington exhibition was widely reviewed, with the *Daily News* of 23 February 1858 calling it 'the great public display of the season'.[19]

The works on view included a great variety of styles and approaches. Some photographers, such as Oscar Gustav Rejlander, attempted to make art; his allegorical tableau *The Two Ways of Life* (opposite) was one of the exhibition's talking points, as it had been when first shown at the Manchester Art Treasures Exhibition in 1857. In what would now be termed the 'fabricated mode', the large composite photograph had been printed from a combination of over thirty separate negatives and measured an impressive 31×16 inches (79×41 cm) in size, although there was also a cheaper, smaller version. It was an allegory of the choice between two paths through life, the righteous and the immoral. On the right-hand side of the picture, Rejlander depicted 'Industry', and on the left-hand side 'Dissipation'. As often, those representing Dissipation seem to be having a better time of it. Some of the women are half naked, and something of a polite orgy seems to taking place. Of course, those who acquired the print - and that included the queen herself, as a gift for her consort - surely did so because of its moral lesson, and not because of the hints of comely breast among those dragged down by vice and laxity.

In complete contrast to mild pornography masquerading as art, the documentary photograph was also well in evidence. Robert Howlett displayed what was to become a famous portrait of the engineer Isambard Kingdom Brunel, cigar clamped firmly in his mouth, and a series showing the ship that he designed, the *Leviathan* (later the *Great Eastern*), under construction in the London shipyards, where Brunel's portrait had been taken. Also included was a group of photographs made by soldiers of the Royal Engineers in Saint Petersburg, Moscow and Singapore, and used by the Ordnance Survey to help with map-making. Noting these images, the *Journal of the Photographic Society* stated that 'in a few years there will be photographic Stations spread all over the world, and having their results recorded in the War Department; and in a short time all the world will be brought under the subjugation of photography'.[20]

The use of the word 'subjugation' is an interesting one - a reminder that, even by the time of the South Kensington exhibition, photography's status was not resolved. Art, science or both? Indeed, it remains a matter of some debate to this day. And, as the whole tone of the journal's statement confirms, the photographic medium, although invented privately, was soon placed at the service of the two major imperial powers in their quest for knowledge about the world. Photography became a way of collating and understanding the material world, and, by extension, of 'owning' it. Furthermore, it was a tool that aided the actual acquisition of territories and resources by the 19th century's colonial powers. Henry Cole was thus both shrewd and prescient when he included photography in the Great Exhibition and in the South Kensington Museum's brief from the very beginning.

It was during the 1850s that photography came of age. In the years between the Great Exhibition and the end of the decade, the medium made astounding progress in Britain and elsewhere. And the three London exhibitions, spanning the decade, played their part. The Great Exhibition had given British photography a wake-up call, which, judging by the evidence of the 1852 and 1858 exhibitions, had certainly been heeded by British practitioners and those who were in a position to support the medium officially.

Like any photographic show, these early exhibitions - and others of the period - had several major consequences, particularly because the decade was such an important one in terms of photographic history. First, they showed work that would inspire present and future practitioners of the art. Second, they placed a new medium before a public that was as yet unfamiliar with it. And third, they suggested ways, both practical and artistic, in which this fascinating medium - half art, half science - could develop over the rest of the century.

In 1853 Queen Victoria and Prince Albert were invited to become the patrons of the Photographic Society of London, an association founded with the aim of promoting the 'art and science of photography'. It was thus that the royal couple met the photographer Roger Fenton, the society's secretary, who the following year was invited to set up a camera obscura at Windsor. Albert was in fact a great enthusiast of the new medium and admired Fenton's work enormously. It was the Prince Consort himself who encouraged the photographer to travel to the Crimea during the war of 1854-56, to carry out what, in effect, was to become the first experiment in photojournalism. The British government had already attempted to send a photographic mission to the forces fighting in the Crimea, but the ship transporting the equipment and team was wrecked, and everything lost. During a second

FOCUS

ROGER FENTON
AND THE CRIMEAN WAR

ALESSIA TAGLIAVENTI

Marcus Sparling on Roger Fenton's 'photographic van', 1855. © Library of Congress Prints and Photographs Division, Washington, D.C.

attempt the officers - having received barely any instruction in the delicate photographic technique of the time (the wet-collodion process) - failed to produce any satisfactory results. It was thus decided to ask the Royal Photographic Society for help. Fenton received financial backing from the War Office, the Crown and Thomas Agnew, a publisher of illustrated books. Once he had transformed a cart into a veritable travelling photographic laboratory, and hired a cook and assistant, Marcus Sparling, in February 1855 he set sail for the Crimea on the HMS *Hecla*.

With great foresight, Prince Albert requested from Fenton 300 or more portraits of British soldiers and officers, with the aim of recording their presence and engagement. In addition, he also commissioned a series of images of the battlefield, skilfully composed and sanitized. Fenton remained in the Crimea from March until June 1855 and took 360 photographs in conditions that were extraordinarily difficult for the time. His photographs never depict the battles, explosions, casualties and devastation of war - not only because of the limits imposed by the photographic techniques of the period, but also because of the government's specific desire to create as 'painless' an image as possible of a war that was unpopular and marked by serious loss of life. On 20 September 1855, an exhibition of 312 photographs of the Crimean War was held in London at the Water Colour Society in Pall Mall, subsequently touring to other British cities.

The British sovereign showed herself to be highly aware of the value of photography as documentary evidence. Images of the Crimean War constituted the first of nine photograph albums of British military campaigns collected by the queen during her reign. The catalogue of the 1855 exhibition stated that Fenton's images were intended to 'illustrate faithfully the Scenery of the Camps; to display prominent incidents of Military Life, as well as to perpetuate the Portraits of those distinguished Officers, English and French, who have taken part in the ever memorable Siege of Sebastopol'.[21] So it was that, scarcely fifteen years since the invention of the new technique, the first exhibition of war photography in history opened, capably demonstrating the potential of the medium as both visual testimony and political propaganda.

Roger Fenton, *Major Burton and officers of the 5th Dragoon Guards*, 1855. © Library of Congress Prints and Photographs Division, Washington, D.C.

FOCUS

THE SOUTH KENSINGTON MUSEUM AND PHOTOGRAPHY

ALESSIA TAGLIAVENTI

On 22 June 1857, the South Kensington Museum in London - what would eventually become the present-day Victoria and Albert Museum - was officially opened by Queen Victoria. The new museum was designed to be a cultural focal point and benefited from the contribution of a number of other institutions: the Museum of Education, the Museum of Animal Products, the Museum of Ornamental Art, the National Art Training School, the Patent Museum and the offices of the Department of Science and Art.

The museum boasts a series of firsts in the history of museums and the arts. The most important aim of the royal couple and of its first director, Henry Cole, was to create a place that would be accessible to the wider public. Not only did it contain a restaurant - the first in any museum, anywhere - but it was also the first museum to be lit by gas lamps, an important feature that allowed the building to remain open during long winter evenings. In addition, the South Kensington Museum has one of the longest and most far-sighted policies as far as the creation of photographic collections is concerned.

When it first opened its doors, the museum already possessed its own small body of images. The photographic collection had been started in 1852, with Henry Cole (1808-82) as its most significant driving force. Cole, who at the time was chairman of the Fine Arts Committee of the Society of Arts, had played a major role not only in organizing the Great Exhibition of 1851, but also in its photographic documentation. This venture represented the most ambitious use of photography to date: a total of more than 200,000 prints produced from 155 negatives taken by 5 photographers, which subsequently illustrated the four volumes of the *Reports by the Juries*. Cole would also be responsible for the British contribution to the Paris Exposition Universelle of 1855, the first international photography exhibition to be held in France.

In 1852 Cole was appointed director of the Schools of Design and the new Department of Practical Art. In this role, he began to acquire photographs, mainly of buildings and works of art. Among the first acquisitions were seventeen images from the series *Égypte, Nubie, Palestine et Syrie*, realized by Maxime Du Camp between 1849 and 1852 during an archaeological expedition under the auspices of the French Ministry for Education. Cole acquired them on 19 April 1853 for the sum of £18. At that time the incipient photographic collection formed part of the Art Library (later the National Art Library). In 1855 the library was further enlarged when Prince Albert donated 150 photographs of a German collection of applied arts.

So it was that Cole began to assemble what would become one of the largest collections in the world. Since 1853, he himself had used photography as part of a programme to document buildings and works of art and design, mainly for educational purposes. In 1856 he took a further step. On 20 July of that year, Cole wrote an enthusiastic note in his diary regarding the possibility of 'making negatives and positives officially'. Cole's enthusiasm led to the creation at South Kensington of the first photographic studio in museum history. The photographer Charles Thurston Thompson was appointed Superintendant of Photography and, aided by soldiers on secondment from the Royal Engineers, began to photograph works of art, selling the

Charles Thurston Thompson,
*Exhibition of the Photographic
Society of London and the Société
Française de Photographie at
the South Kensington Museum,*
1858. © Victoria and Albert
Museum, London

prints at a reasonable price to scholars or anyone else who might require them. Thompson thus provided a great stimulus to photography within the museum; he even began to teach photography courses for the soldiers - an initiative the museum continued and expanded over the next few years. After all, Fenton's exhibition had shown how useful photographic documentation could be for the armed forces right across the empire.

The novelty of the museum's photographic studio caused a sensation - and also much debate. Professional photographers were strongly opposed to the creation of a studio within an institution that, since it received public funds, was able to produce and sell prints at competitive prices. In 1860 a special commission was set up by the House of Commons to look into the studio's activities. As John Physick reports, when Cole was asked to explain the photographic collections by the president of the commission on 5 July 1860, he replied: 'The Photographic Department of the South Kensington Museum has arisen from a desire expressed by the various schools of art throughout the country to obtain specimens of the highest objects of art at the cheapest possible rate. During the Paris exhibition the Emperor of the French was good enough to allow the British authorities there to have practically almost unlimited access to the collections of the Louvre, the Musée d'Artillerie, and elsewhere, and hardly any restriction whatever was placed upon the reproduction of any objects in those museums ... The Committee is perhaps aware that the collection at the Louvre is the richest in the world in objects of the class of enamels and crystal, and of course it may be presumed to be not at all likely that they will ever go out of Paris. By the good nature of the Emperor of the French, we were allowed to photograph and colour those objects, so that we are enabled to give our people the benefit of them at a comparably insignificant rate ... A facsimile of this drawing, by the agency of photography and by the action of the department, any working man in the country may get for 5d. I would apologise for the department being something that looks like a trader, but I am afraid that it is Hobson's choice; either the department must be a trader, or the public cannot have the copies.'[22]

Thanks to Cole, Thompson and the photographic studio, for the first time ever the educational value of photography to a museum was recognized. Cole did not stop there, however. As an admirer of photography, he also considered the new medium as the herald of great creative opportunities. It was this conviction that led him to acquire, on 22 January 1856, the first artistic photographs in the collection. Cole and Thompson were visiting an *Exhibition of Photographs and Daguerreotypes*, the Photographic Society of London's annual exhibition at the gallery of the Society of Painters in Water Colours. Cole acquired twenty-two of the images on display, including examples of genres typical of fine art: the nude, represented by a photograph by John Watson entitled *Academic Study*; still life, in the form of *Christmas Fare* by V. A. Prout and *The First of September* by William Lake Price; and landscape, with views taken by Robert Howlett at the Valley of the Mole, Surrey.

In 1862, after lengthy and considered reflection, the directors of the International Exhibition held at the South Kensington Museum came to the conclusion that photography could be classified as 'an independent art'. Three years later, the museum was the first to exhibit and acquire the innovative photographs of Julia Margaret Cameron, to whom Cole also offered a space within the museum to use as a studio for her portrait work. As Mark Haworth-Booth, curator at the Victoria and Albert Museum from 1970 to 2004, has pointed out, this was another innovation that anticipated the idea of the artist in residence.[23]

Ten years after its foundation, the museum's photography collection amounted to a total of 7,878 images, many of which were exhibited periodically in the museum or at the Schools of Art. The institution's long connection with photography continues right up to the present day: in 1977, the Victoria and Albert Museum became officially responsible for 'the UK's national collection of the art of photography'.

1858: THE FIRST INTERNATIONAL EXHIBITION OF PHOTOGRAPHY TO BE HELD AT A MUSEUM

Another significant achievement of the South Kensington Museum was its hosting of an international exhibition of photography in 1858. Cole decided to present - for the first time within a museum - the annual exhibition of the Photographic Society of London and its French counterpart, the Société Française de Photographie. A total of 1,009 photographs were included, with both countries highlighting work by the greatest photographers of the time. Among the British photographers on display were Francis Bedford, Lewis Carroll, Roger Fenton, Lake Price, Oscar Gustav Rejlander and Henry Taylor. The French, who exhibited an ample selection of approximately 250 images, showed works by Gustave Le Gray (particularly portraits), Nadar, Édouard Baldus and Charles Nègre, among others.

On 12 February 1858, Cole noted in his diary: 'Museum: Queen &c came to private view of the Photographic Socy., being the first exhibition in the Refreshment upper room.'[24] The display - praised by the critics and inspired by those of the 'watercolour exhibitions' - is recorded in a photograph by Thompson, the museum's official photographer. The image reveals a tightly packed arrangement of photographs of various genres, including landscapes, architectural views and reproductions of works of art. In the middle of the gallery several stereoscopes were crammed onto tables. At the centre of the exhibition was Lake Price's image of *Don Quixote in his Study*, alongside images of classical busts photographed by Fenton in the British Museum. The show also included Rejlander's *The Two Ways of Life* (p. 48), which was on sale for 10 guineas or, for a 'Small Copy', 12 shillings and sixpence. Of all the images exhibited, Cole acquired only eight: photographs of drawings in the Uffizi taken by the Alinari brothers.

Despite the *Daily News* having praised the exhibition as 'the great public display of the season', there was also much criticism. For example, the *Art Journal of London* (vol. 4, 1858) declared: 'We cannot discover a novelty in the exhibition: the instantaneous pictures, giving us the breaking waves, have been familiar to us since the very first evening meeting of the Photographic Society. ... Why do we miss the names of so many excellent amateur photographers who have hitherto been regular exhibitors? Why have we so many pictures which have already been seen in this or in other exhibitions?'

As Mark Haworth-Booth remarks, despite the fact that the display was admired and copied, the first international exhibition of photography at the South Kensington Museum was not considered a great success. Contributing to its mixed reception was perhaps the high ticket price of one shilling, or simply the fact that the South Kensington Museum was in an inconvenient location too far from the centre of London. On 21 May 1858 the *Journal of the Photographic Society* declared: 'We must say that a more out-of-the-way place could not well have been chosen. It would be a very curious calculation to know how many of the few who visited that really admirable Exhibition, went there for the sake of the photographs themselves - pilgrims to the shrine of photography, - as distinguished from those visitors who made a "day out" of it and "did" the Kensington Museum at the same time.' Whatever their reasons for coming, the number of visitors was considerable: approximately 456,000 visited within the space of a year.

Isabel Agnes Cowper, *South Kensington Museum, Educational Collection, showing School Furniture and Apparatus, c. 1868.*
© Victoria and Albert Museum, London

NOTES

1. Several different people in England and France were involved in photographic experiments, including Thomas Wedgwood and Joseph Nicéphore Niépce.

2. Y. French, *The Great Exhibition 1851* (London: Harvill Press, 1950), p. 29.

3. J. Szarkowski, *Photography Until Now* (exh. cat., New York: Museum of Modern Art, 1990), p. 57.

4. W. H. Fox Talbot, *The Pencil of Nature* (London: Longman, Brown, Green & Longmans, 1844–46). The work consisted of twenty-four calotypes published in six separate volumes with commentary. Part I (containing five calotypes) was published on 29 June 1844; Part II (seven calotypes) on 31 January 1845; Part III (three calotypes) on 10 June 1845; Part IV (three calotypes) on 2 August 1845; Part V (three calotypes) on 7 January 1846; Part VI (three calotypes) on 23 April 1846. W. H. Fox Talbot, *Sun Pictures in Scotland* (London: n.p., 1845).

5. W. H. Fox Talbot, letter to Constance Talbot, October 1851; Talbot Collection, British Library, London, LA51-45.

6. R. Taylor, *Impressed by Light: British Photographs From Paper Negatives, 1840-1860,* (New Haven, Conn.: Metropolitan Museum of Art and Yale University Press, 2007), p. 37. I have relied a great deal on Roger Taylor's catalogue of English calotypes; even if it concentrates on that particular photographic process, it contains a wealth of information about British photography in general, including exhibitions of the period.

7. The publication of *the Reports by the Juries* has a complex story. Originally there were two different publications: the *Official Descriptive and Illustrated Catalogue (of the Great Exhibition of 1851)* (London: Spicer Brothers and W. Clowes and Sons, 1851) in three volumes, and *Reports by the Juries on the Subjects in the Thirty Classes into which the Exhibition Was Divided* (London: Royal Commission/William Cowes & Sons, 1852), composed of four volumes. They were brought together, along with two supplementary volumes, in a luxurious publication intended for an affluent readership. See Taylor, pp. 39–42 and corresponding notes.

8. J. Glaisher, 'Class X: Philosophical Instruments and Processes depending on Their Use', in *Reports by the Juries*, p. 244, cited in Taylor, p. 244.

9. Ibid.

10. W. H. Fox Talbot, letter to Sir David Brewster, 20 October 1851; National Media Museum, Bradford, 1937-4989.

11. *Reports by the Juries, vol. II: Exhibition of the Works of Industry of All Nations*, p. 520. Cited in M. Haworth-Booth, *Photography, an Independent Art: Photographs from the Victoria and Albert Museum 1839-1996* (London: V&A Publications, 1997), p. 25.

12. Haworth-Booth, p. 29.

13. W. H. Fox Talbot, letter to Lord Rosse, 30 July 1852; Royal Photographic Society Collection, National Media Museum, Bradford, T/2 1274-A.

14. 'Exhibition of Photographs', unnamed article in *The Times*, 31 December 1852. Other notices also covered the exhibition, which received full and positive reviews: see, for example, 'Exhibition of Photographs at the Society of Arts', *Athenium*, 1 January 1853; 'Exhibition of Photography', *Literary Gazette*, 15 January 1853; and 'Photographic Exhibition at the Society of Arts', *Art-Journal*, 1 February 1853.

15. F. Zanot, 'Exhibition of Recent Specimens of Photography', in W. Guadagnini (ed.), *Photography: The Origins, 1839-1890* (Milan: Skira, 2010), p. 58.

16. Taylor, pp. 54-55.

17. Ibid., p. 55.

18. The South Kensington Museum formally became the Victoria and Albert Museum on 17 May 1899, when Queen Victoria laid the foundation stone of Aston Webb's building. It was her last official public appearance and took place a week before her eightieth birthday.

19. 'Fine Arts - Exhibition of the Photographic Society', anonymous article in the *Daily News*, 23 February 1858.

20. *Journal of the Photographic Society*, vol. 5, no. 68 (21 July 1858).

21. See *Exhibition of the Photographic Pictures Taken in the Crimea, by Roger Fenton, Esq., during the Spring and Summer of the Present Year* (exh. cat., Water Colour Society, Pall Mall, London/Manchester: Thomas Agnew & Sons, 1855).

22. John Physick, *Photography and the South Kensington Museum* (London: V&A Publications, 1975).

23. Mark Haworth-Booth, *Photography, an Independent Art: Photographs from the Victoria and Albert Museum 1839-1996* (London: V&A Publications, 1997).

24. Cited in ibid., p. 42.

Jean-Baptiste-Louis Gros,
The Salon of Baron Gros,
c. 1850–57, daguerreotype.
© Metropolitan Museum of
Art, New York

3

Between Pride and Prejudice:
Exhibiting Photography in the 19th Century

Paul-Louis Roubert

It would have been highly surprising if the 19th century neglected to include photography in its exhibitions, since the technique fitted so well with the century's visual and commercial drive - of which exhibitions themselves were so emblematic. Windowed shopping arcades and glass palaces devoted to international expositions proliferated and became the privileged settings for displaying photography. Within these light and airy spaces, the mechanical image reflected the period's narcissistic dream of reproducing itself on an industrial scale in a manner accessible to all. In the first two decades of its public life, photography was the subject of a public debate surrounding its status in relation to the spaces in which it was shown. But for this debate to take place, and for new territories to be conquered, the medium had to structure itself around institutions that were capable of supporting its evolution and, above all, its ever growing ambition to achieve the status of art. The concept of the photography exhibition is part of the medium's history, as it sought to define itself in the face of prejudice. In the event, photography shaped its own destiny by adopting a different approach and through the tireless campaigning of a few pioneering figures.

Philistine exhibitions

François Arago had presented Daguerre's invention to the Académie des Sciences and the National Assembly in 1839 with great scientific, artistic and social plans in mind: he thought that these precise images might eventually replace the fallible human hand in all domains. This utopian dream was quickly set aside in favour of a far more prosaic, commercial application: the development of the photographic portrait. With free access to the daguerreotype process, a large number of enthusiasts, opticians and chemists set about improving upon it - particularly the amount of time required for posing, which was reduced from dozens of minutes to just a few seconds. During the 1840s the professional daguerreotype portrait became the spearhead of photography. And so, alongside the expert amateurs - still few in number - there arose a new profession, that of the daguerreotypist, and the first generation of photographers was born. As trade blossomed the price of the daguerreotype fell - so much so that, by the end of the decade, the daguerreotype portrait had become financially accessible to a far wider public than just the middle classes. The dominance of the daguerreotype portrait in the 1840s made a huge contribution to the social impact of photography

and hence, in all senses of the term, to its image. It rapidly became a modern consumer item and, in contrast to its 1839 status as an 'event', now found its way into people's homes and everyday lives. It had simply become part of the decor. However, this disappearing act was accompanied by a degree of standardization in studio portraiture. As is often the case with industrialization, the product generally became monotonous, unoriginal: the poses, the lighting, the backgrounds all seemed to emerge from the same production line, and for the most part were mediocre. This standardization was largely responsible for giving photography a poor reputation and, indeed, photographers too, who were seen as money-minded charlatans or failed painters.

Another feature was crucial to the diffusion of the image in urban surroundings. This was the shop window, usually in the same building as the studio, where a few daguerreotypes were displayed in order to attract new customers. As the novelist Charles Paul de Kock noted: 'There are many people in the city who say they will do your portrait by this new process. A display case placed at the entrance tells you that the building houses a daguerreotypist ... for there is no way they can talk here of a painter ... The painter is giving you a slap in the face.'[1] This short extract from a satirical text mocking the daguerreotypists' naive clientele tells us all we need to know: outside the carriage gates on all the great Parisian boulevards were generally unflattering galleries of characters all chasing photographic glory. This view is mirrored in fiction, where the figure of Madame Bovary's husband wants to have his portrait done in Rouen - a plan that Gustave Flaubert describes with some cynicism: 'Finally Charles ... asked [M. Léon] to find out what the cost of a good daguerreotype might be in Rouen; this was to be a sentimental surprise especially for his wife - a most thoughtful gesture - his portrait in black.'[2] This trade flattered both the photographer and his model, both of them acting out the comedy of art and good taste that now pervaded the city streets, as the Parisian *flâneur* Victor Fournel complained:

The studio of a daguerreotypist, illustration from Charles Paul de Kock, *La Grande Ville. Nouveau tableau de Paris, comique, critique et philosophique*, vol. 1, Paris: Publications Nouvelles, 1844.
© Bibliothèque Nationale de France, Paris

What I resent most is the daguerreotype - the daguerreotype, which pursues and fills your gaze wherever you go ... In the streets, the through roads and the cul-de-sacs, wherever there is any kind of traffic, whether they're on a wall, in a window, on a shop front - there, spreading themselves out with unbearable self-satisfaction, you will see these daguerreotype trophies reflecting the myriad bourgeoisie in all ages and all shapes. Oh, you bourgeois of Paris and elsewhere, if only you would realize that, if you are not beautiful in flesh and blood, you are extremely ugly when you have yourselves painted, especially by an unintelligent machine that does not even have the wit to throw a bit of gold dust over your physical imperfections, but instead brutally sticks your colourless, lifeless replica on the plate![3]

The result of this dominance by the daguerreotype and the portrait studios was the imposition of a very poor aesthetic, which flattered the 'barbaric'[4] taste of a public unaware of what photography could achieve.

An industrial product

Nevertheless, from the beginning of the 1840s photography benefited from official promotion. Created at the end of the 18th century, the Expositions de l'Industrie Nationale were designed not only to reflect, but also to stimulate, French industrial creativity in the context of fierce competition, above all with England. In line with the triumphant march of industry during the 19th century, this exhibition of industrial products was divided into several categories, ranging from weaving to machinery and agricultural tools, and from precision instruments to chemistry. An exhibition of this type was held in 1839 but finished too soon (on 31 July) for the new daguerreotype to be included. It was not until the next, in 1844, that Section VII, 7th Class ('Imprimerie, Lithographie, Gravure, etc.') included a subsection entitled 'Photographie'. More specifically, Section VII was called 'Beaux-arts', and it grouped together industrial applications of the fine arts: porcelain, earthenware, goldsmithing, etc. The subsection on photography followed the same general pattern, but also revealed recent technical advances: 'Photography, this ingenious invention that fixes the image produced by the objects themselves on metallic plates, has already undergone numerous improvements. The apparatus has been simplified, the processes have advanced, and the images obtained have far outstripped the first ones that were put before a curious public. Nevertheless, photography is very far from being the finished product, and we can expect new discoveries as a result of the continuous research of which it is the subject.'[5]

Although it was recognized that technology was developing quickly, the 1844 exhibition still reflected the basic state of the profession at that time: seven out of the eight photographers it included were daguerreotypists. Reviewers, therefore, mostly focused on improvements in portraiture: 'We know that, even though M. Daguerre's process reproduces with remarkable fidelity the images of monuments in all their finest details, the portraits by contrast leave a great deal to be desired in terms of their general effect and their models. M. Sabatier-Blot is one of those whose daguerreotype portraits are the most successful.'[6] The only exception was the French photographer Antoine Claudet. Claudet had settled in London in 1841 and was one of the few to make daguerreotype portraits there, under licence from Daguerre. But in 1844 he also began to use the calotype process invented and patented by William Henry Fox Talbot,[7] which involved paper negatives: 'M. Claudet is licensed to make daguerreotype prints on paper using the Talbot process. The results are the same (although produced by different methods) as those obtained a few years ago by M. Bayard.'[8] Nevertheless, this kind of technical presentation, with its focus on the portrait business, did little to challenge the classification of photography as an industrial product, as was pointed out by the reviewer in *Le Moniteur Universel*: 'It is no longer science, it is no longer art, it is commerce, it is industry.'[9]

By 1849 and the industrial exhibition, the photographic scene had undergone a transformation. In 1847 a draper in the north of France had succeeded in adapting the calotype formula patented by Talbot in a way that made it freely accessible in France. From that moment on, the improvements that had been made to the daguerreotype could also be applied to the other technique. The practice of photography on paper was now seen as offering a genuine alternative, since it had a number of advantages: quite apart from the fact that the images were reproducible, the use of paper as both negative and positive made it possible for them to be arranged in portfolios, stuck in albums, touched up or cut out. In sum, they took up less space, were far lighter and could be produced much more cheaply than the daguerreotype. Furthermore, the arrival of this new process attracted the interest of a new generation of photographers who had turned away from the daguerreotype, which, even though it was superior in terms of detail and precision, no longer seemed to interest anyone but commercial photographers and their boulevard customers.

For the 1849 exhibition, photography on paper found a true champion in the person of Léon de Laborde. Senator, archaeologist, curator and also a member of the jury for the exhibitions of 1839 and 1844, Laborde was appointed the event's official recorder. He devoted several pages to photography in his jury report, and what he wrote marks an important milestone in the recognition of photography within an institutional framework. Although eight out of the thirteen photographs shown in the division were still daguerreotypes, Laborde did not hesitate to argue in favour of more recent developments, referring to the calotype in France, and also to the very latest process, which used a glass support for the negative. Only three of the exhibitors used one of these new techniques. While recognizing the commercial importance of the daguerreotype,[10] Laborde landed on the side of technical and aesthetic innovation: 'These advantages seem clear to us: they transform into a practical art what had been previously been subject to certain conditions of good fortune: thus they render a marvellous resource accessible to all artists by making the necessary equipment inexpensive, transport convenient and preservation simple, whereas before all this was expensive, cumbersome and fragile.'[11] This report thus describes photography in terms of its practice rather than commerce and consumerism, and Laborde's focus was on making the practice of photography available to everyone, and in particular to artists:

Charles Marville and Michel, *Floor plan and façade of the Palais de l'Industrie*, 1844.
© Charles Marville/Musée Carnavalet/Roger-Viollet/ Alinari Archives

Cliché bitumineux par Michel. — Exposition de 1844.

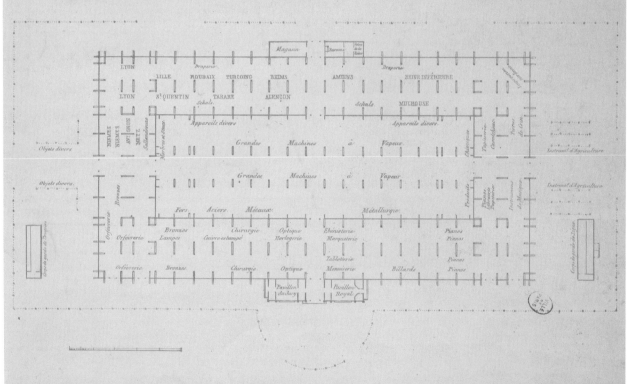

Challamel, éditeur, 4, rue de l'Abbaye-St-Germain.

Typogr. Ducessois. — Lith. Grégoire et Deneux.

PLAN ET ÉLÉVATION DU PALAIS DE L'INDUSTRIE
(CARRÉ MARIGNY, CHAMPS-ÉLYSÉES).

If ... by placing a camera obscura in front of the objects he wishes to study, the artist can reproduce them in ten seconds rather than the weeks required for a drawing by hand; if he can reproduce with great precision and matchless charm all the details that he has cleverly combined within his composition - here the leaves on the trees, with all the clarity of their forms, with all the delicacy of their fibres; there the flowers and the fruits ... if he can do all that in his moments of leisure, almost instantaneously, who will benefit? Industry first, but also the artist himself, because his *mechanical* studies will shape his museum.[12]

Laborde is describing here an artist of a new kind: the amateur photographer who wishes to use photography not in competition with art but as an aid to his artistic practice. Although the jury gave some awards to the daguerreotypists - mainly honourable mentions - the highest distinction, a silver medal, went to Hippolyte Bayard, who since 1839 had championed the use of paper. However, to Laborde, the person who best represented the hopes of the new generation was a young artist aged 29, Gustave Le Gray, with whom Laborde had already taken some photography classes:

This young artist has applied himself to subjects that played a role in his early studies ... The pictures he has copied, and the objets d'art he has reproduced, are masterpieces that are beautifully finished ... M. Legray [*sic*] is not an inventor, and he specializes in no particular process; but he is gifted with a rare intelligence and an invaluable thoroughness; he happily combines all those things that will enable his art to develop, but, even more importantly, he very freely communicates to others the methods in which he is successful, thus gaining the respect of his fellow artists and the favour of the jury, which has awarded him a bronze medal.[13]

Technical excellence, photographic intelligence and stylistic freedom are the three essential characteristics the report ascribes to Le Gray. He belonged to a generation that wished to lead photography away from the focus on representation that had been its hallmark during the 1840s, particularly when it came to exhibitions. Yet there was one space that seemed totally inaccessible to photography: the Salon des Beaux-Arts. This annual or biennial exhibition of painting and sculpture enabled art lovers, critics and ordinary members of the public to inspect the latest artistic developments. Each salon - organized according to the well-established codes of the Académie des Beaux-Arts - was devoted entirely to contemporary art, allowing artists to display their work, bring it to the attention of art critics, meet clients, and perhaps even have it purchased by the state. Even if no one had yet asked the question, it was nevertheless clear that, for photography - a mechanical and not a manual art - the Salon des Beaux-Arts was forbidden territory.

New tools

It was precisely this situation that Gustave Le Gray set out to highlight a few months later when he sent the selection panel of the 1850 Salon des Beaux-Arts nine prints on paper, including views of the forest of Fontainebleau and reproductions of two paintings. Owing to a degree of indecision - and possibly also myopia - on the part of the committee, the prints were initially accepted for the lithography section, only to be rejected a few days before the Salon opened. Nevertheless, this attempt clearly demonstrates the ambitions of photographers such as Le Gray: not satisfied with having their work exhibited as an industrial product, they were targeting the realm of the fine arts, in order to benefit from increased visibility and to encourage a critical discourse that treated the photograph as a form of artistic expression. Out of this ambition arose the idea of creating a society of photographers, which would both circulate information among practitioners and work as a pressure group to advance the cause of the medium. Thus at the beginning of 1851 the Société Héliographique was formed in Paris, with the principal aim of supporting and promoting photography on paper. The term 'héliographique' was a reference to Nicéphore Niépce's original research on photographic reproducibility; any mention of the daguerreotype technique was omitted.

The new society immediately established its own magazine, entitled *La Lumière*. The first periodical devoted to the photographic image, it discussed technique, aesthetics and the history of photography, reviewed the current art scene and offered translations of foreign articles. The art critic Francis Wey, one of its most active writers, supplied the first articles to defend the idea of an alternative to the daguerreotype. His very first piece opened with the tale of how Le Gray's prints were rejected by the 1850 Salon, and concluded as follows:

> In certain respects photography provides a link between the daguerreotype and art in the true sense of the word. It seems that, by being transferred onto paper, the mechanism comes alive; the camera is elevated to an intelligence that combines effects, simplifies execution, interprets nature, and adds to the reproduction of lines and layouts the expression of feelings and faces ... There can be no doubt that other genres will disappear: a revolution will take place, slow but deep, and salutary ... Let us briefly sum up the definitive outcome: truly original artists, far from being under threat, will extract unexpected resources from this new invention and will expand their repertoire. It is the *journeymen, the mechanicals* as they used to be called, who will be downcast ... [It] will lead to the destruction of the lower echelons of art. Comparison between their feeble works and the pure, true-to-life reproduction of nature will regenerate public taste and make it discriminating.[14]

Wey and the members of the society had already assigned two basic roles to photography on paper: to clean up the profession by getting rid of photographers whose sole motivation was profit and who were not interested in art; and to educate the public about photography and questions of quality, to the detriment of 'the journeymen, the mechanicals'.

The new society consisted of photographers including Bayard, Le Gray, Baldus and Le Secq, artists including Eugène Delacroix and Jules Ziegler, critics such as Étienne-Jean Delécluze, and people who were simply supporters and amateur photographers themselves, such as Laborde, the banker Benjamin Delessert and the chemist Henri Victor Regnault. It was, in effect, a club dedicated to lobbying on behalf of the profession. Since the fine art exhibition would not give space to photography, in the spring of 1851 the society created an *Album de la Société Héliographique*, to which each member was expected to contribute his best prints. Wey described it as follows: 'In every season, newspapers devote detailed articles that analyse painting exhibitions. Our albums are our *salons*; they provide theory with new perspectives concerning art, and ... they offer to the descriptive imagination subjects that are all the more productive and all the more satisfying because the work that is to be interpreted comes very close to nature, of which it is the most immediate translation.'[15] As both a salon and a museum of contemporary photography, the album would serve to sharpen the public's taste for photography: 'Enriched by the best prints obtained by the most skilful practitioners, this large, original and remarkably diverse collection will offer to those curious enough to wish to explore it a vast field of observation... It will introduce [the amateur] to the very best products of French photography as well as enlightening him in his selection of acquisitions.'[16] Once again, the exhibition was to serve the dual purpose of giving photography a voice and influencing public taste. In the event, the Société Héliographique was dissolved at the end of 1851.[17] Already, however, it had established the aims of the profession: to secure a means of distribution (*La Lumière* survived, having been taken over by the publishing house of Gaudin), to organize exchanges and social events, and to stimulate the interest and influence the taste of the public through exhibitions.

Photographic activity on the other side of the Channel served only to strengthen this commitment. The French were not alone in their quest for institutional recognition: since 1839 the English had been courteous but resolute rivals, and one particular event unquestionably gave them a head start. The popularity of industrial exhibitions created healthy competition throughout Europe, spurring countries into organizing world fairs, the very first of which took place in London in 1851. Beneath the glass roof of the Crystal Palace was assembled everything that the Western world could conjure up in the form of innovations, techniques and practical knowledge. There were over 17,000 exhibitors from 94 countries. The fine arts as such were not represented (though some sculpture was allowed), so photography found itself pigeonholed into different sections, principally Section II, 'Machinery for Agricultural, Manufacturing, Engineering, and other purposes and Mechanical Inventions', Class X, 'Philosophical Instruments',[18] Subclass D, 'Application of Mechanical and Physical Science to Useful Purposes', Section 3, 'Instruments to assist Vision'.[19] Aside from the fact that this grouping mixed photographers and manufacturers together, the exhibition was also divided up by country. On display were 772 prints from 6 different nationalities, of which Britain, the United States and France provided the majority.[20] This dispersal made it impossible for a visitor to gain an overall view of contemporary photography - a situation exacerbated by conditions that were sometimes far from ideal, as Jules Ziegler remarked:

> It is quite difficult to examine the American daguerreotypes; they have been placed under a kind of awning or canopy that drastically affects the light, in such a way that in order to avoid reflections one is put to a great deal of inconvenience; visitors can see themselves in the plates, as well as everything else around them that is white or bright ... M. Bayard is fixed on the outermost walls, in a place where for the sake of ventilation they have cut short a particular section of the glass wall, so that the refreshing breeze from Knightsbridge somewhat

distracts one from the contemplation of the fine Gothic portals ... M. Martens is perfectly exhibited, as are MM. Lesecq [*sic*] and Le Gray.[21]

In spite of all this, the Great Exhibition ranks as the first photography exhibition with an international scope. It demonstrated the wide variety of forms that photography had already assumed: adaptations of Talbot's process in England, the spread of the daguerreotype in the United States and the vitality of photography on paper in France - the country that appears to have won the day, judging by the number, quality and organization of its photographers. For British photography this was a hard blow - especially on its home turf, which had witnessed the birth of the calotype - and it was to have concrete consequences.

Britain was home to the earliest photography associations, but they were somewhat informal in character and did little to shape the role of the medium. Consisting mainly of amateurs wedded to photography on paper, they came under pressure following the setback that British photography had suffered at the Great Exhibition. In an initiative led by the photographer Roger Fenton and the then director of the National Gallery, Charles Lock Eastlake, a committee was formed to create a photographic society. Far more than a simple, friendly get-together of people who shared a pastime, it would have the status of a learned association like the many others that existed at the time. However, before the society was created, the priority of its main figures was to organize an exhibition that would display the state of British and European photography, erase the disgrace of 1851 and highlight the capabilities of English calotypists. And so on 22 December 1852, at the prestigious Society of the Arts in London, the very first exhibition devoted exclusively to photography took place. Featuring some 800 prints by 76 different photographers, most of them British amateurs, this exhibition (called *Recent Specimens of Photography*) signalled the 'return' of British photography and showed the need for proper organization. The French photographers invited to take part - including Maxime Du Camp, Gustave Le Gray, Frédéric Flachéron and Henri Le Secq - found themselves participating in an exhibition of high-quality works, presented in suitable surroundings, but for which not a single daguerreotype had been accepted. The committee was determined that the event should reflect the interests of a learned society rather than those of a trade association. Once it had ended, on 20 January 1853, the Photographic Society was founded. In June 1853 the society received the patronage of Queen Victoria and Prince Albert. The following year it launched the *Journal of the Photographic Society*,[22] and by the mid-1850s the calotype process was fully established on British soil.

The Paris Exposition Universelle of 1855

Following the demise of the Société Héliographique, there were several attempts in France to restructure the field of photography, culminating in the foundation, at the end of 1854, of the Société Française de Photographie (SFP). This brought together some of the most active members of the defunct Société Héliographique and incorporated its basic principles, but it also followed the example of the Photographic Society by drawing up statutes in keeping with the precepts of a learned society. At the beginning of 1855 it launched the *Bulletin de la Société française de photographie*, with the aim of promoting its work. In addition - no doubt influenced by the experience of the Great Exhibition in London - the founders made the organization of exhibitions part of its constitution: 'Art. 42: Every year, under the auspices of the administrative committee, a public exhibition of works and photographic instruments may be organized.'[23] In February 1855 the committee announced that it was organizing its first exhibition; among the rules governing submissions we read that 'nudes in general and without exception will be rejected', and also the requirement that photographers accompany their prints with the original negatives.[24] The exhibition was to be open to the public on the premises of the Société Française de Photographie, Rue Drouot, on Wednesday, Friday and Sunday every week from 10 am until 5 pm. Its provisional launch date was 1 June, but this had to be postponed for two months owing to the inauguration of the Paris World Fair.

The Exposition Universelle opened on 15 May in a brand-new 'Palace of Industry' on the Champs-Elysées. As with the Great Exhibition in London, works were divided up according to country. Although photography seems to have been well represented in terms of quantity (there are no precise figures for the number of prints included), once again the layout did not allow visitors to gain an overall view - as Jules Ziegler complained, with a dash of irony:

> One fears that soon the thousand twists and turns in this vast city of exhibitors in daily competition with one another will form a network whose development will be out of all proportion to the strength of the human knee, and the route one needs to take in order to see everything will be of the kind one can only travel by carriage ... If you aspire to see everything, you risk embracing too much and grasping nothing. And so everyone has a little selection work to do ... In order to bunch together the scattered blooms of heliographic art, we covered vast areas, squares, streets, lanes, dead-ends, the pavilions and the shops of this huge metropolis of industrial nations, and still we are not sure that we saw everything.[25]

For the first time a world fair offered a genuine exhibition of the fine arts, comprising a general retrospective of works from the beginning of the century, plus two separate displays of Ingres and Delacroix. Photography, on the other hand, once again found itself classified as an industrial product in Group VII (furnishings and decorations, fashion, industrial design, printing, music), Class 26 (industrial applications of design and plastics, letterpress and intaglio printing), 4th Section. Furthermore, the way in which it was shown was thought to be unsuitable, as Ferdinand de Lasteyrie complained: 'One can see that French photography is quite well represented at the Palais des Champs-Elysées. Nevertheless, this part of the exhibition leaves a great deal to be desired, firstly because of the location (it would have been difficult to find one that was worse and more disadvantageously lit) and secondly because of the many annoying gaps that one notices.'[26] The lack of care and consideration shown to photography was naturally deplored by the leaders of the new SFP:

> In one of the first corridors ... one comes upon four or five compartments, cubbyholes or booths, onto the four sides of which are squeezed the finest examples of French photography,

fighting for the slanting rays of an ever changing, uncertain day. Certainly, if we have reason to be proud of our art in this exhibition, it is not on the grounds of the hospitality meted out to us ... Many of us right from the start felt disorientated amid all the products of cosmopolitan industry, marvellous though they may be. The gloriously rich results of an invention that surpasses and threatens the survival even of lithography, engraving and certain areas of painting seemed to us worthy of a place in the sanctuary of *the arts*.[27]

Paul Périer and Ferdinand de Lasteyrie became spokesmen for the SFP, whose call for action was very clear: separate the wheat from the chaff, and allow photography to be represented in the sphere of art: 'Artistic works would have been made welcome and humbly laid out beneath those of the creative geniuses. As for those who, under cover of photography, direct factories that make lighting equipment ... they would have had the means of displaying their wares in this - incidentally very honourable - location where we are, that is to say in the midst of manufactured goods from all over the world.'[28] For the champions of artistic photography, the enemy was as much without (the authorities who had to be convinced of its worthiness) as within (the photographers who dishonoured the practice): 'Those ... the public can already recognize by the permanent exhibitions they hold all along the boulevards ... It is a trade that has undergone an amazing development over the last few years. But the photography there is worth next to nothing.'[29]

This disappointment spurred the SFP to promote its own display methods: 'This relatively inferior location [i.e. the space that the Exposition Universelle devoted to photography] becomes all the more striking if one goes to see the charming exhibition now open at no. 11 Rue Drouot, at the premises of the photographic society.'[30] The exhibition had finally opened on 1 August and, although modest in scale, it showed how capable the society was of organizing such an event: 'The Société Française de Photographie has launched the first of a series of annual exhibitions in its salons in Rue Drouot. Now open, it offers one of the richest and most complete collections of photographs ever assembled ... some of the works deserve special attention, being quite successful and perhaps better displayed than at the Palais de l'Industrie.'[31] Far from competing with the exhibition in Rue Drouot, then, the display at the Exposition Universelle helpfully highlighted the former's superiority:

> The call of our nascent society to all who practise or love photography has been greeted with an enthusiasm that, even if anticipated, has nevertheless moved us deeply ... One felt that this exhibition, in a purely photographic milieu, was going to be a kind of firm expression of the state of a science and an art appreciated for their results; and that this appreciation, formulated in the press releases by a gathering of men personally devoted to the practice of photography, and above all to the cause of progress, would take on an irresistible authority.[32]

Thus the SFP gave its full support to a vision for photography that aimed to eliminate 'those deplorable illuminations that shame our crossroads and our boulevards', ensuring that 'those whose concern is with the true advancement of photography should of necessity exclude appreciation of works that, under the guise of art, can only corrupt the taste of the public and are a disgrace to photography when they are produced in its name'.[33] The idea of an official exhibition supported by the state now had a solid basis, as envisaged by Le Gray:

> Photography is in effect both a science and an art … two good reasons for it to be encouraged by the government. If one of the rooms in the Louvre were to be devoted to it, that would be an act of justice, courtesy and awareness. By calling on the crowd to make its own judgment, one could develop its future potential. The feet of the public always fertilize the soil on which they tread. Being seen makes the work stir. Photography is something other than an industry.[34]

The myth of the photography salon

After this first successful experience in 1855, and in the face of little support from the public authorities, the SFP fought on throughout the second half of the decade. In order to strengthen its reputation, the society set itself up as an intermediary for all questions relating to the exhibition of photographs. And so, in the run-up to the Brussels World's Fair of 1856, it was the SFP that organized the French selection by centralizing submissions. Articles published in the *Bulletin de la SFP, La Lumière* and *Le Moniteur Universel* praised the quality of the Brussels presentation, the comfort provided to visitors and the felicitous presence of a catalogue. When the next SFP exhibition was being prepared in Paris, the photographer Félix Tournachon (better known as Nadar), who was fighting for recognition as an artist, approached the society's leading figures for the first time:

> Gentlemen, until now photography has been forgotten in the programme for the exhibition of fine arts in 1857. This neglect seems to me detrimental both to the art and to the interests that you represent. No doubt you have already had the same thoughts as I have, and in all likelihood I am a little late in calling your attention to the influence that an official intervention by your society might have in this matter. Such a collective course of action would come to unite - by giving them a very real power - the individual influences that each of us must bring to bear in the common cause.[35]

On account of his political leanings Nadar was somewhat detached from the members of the SFP, but they shared a common ambition. Once again, the question was asked whether photography should feature in the Salon des Beaux-Arts - an issue that extended beyond the SFP itself. If, however, it was to be resolved, the SFP would need to develop a strategy that went a good deal further than its expertise in organizing exhibitions.

The second annual SFP exhibition - officially dated 1857, though it opened at the end of 1856 - immediately followed the Brussels World's Fair in order not to double the photographers' workload. As the society's rooms in Rue Drouot were too confined, the event moved to Gustave Le Gray's new studio on the Boulevard des Capucines. It displayed the work of 168 practitioners, including foreign photographers, and a catalogue was produced. It benefited considerably from eulogistic articles in the press, which emphasized the serious and the pedagogical aspects of the work as well as the high quality of the presentation. Art critics such as Théophile Gautier for *L'Artiste* and Étienne-Jean Delécluze for the *Journal des Débats* contributed special features. The photographer Paul Périer, in his review in the *Bulletin*, felt able to congratulate himself on the progress that had been made:

> Let us recall the unfavourable impression ... conveyed by those artists who for so long knew nothing of photography save those sad roadside exhibitions. Those products of the lens, dull, dreary, characterless ... well deserved to arouse the most profound disdain of true artists for these curious machines that seemed to have drained all individuality from their operators. Today, we can say that, thanks above all to the exhibitions mounted by our society, the public is now able to recognize that the true artist-photographer knows how to master his instruments and his processes in such a manner as to give his work a style, a personal character which, even without a signature, will make it perfectly distinguishable from all those around it.[36]

On the strength of this success, the SFP was now far more than a mere private members' club. Recognized internationally, it was an authority on media coverage, distribution and the devulgarization of photography. Thanks to the SFP, the medium had emerged from its boulevard rut and became respectable.

In addition to this long-term strategy, the society's principal activists used all their contacts to exert pressure on the fine arts administrators. A report in the *Revue photographique* gives us a good idea of the approach adopted at its general meeting on 17 April 1857:

> The society previously appointed a committee from among its own members to study the question of how to get photography admitted to the exhibition of fine arts. Today the committee issued its report through M. Paul Périer. It agrees and maintains that photographic works, or at least certain photographic works, are genuine works of art and that as a consequence they have the right to appear in the galleries of the exhibition of fine arts that is currently being organized ... The conclusions reached by the report gave rise to a very long discussion, in which the majority of members were of the view that photography should not continue to tag along behind the industrial arts; its rightful place is clearly alongside drawing, painting, engraving and lithography, and it cannot be denied this place without injustice ... M. Regnault, honorary president of the society, was therefore asked to make an official approach, prior to the next meeting, to the president of the jury and even, if possible, to the minister of state.[37]

Thanks to the management skills of its most prestigious members, the SFP moved from aspiration to negotiation. The conclusion was not long in coming. The *Revue photographique* reported on the extraordinary meeting of the SFP on 1 May: 'M. Regnault announced that he had fulfilled the official mission entrusted to him by the society and had approached the general director of the Beaux-Arts, M. de Nieuwerkerke, and he was told that the minister of state had authorized the director general to issue an outright refusal to admit any photographs, so that there was absolutely no hope for this year. However, nothing stopped the society from seeking success another year.'[38]

The SFP did not organize an exhibition in 1858, since they needed time to negotiate their aims. Instead they left the field clear for the Photographic Society in London, which for the first time held its exhibition at the prestigious South Kensington Museum (later

Olympe Aguado, *Room in the Château de Sivry*, c. 1856, albumen print. Musée d'Orsay, Paris © RMN – Grand Palais

the Victoria and Albert Museum). More than 1,000 prints were put on display, including a large French contribution organized entirely by the SFP. Finally, on 1 April 1859, the Société Française de Photographie held its third exhibition in the Palais de l'Industrie, in the same building, and on the same dates, as the Salon des Beaux-Arts. La Gavinie, the columnist for *La Lumière*, reported: 'Today, in its exhibition hall, [the government] opened rooms specially devoted to photography. This serious encouragement, which has been withheld for several years, surely signifies a complete vindication of the view in favour of art, of which the journal in which we are writing these lines was the first popularizer.'[39]

What, precisely, did the negotiations undertaken by the society's leading figures - men such as Regnault, Laborde and Olympe Aguado, the fabulously wealthy banker and friend of Princess Eugénie - achieve? The administration had authorized the SFP to organize an exhibition *parallel* to that of the Salon des Beaux-Arts, from which it was separated by a barrier. The entrance to the SFP exhibition in the Palais de l'Industrie was well away from the entrance to the Salon. The display was not mentioned once in the official publicity. All the costs for hanging the works, producing the catalogue, etc. had to be paid by the SFP. In effect, then, photography was entirely absent from the Salon des Beaux-Arts in 1859: it was concealed next door, a curiosity visited by a few enthusiasts or lost souls who would complain at having to pay an entrance fee considerably higher than for the Salon itself. As far as the Beaux-Arts administration was concerned, this apparent concession had preserved the status quo: by coming up with such a solution, they had flattered the SFP and recognized its ability to organize high-quality exhibitions without having to pass any real judgment on the question of photography as art. The critic Maurice Aubert recognized and supported the need for caution:

Some have wished that [the photography exhibition] had not been shut away, so to speak, in a separate location from the ... works accepted by the Salon, and the wish has been expressed that it should not be separated in future. The fulfilment of this wish would undoubtedly create a justified feeling of pride; but would it really be in the interests of this new branch of art? ... Without in any way wishing to reduce its undoubted value, the interests of photography itself obviously lie in its being exhibited in isolation. It needs to be contemplated at leisure, without the eye being distracted by other objects, even those of lesser artistic merit.[40]

It would take several years for photographers to view the photograph as an independent means of expression without reference to the world of the fine arts. The status quo established in 1859 continued in the exhibition that followed in 1861 and lasted up until 1876, maintaining a clear distinction between the photograph in the shop window and the photograph on the picture rail.

Charles Michelez, *Fifth exhibition of the Société Française de Photographie, Palais de l'Industrie, South-East pavilion*, 1863.
© Collection Société Française de Photographie (SFP), Paris

NOTES

1 Charles Paul de Kock, *La Grande Ville. Nouveau tableau de Paris, comique, critique et philosophique*, vol. 1 (Paris: Publications Nouvelles, 1842), pp. 193-94.

2 Gustave Flaubert, *Madame Bovary*, in *Oeuvres*, vol. 1 (Paris: Gallimard/ Bibliothèque de la Pléiade, 1951), p. 397.

3 Victor Fournel, *Ce que l'on voit dans les rues de Paris* (Paris: Adolphe Delahays, 1858), pp. 397-400.

4 See Pierre Bourdieu, *Un Art moyen: Essai sur les usages sociaux de la photographie* (Paris: Éditions de Minuit, 1965). Bourdieu took the concept of 'barbaric taste' from Immanuel Kant, *Critique of Pure Reason* (1790): 'Taste always remains barbaric when it needs the mixture of *charms* and *emotions* to satisfy itself.'

5 Jules Burat, *Exposition de l'industrie française: Année 1844*, vol. 2 (Paris: Challamel, 1845), p. 48.

6 Ibid.

7 Derived from the 'photogenic drawing', the calotype process, invented in 1841, allowed the creation of a negative image on a sheet of paper exposed in the camera obscura, from which one could make as many positive images as necessary. See chapter 2 of this book.

8 *Exposition des produits de l'industrie française de 1844: Rapport du jury central*, vol. 3 (Paris: Fain et Thunot, 1844), p. 385.

9 A. C., 'Exposition des produits de l'industrie', *Le Moniteur Universel*, 7 July 1844, pp. 2073-74.

10 De Laborde calculated that 100,000 'portraits and views ... are preserved every year, without counting a considerable number of unsuccessful operations'; see Léon de Laborde, 'Septième section. Héliographie', *Rapport du jury central sur les produits de l'agriculture et de l'industrie exposés en 1849*, vol. 3 (Paris: Imprimerie Nationale, 1849), p. 530.

11 Ibid., p. 532.

12 Ibid., p. 534.

13 Ibid., p. 539.

14 Francis Wey, 'De l'influence de l'héliographie sur les beaux-arts', *La Lumière*, 9 February 1851, pp. 2-3.

15 Francis Wey, 'Album de la Sociéte héliographique', *La Lumière*, 18 May 1851, p. 57.

16 Ibid.

17 See André Gunthert, 'L'Institution du photographique: Le roman de la Société héliographique', in *Études photographiques*, no. 12 (November 2002), pp. 37-63.

18 *Official Descriptive and Illustrated Catalogue of the Great Exhibition* (London: Spicer Brothers and W. Clowes and Sons, 1851), Part I, p. 23.

19 Ibid., p. 95.

20 See J.-J. Arnoux, 'Exposition Universelle (premier article)', *La Lumière*, 19 June 1851, p. 82.

21 Jules Ziegler, 'Exposition Universelle', *La Lumière*, 20 July 1851, p. 93.

22 See R. Taylor, *Impressed by Light: British Photographs From Paper Negatives, 1840-1860* (New Haven: Metropolitan Museum of Art and Yale University Press, 2007)

23 'Statuts de la Société française de photographie. Fondée le 15 novembre 1854', *Bulletin de la Société française de photographie*, vol. 1 (1855), p. 13.

24 'Première exposition publique dans les salons de la société', *Bulletin de la Société française de photographie*, vol. 1 (1855), p. 40.

25 Jules Ziegler, *Compte rendu de la photographie à l'exposition universelle de 1855* (Paris: Douillier, 1855), p. 32.

26 Ferdinand de Lasteyrie, 'Exposition universelle. Photographie. 2ème article', *Le Siècle*, 6 November 1855, p. 3.

27 Paul Périer, 'Exposition universelle. 1er exposition', *Bulletin de la Société française de photographie*, vol. 1 (1855), p. 146.

28 Ibid.

29 Ferdinand de Lasteyrie, 'Exposition universelle. Photographie. 2ème article', *Le Siècle*, 25 October 1855, p. 3.

30 Ferdinand de Lasteyrie, *Le Siècle*, 6 November 1855, p. 3.

31 Henry de Saint-Didier, 'Mosaïque', *Revue des beaux-arts*, vol. 6 (1855), p. 420.

32 Eugène Durieu, 'Rapport [sur la première exposition de la SFP]', *Bulletin de la Société française de photographie*, vol. 2 (1856), p. 38.

33 Ibid., p. 39.

34 Henri de la Cretelle, 'Revue photographique. II', *La Lumière* (20 March 1852), p. 49.

35 General Assembly of the Société Française de Photographie held on 21 November 1856; see *Bulletin de la Société française de photographie*, vol. 2 (1856), p. 326.

36 Paul Périer, 'Rapport sur l'exposition ouverte par la société en 1857', *Bulletin de la Société française de photographie*, vol. 3 (1857), p. 262.

37 *Revue photographique*, no. 19 (5 May 1857), pp. 293-94.

38 Ibid.

39 La Gavinie, 'Chronique', *La Lumière*, 26 March 1859, p. 52.

40 Maurice Aubert, *Souvenirs du Salon de 1859* (Paris: Jules Tardieu, 1859), pp. 349-50.

Exhibition by the Photographic
Society of Vienna, 1904, in the
main hall of the Imperial Royal
Austrian Museum of Art and
Industry, now the Museum
for Applied Arts (MAK), Vienna.
© MAK

4

The 1891 Vienna International Exhibition of Artistic Photography: The Birth of Picture-Making and an End to Prejudice and Misunderstanding

David Spencer

In 1905 the British photographer, editor and critic Alfred Horsley Hinton (1863-1908) wrote perhaps the most forceful and prescient account of why the 1891 Vienna International Exhibition of Artistic Photography was so important in the history of the medium:

> The present day Pictorial movement in photography which is exhibiting so much activity in nearly every country of Europe and also in America, may be said to have taken definite shape somewhere about 1891, when the Vienna Camera Club organised its first Exhibition, an entire innovation as regards photographic exhibitions of that time inasmuch as the competitive element was quite absent, and the principal exponents of the artistic side of photography in various countries were invited to exhibit; from which it will be seen that there were not wanting a considerable number of scattered and isolated workers striving in the face of preju-dice and misunderstanding to apply photographic means to the expression of personal ideas. Lost sight of amidst their more numerous technical and scientific contemporaries they lacked organisation and the opportunity of demonstrating their aims, and needed an exhibition in which interest in the picture could be invited apart from the consideration of the means employed in its making.[1]

A talented artist specializing in landscapes, who had five of his own photographs in the 1891 show,[2] Hinton may have got only one thing wrong. In fact, the Vienna Camera Club - then known as the Club of Amateur Photographers in Vienna - had already mounted its first international photography exhibition, in 1888. However, in common with other exhibitions of its day, the earlier show had highlighted and judged works on the basis of technical achievement - in other words, choosing sharply focused photographs rather than considering artistic intent. Hinton did not mention the 1888 show for good reason: the true photographic revolution was spawned in 1891. By 1905, fourteen years had passed since the last of the 600 photographs had been removed from the museum's main hall and galleries (today the home of the Museum of Applied Arts in Vienna, known as MAK[3]), but the exhibition's effect on shows mounted after this period - the silencing of what Hinton described as 'prejudice' and 'misunderstanding' - remained. In essence, Hinton was saying that 'art photography' was not only possible, but had become a true and accepted form of the camera arts. In addition, he implied that this type of photography was no longer something to be ashamed of, hidden or gazed upon only by the lone photographer working without an audience; instead, this creative endeavour could now be celebrated in the form of framed photographs on public walls.

The big show opens

Although advertised in the international photographic press as 30 April 1891,[4] the exhibition's formal launch took place a few days later, on 4 May. It was presided over by Archduchess Maria Theresa of Austria (1855-1944) and took the form of an elaborate, solemn ceremony that began precisely at 11 am in the magnificent columned court of the Vienna museum. The archduchess certainly had reason to attend: she was an amateur photographer and had four of her own photographs in the exhibition - including a view of the Ca' Vendramin Calergi palace in Venice, owned at the time by Prince Henry of Bourbon, Count of Bardi (1851-1905), himself a fellow exhibitor.[5] Originally scheduled to run until 31 May, the show was deemed such a success that it was extended by an additional two weeks until Sunday 14 June, according to documentation in the annual museum register.[6]

At the appointed hour, in a show of pomp and ceremony, the archduchess was helped from her elaborately detailed horse-drawn carriage outside the entrance to the Imperial and Royal Museum. This, the first museum on the famed Stubenring, had opened twenty years earlier, in 1871, and was designed in the Renaissance style after London's present-day Victoria and Albert Museum. The event was noted in the *Wiener Abendpost*[7] and received the following write-up in the May issue of the *Photographische Rundschau* ('Photographic Review', the journal of the Club of Amateur Photographers):

> On 4 May at 11 o'clock in the morning, the ceremonial opening of the exhibition by the archduchess took place. At the stroke of 11 o'clock, the empress, accompanied by Countess Schönfeld and the Lord High Steward Count Pejačević, arrived before the Imperial Austrian Museum on the Stubenring where they were received at the front entrance by the museum's director, Jacob von Falke; the president of the Club of Amateur Photographers in Vienna, Carl Srna; and members of the exhibition jury, overseen by Professor Fritz Luckhardt, himself the imperial court photographer to Austrian Emperor Franz Joseph I. Inside the cavernous main hall, decorated for the occasion with "glorious" floral bouquets, a crowd numbering 400

people had gathered to greet the duchess, including the camera club's board members, the exhibition jury made up of ten distinguished artists (with Luckhardt acting as jury spokesman and technical adviser), as well as many exhibitors.[8]

Setting the stage for 1891: The founding of the Club of Amateur Photographers in Vienna

Most great exhibitions have precedents, and the Vienna International Exhibition of Artistic Photography became a reality following the formation of a new organization four years earlier: the Club of Amateur Photographers in Vienna. The idea for a newly independent group based in the Austrian capital took form in December 1886 and was promoted by the enthusiasm of Carl Srna, who would eventually be elected president, Dr Federico Mallmann, who became the club's librarian, and photographers including Charles Scolik, Ludwig David, Carl Graf Brandis, Otto Krifka, Dr J. C. Lermer, Carl Nedwed, Ernst Rieck, Amadeus Szekulicz, Victor Tóth, Friedrich Vellusig and Alfred Werner.[9] A formal constitutional assembly to establish the club took place three months later, on 31 March 1887, at the Austrian Engineers and Architects Association in Vienna. The author Manon Hübscher notes the cultural context in which this new and independent voice appeared: 'Imperial Vienna, already in political decline owing to the failures of liberalism and the rise of nationalism, had become the symbol of a rich and diverse center for literature, music, other arts, and the sciences, a phenomenon that was often encouraged by the authorities.'[10] Photography was not neglected, its development in Austria 'stimulated by rapid industrial expansion and the accompanying rise of a bourgeois class that had the wealth and resources to pursue such leisure activities ... [It] was also supported by political, military, and scientific circles, which had been quick to grasp its significance.'[11]

In its first year, the amateur club grew to include 104 members, eventually finding a home in 1888 at 4 Walfischgasse, a brisk ten-minute walk from the museum that would soon host the club's two most important exhibitions. At the time of its inception, the club had the fortune to acquire a rich library, purchasing several hundred volumes for very little money from the library of Dr Emil Hornig (1828–90), past president of the Photographic Society in Vienna.[12] Through large donations made by Mallmann and Srna, the club established its own organ in late 1887, the *Photographische Rundschau*, which was first published and edited by club member Charles Scolik.[13]

The 1888 International Exhibition: Photography as a versatile tool of the sciences

The template for the 1891 exhibition was the happy circumstance, in 1888, of the Club of Amateur Photographers in Vienna's first international exhibition: a dry run, so to speak, held at the Imperial Royal Austrian Museum of Art and Industry on the occasion of the

40th jubilee of the Austrian emperor, Franz Joseph I. For this first show, which ran from 1 October 1888 to 4 November 1888, Dr Mallmann and Carl Srna once again dug into their own pockets, donating the sum of 10,000 florins to cover the exhibition's costs. Some 25,000 people attended, including the emperor himself and 'almost all the members of the imperial family'.[14] Although it showcased the contemporary state of amateur photography, professional photographers also took part; the exhibited photographs were for the most part consistent with the practice of the day, with all details of the chosen subjects reproduced in sharp focus. The following solicitation for the exhibition, dated March 1888, was addressed to the editor of the American journal *The Photographic Times* and published in its April issue:

> Dear Sir: The Club of Amateur Photographers in Vienna intends celebrating the Jubilee of H.I. and R. Majesty the Emperor by holding an International Exhibition at the I. & R. Austrian Museum of Arts and Manufactures here. This Exhibition, which will be open from September 15th till October 25th of this year, will serve to show to the public photographs taken by amateurs, as also chemicals, apparatus, and other photographic requisites. To the various clubs and societies of amateur photographers and to firms manufacturing and dealing in the above named articles has been forwarded an invitation to send exhibits. Further particulars may be obtained of the club on application.[15]

Though scheduled to start on 15 September, the exhibition was delayed until 1 October owing to Archduchess Maria Theresa's travels in Transylvania, as well as the late inclusion of additional exhibitors.[16] A summary of the show appeared in the December issue of *The Photographic Times*:

> The International Photographic Exhibition, held by the Club of Amateur Photographers of Vienna, has created quite a sensation, not only in photographic circles of Europe, but also among many of the members of the Hapsburgh family, princes and princesses of the realm, and high dignitaries of the court.
>
> The international character was well sustained by many exhibits from foreign countries, three from England being the most numerous. France and Germany were also well represented, but less was seen from America, Russia, Belgium, Switzerland, etc. Local reports speak very highly of the artistic merits of the English exhibits especially in landscape and genre pictures, and partly because of platinum printing employed which is so much appreciated by connoisseurs and critics. Instantaneous photographs were exhibited in countless numbers; portraiture from original negatives and bromide enlargements represented professional artists, and many photographs of a strictly scientific nature created much interest. There were astronomical and astrophysical specimens of photogrammetric and medical objects to be seen. Archaeology and geography, spectrum-photography, and other branches fairly well represented. Photographic literature, apparatus and implements completed the show.
>
> Emperor Francis Joseph and his court visited the hall. The exhibition was held under the special patronage of an archduchess, and the scientific, artistic and technical value of the exhibition did not fail to make it a brilliant success.'[17]

The 1888 International Exhibition: amateurs vs. professionals

In the context of the 1891 exhibition and the Vienna club's stipulation that submitted photographs from around the world should be judged only on an artistic basis, a few observations from the *Photographische Rundschau*'s review of the earlier show are worth mentioning. The Vienna club expressed their viewpoint as follows:

> It was not intended in this exhibition that the achievements of amateur photographers should be measured against those of professional photographers. It was long ago settled that the purpose of the two diverge, and in addition they do not work with the same resources, for which reason a competition between the two cannot be considered. Rather, the work of amateurs should be compared only among other amateurs.[18]

Since this was the view of an amateur body, it was natural for the subject to be discussed further, and an interesting question was raised:

> It is not the role of amateur photography to compete with the professional photographers, to press into their very own territory, which is also their means of subsistence. The amateur photographer will, rather, seek to achieve goals that are naturally out of the sphere of professional photographers, to which he will never aspire, since he lacks this time and resources ... Where is the line between professional and amateur photographer? We want to see!'[19]

On 1 October 1888, while addressing the archduchess during the opening ceremony, the club's president, Carl Srna distilled to those assembled the reasons for what would become the club's mission: 'By holding an international exhibition, they would promote the benefits of amateur photographers in a most complete way in order to show how photography could be used in the service of science and art.'[20]

The 1888 show demonstrated what photography could achieve for Austria-Hungary. As was noted in the *Photographische Rundschau* article, England had the largest number of images in the show of any foreign country; this was instructive, because at the time it was considered the foremost laboratory of amateur photography, followed by Germany, then France and Italy. Although a disclaimer stating geographic remoteness and a tight submission deadline may have been to blame, the article's author seems to throw out a challenge, deeming work from Russia, Switzerland, Belgium, Holland and America to be 'very poorly represented'.[21] Instantaneous photographs, taken by so-called 'detective cameras', were in abundance at the show, but earned the following rebuke: 'These genre pictures, in which the machine does everything itself, give no benchmark for the skills of an amateur. They have their full rights, are of great value for the traveler, but they do not form suitable exhibition objects.'[22] Aside from the various photographic styles, vanity was also on display. Visiting the show on 21 October, the emperor made a humorous observation: while gazing at a photograph of himself outfitted in hunting attire taken by the club president, he smilingly remarked: 'They have enlarged me.'[23]

The opening of the 1891 Salon and a formal revolution
for Austrian amateur photography

Infanta Maria Theresa of Portugal (1855-1944) became an archduchess of Austria through her marriage to Archduke Karl Ludwig, brother to Emperor Franz Joseph I. As an amateur photographer and exhibitor, albeit one judged *hors concours* (separately from the other competition entrants), she agreed to be special patron for the 1888 international exhibition and was described as an enthusiastic advocate for the photographic arts.[24] Her own work depicted Bavarian royal castles, original children's groups, portraits and 'Transylvania types' (portraits of peasantry); it showed complete familiarity with photographic technique and revealed a good amount of artistic talent.[25] Following the success of this first international exhibition, the following year Maria Teresa officially took over as royal patron of the Vienna club, and five members of the imperial family were given honorary membership.[26]

Organized, international exhibitions of so-called 'artistic photography' had taken place many times around the world before the ground-breaking 1891 Vienna International Exhibition of Artistic Photography (Internationale Ausstellung Künstlerischer Photographien in Wien). In 1886 the Photographic Society of Philadelphia at the Pennsylvania Academy of Fine Arts had organized an 'International Exhibition of Photography', which, in turn,

Carl Ulrich, displays at the 1888 exhibition in Vienna. © MAK

'led to a series of annual salons that rotated among Philadelphia, New York, and Boston; they were a key factor in the flowering of American art photography in the 1890's'.[27] In 1889, photography celebrated fifty years since the miraculous discovery of permanent photographic imagery following the work of Louis Daguerre and William Henry Fox Talbot; the anniversary was marked by 'the first exhibition of the kind ever held in Germany' - an international show in Berlin sponsored by the German Society of Friends of Photography.[28] In 1891 two noteworthy international exhibitions were held in England: one in Liverpool, running from March to April, and another under the direction of the Glasgow and West of Scotland Amateur Photographic Association in September.[29]

The second international Viennese exhibition, organized in 1891, was once more held at the Imperial Royal Austrian Museum of Art and Industry (today the MAK). It is considered one of the defining exhibitions in the history of photography owing to the fact that entries were accepted solely on the basis of their aesthetic virtues for the very first time. Some 4,000 photographs were submitted for consideration by photographers from around the world. Acceptance was considered a great achievement given the level of worldwide competition. A fascinating overview of how participation was perceived in America appeared in *The American Amateur Photographer*, having been lifted from the local newspaper of one George A. Nelson (1858-1913) of Lowell, Massachusetts. Secretary of his local camera club and an engineer by training, Nelson displayed a work entitled *The Village Cobbler*.[30] There were ten judges, all artists, in addition to Fritz Luckhardt (1843-94), the official court photographer. Luckhardt's role did not include voting rights, however: he is named in the published catalogue as acting technical adviser and spokesman for the collective jury. Ultimately, 600 photographs were chosen for admission and display following a rigorous two-thirds majority vote, and the exhibition ran for nearly six weeks.

The Vienna club - newly energized by its success in 1888, a growing membership list, the active patronage of Archduchess Maria Teresa, and a solidarity of purpose in advancing the artistic virtues of amateur photography - began promoting and soliciting for a second exhibition in earnest in 1890. In America, the October issue of *Wilson's Photographic Magazine* spelled out in detail some guidelines for the prospective show:

> We have received further particulars of the Photographic Salon which is to be held in the Imperial Museum of Arts, Vienna, Austria, during May, 1891. We present the circular as received, and would urge the fraternity to give it their special attention - because of the honor which attaches even to the admission of a photograph in the proposed Salon. Details of the circular, with club president Carl Srna listed as contact, are as follows in part:
>
> 'The Club of Amateur Photographers in Vienna intends holding an International Photographic Exhibition at the Imperial and Royal Austrian Museum of Arts and Manufactures, which differs from the former Vienna Exhibition of 1888, by exhibiting only such photos as have artistic value.
>
> The admission of pictures will be subjected to the decision of a competent jury of artists and photographers, which admission is an honor and will be certified by special diploma

bearing the signature of the Patroness of the Exhibition, Her Imperial and Royal Highness the Archduchess Maria Theresa.

The jury has the privilege of recommending competitors for special good work for the Vermeil Maria Theresa Medal, which will be awarded by Her Imperial and Royal Highness. The number of these medals is not to exceed ten and must be awarded unanimously.

The approval of two-thirds of the jury is required for admission.

No scientific section can be admitted this time.

All photographs of artistic merit will be admitted, including: Landscapes, studies of flowers and of animals, genre pictures, portraits, etc., besides diapositives, lantern-slides, and stereoscopes. Every picture, not smaller than twelve centimeters by nine centimeters, must be mounted on a separate cardboard, with or without a frame. Suitable frames will be supplied by the Club free of charge. The subject and artist's name must be on each picture. Pictures already exhibited in Vienna, 1888, cannot be sent in again.'[31]

Thus far, no actual installation photographs of the 1891 exhibition have been located in the archives of the MAK, the Albertina Museum or the Austrian National Library in Vienna, nor among hundreds of likely volumes online. However, an idea of how works might have been mounted and displayed can be gleaned from several photographs taken by Vienna club member Carl Ulrich for the 1888 international exhibition and published in the *Photographische Rundschau* (p. 84). A history of the Vienna club, published in the same journal in 1893, confirms that the 1891 exhibition 'was installed like the first at the Austrian Museum of Art and Industry, [and] had a large number of visitors, including once again His Majesty the Emperor Franz Joseph I and many members of the imperial family.'[32]

Ulrich's photographs of the 1888 exhibition halls are fascinating to look at, especially alongside modern-day views of the same spaces within the MAK (p. 89). Today we are familiar with museum collections displayed in large, often white rooms with high ceilings, lit by carefully positioned electric lighting that showcases works arranged on walls in a limited and deliberate fashion. In fact the opposite was true for the 1891 exhibition. The main focus of the exhibition - the display of amateur work - was housed in a large hall on the ground floor, perhaps 35 m (115 ft) in length, illuminated solely by a large bank of windows on one side. Remodelled in 1910 and today housing the museum's library and archive of works on paper, the space - one of several galleries used in 1891[33] - was literally crammed full of photographs. Arranged in distinct grid-like assemblages according to country and photographer, the works - both framed and unframed - were individually mounted on cardboard and displayed on walls and dividing partitions. Tables were temporarily installed between these partitions. As is known from the 1890 invitation reproduced in *Wilson's* magazine, entrants had the option of supplying their own frames or using frames supplied by the club itself, so the overall presentation would have included several styles. The relatively few diapositives that the official catalogue listed as being acceptable for exhibition (lantern-slides, in effect) would have been displayed near, or in front of, the large bank of windows, just as they were in 1888. Additionally, easels were arranged in the corners of the room for displaying works,

Baron Nathaniel von Rothschild,
Children's tea time, 1891.
© PhotoSeed Archive

and in the centre a plush seating area gave visitors an opportunity to rest while taking it all in.[34] Unlike its 1888 predecessor, the 1891 exhibition room would have lacked the imperial canopy, made of heavy red fabric decorated with gold, that had been installed for the 40th anniversary jubilee, but almost certainly a bust of the emperor would have been on display somewhere. Embellishments of red fabric would surely also have covered at least some of the walls, in tribute to Archduchess Maria Theresa's patronage.

Crowds in Vienna and Salon reviews

The exhibition was well attended, although visitor numbers were not nearly as high as for the first, which was viewed by 25,000 people. It seems likely that approximately 15,000 visitors attended the 1891 Salon; official attendance records kept by the museum and printed in their journal at the end of 1891 show that 12,625 visitors toured the museum in May, and that an additional 4,485 came in the first two weeks of June.[35]

    Written commentary about the significance of the exhibition shows how far opinions differed. On the Austrian side, deference to royalty seems to have coloured the reporting - inevitably so, considering the venture's imperial patronage and the possibility that the idea for the exhibition came from none other than Archduchess Maria Theresa herself. The attendance of royalty was always noted in the literature; after reading that Emperor Franz Joseph finally attended twenty days after the show's official opening, on 24 May, we also

Above: **The exhibition room used in 1891, after restoration, Vienna, 1914.** © MAK

Opposite: **The MAK library archives today.**
© MAK/Georg Mayer

learn that the archduchess had attended yet again, on 14 May, this time accompanied by her husband, Archduke Karl Ludwig.[36] The museum's director, Jacob von Falke, did his part for posterity, describing the artistic photographs on display as having a 'striking new appearance' and conjuring up, perhaps unknowingly, the idea of selective focus espoused by the new school of naturalistic photography championed several years earlier in England by Peter Henry Emerson (1856-1936). Falke describes the new artistic photography as requiring 'concealment and disappearance of the details … the art will represent how the human eye sees'. Perhaps not coincidentally, he goes on to state that 'this new school of photography originates in England, and England has also sent a number of representatives, a number of names, each with a large number of most excellent photographs'.[37]

Some more strident voices were unafraid to take a stand over perceived exhibition improprieties. In his 'Letter from Germany', published in New York's *Anthony's Photographic Bulletin*, the pioneering German photochemist Hermann Wilhelm Vogel (1834-98) - a professor at the Technical University of Berlin who championed photography as a field of study - stated an opposing view of the 1891 exhibition, remarking that the so-called 'artistic photography' on display showed 'careless technical execution'. But that was not all. Vogel was particularly intent on conveying his disdain for the jury itself:

> We have now a photographic exhibition in Vienna, and the newspapers are speaking in the highest terms of praise about it. But, nevertheless, there is a strong opposition to the jury selected. It has always been the custom to admit artists to such a jury, but only in the minority.

In Vienna, however, the jury is composed entirely of artist-painter and sculptors, with the single exception of expert Mr. Luckhardt. Is that correct? I believe that a general cry of indignation would be raised if the jury for an exhibition of oil paintings consisted of professional photographers only. Is it therefore to be wondered at if similar feelings are expressed by the photographers? It is even not necessary to refer to photography ...

The exhibition in Vienna may be called a very good one. The too high requirements have led to a still more careful selection. But at the same time exhibits are said to have been admitted, which, by their careless technical execution (under exposure), etc., etc., were much commented on by practical photographers. I am not astonished about this. When I directed in 1864 the first international photographic exhibition in Berlin, I was surprised, how the artists passed some of the English pictures which our photographers failed to admire. They succeeded even so that some of those actually carelessly executed pictures (Miss Cameron's) received a diploma. One picture among those showed only the back part of the head of an old woman, with side-light similar to the later Rembrandt effect. Everything else was shrouded in darkness. The artist, Gustav Richter, admired this picture particularly. Why? After years I recognized this figure in his well known picture: *The Building of the Pyramids*, for which he had used it. The figure is in the foreground.[38]

But there were also champions for the emerging artistic photography movement - a direct result of the Vienna exhibition, which spawned many disciples. In England, the leader of the new school, and the most important voice to emerge in the wake of the 1891 Salon, was George Davison (1854-1930). An amateur photographer, the wealthy managing director of the British arm of the mighty Kodak Corporation and a founding member of the Brotherhood of the Linked Ring, Davison was a staunch defender of this new so-called 'picture-making' and style of creative pictorial expression. In July 1892, a year after Vogel's remarks, Davison's speech to those attending the 1892 Edinburgh Photographic Convention offered a completely different viewpoint on the subject of artistic photography.[39] Having first dispensed with those convention-goers more aligned with photography's scientific benefits ('I felt I could say nothing in technical criticism of recent purely scientific advances or inventions in photography which would not have been already better summarized and explained'), he then let them know his true feelings: 'I propose to direct my remarks chiefly to one particular aspect of our progress in photography, namely, the art aspect.' Later commenting on this artistic standpoint in relation to photographic exhibitions, he brought up the 1891 Vienna Salon, among others:

The best argument to be adduced in support of this view is the success which has attended the International Exhibition at Vienna, the English Exhibition at Brussels, and the practical repetition of this latter at Lincoln, in all of which, by selection and invitation, a better average of excellence and a far greater credit to photography have been the result. In this connection it will be remembered it has been a frequent custom to divide the art section of photography exhibitions into amateur and professional classes. For this, I think, there can be absolutely no defense if the exhibition has any pretensions whatever to be called an art exhibition.

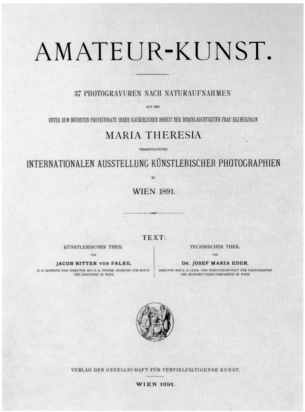

AMATEUR-KUNST.

37 PHOTOGRAVUREN NACH NATURAUFNAHMEN

AUS DER

UNTER DEM HÖCHSTEN PROTECTORATE IHRER KAISERLICHEN HOHEIT DER DURCHLAUCHTIGSTEN FRAU ERZHERZOGIN

MARIA THERESIA

VERANSTALTETEN

INTERNATIONALEN AUSSTELLUNG KÜNSTLERISCHER PHOTOGRAPHIEN

ZU

WIEN 1891.

TEXT:

KÜNSTLERISCHER THEIL	TECHNISCHER THEIL
VON	VON
JACOB RITTER VON FALKE,	DR. JOSEF MARIA EDER,
K. K. HOFRATH UND DIRECTOR DES K. K. ÖSTERR. MUSEUMS FÜR KUNST UND INDUSTRIE IN WIEN.	DIRECTOR DER K. K. LEHR- UND VERSUCHSANSTALT FÜR PHOTOGRAPHIE UND REPRODUCTIONS-VERFAHREN IN WIEN.

VERLAG DER GESELLSCHAFT FÜR VERVIELFÄLTIGENDE KUNST.

WIEN 1891.

In art there can be no division of amateur and professional in the common acceptance of the terms ... but in art there is only quality - the good and the bad - whether the pictures be for sale or not.[40]

A lasting legacy

Late in 1891, on the 20th anniversary of its founding, the Vienna publishing house Gesellschaft für Vervielfältigende Kunst[41] issued *Amateur-Kunst* ('Amateur Art'), a sumptuous portfolio of hand-pulled photogravures containing selected memorable images - landscapes, genre work and portraits - by the amateur and professional photographers whose work lined the walls of the 1891 Salon. Jacob von Falke provided an essay giving context and credibility to the artistic work: 'The second international show was all about the artistic side. Only those work were shown that seemed artistic, colourful and beautiful,' he said. Dr Josef Maria Eder (1855-1944), who had established Vienna's Imperial and Royal Graphic Arts Institute in 1888, supplied a technical overview as well. This was significant since the institute - one of the world's most innovative schools, combining study of 'scientific photochemistry, applied photography and its artistic development' - would soon shape the education and ambitions of student photographers, encouraging not merely technical skill, but also an understanding that nuance in the form of photographic artistic expression could be a powerful tool in its own right.

Cover and title page of the portfolio *Amateur-Kunst*, Vienna, 1891.

Lyddell Sawyer, *Waiting for the Boats*, **1889.**
© PhotoSeed Archive

In conclusion, let us hear a few more thoughts from Alfred Horsley Hinton, who in his 1905 essay observes the rise of pictorial photography and the birth of the Photographic Salon - but one offshoot of the Vienna Salon.[42] Other secessionist schools were the Photo-Club de Paris, founded in 1894, and the Photo-Secession in America, founded in 1902,[43] both of which confirmed for all time the significance of the 1891 exhibition:

> Almost immediately the example of Vienna was followed in England, and The Photographic Salon founded in London in 1892 has been maintained annually with obvious success. From thence onward is, then, the period during which Pictorial Photography has developed, shaking off the swaddling clothes of technical tradition, as its growth and desire for independence demanded greater freedom.[44]

There will always be ground-breaking moments when it comes to art, and of course that includes photography. How could it be any other way? The idea of art as a form of active communication might be an old one, stretching as far back as carbon smudges on cave walls that delight us even today; but for these conversations to remain vibrant, there must be resolve, and a willingness to change the rules in order to make it happen. Fortunately, part of the mission of the newly formed Club of Amateur Photographers in Vienna was to change an established mindset and to break these rules, thus altering our collective conversation for the better.

FOCUS

THE CATALOGUE OF THE 1891 VIENNA INTERNATIONAL EXHIBITION

The best way of learning about the 1891 exhibition is by dissecting the published catalogue to discover what was accepted by the jury and subsequently displayed.[45] Since the competition criteria, published the year before in photographic journals around the world, specified that 'all photographs of artistic merit will be admitted' and that no scientific photographs would be considered, prospective entrants were immediately confronted with the need to break with any preconceived ideas or adherence to accepted schools of photography if they were to have work accepted.

The *Catalog der internationalen Ausstellung künstlerischer Photographien* ('Catalogue for the International Exhibition of Artistic Photography') was a small, thirty-page brochure 23 cm (9 in.) tall, priced at 20 Kreuzer. It lists titles for all 600 accepted photographs, although closer inspection reveals skipped numbers in the pagination and a total of 586 exhibited photographs. The authors of these works are credited along with the name of their city, town or country of origin; there were 174 named photographers in all, including four members of royalty, from a total of twenty countries. In addition, eight frames, including a diptych, were attributed to an unknown number of student photographers from the Teaching and Research Institute of Photography and Graphic Arts, Vienna, who specialized in portraiture and retouching.[46] The catalogue cover prominently displays the name of Maria Theresa as patron of the Club of Amateur Photographers in Vienna, as well as the name of the exhibition itself, its location and dates. The catalogue states that the show was a fund-raising effort for the establishment of a hospital and children's asylum in Vienna, Maria Theresa's favoured charity. Other than a full-page advertisement for Vienna club member Charles Scolik, who maintained a photographic studio at 48 Piaristengasse, no other advertisements were included in the particular catalogue consulted; it seems likely they were merely missing from this copy, however, since they were included in the 1888 catalogue and would have provided a source of revenue for the fledgling club.[47] Purchase of the catalogue most likely also gave its bearer admittance to the exhibition. Aside from listing the works on display, the document also includes an essay by Fritz Luckhardt covering three-and-a-half pages. At the time Luckhardt was known as the official court photographer to Emperor Franz Joseph I, but he was also an imperial councillor and, later, Knight of the Imperial Austrian Order of Franz Joseph and member of the French Legion of Honour. A portrait photographer by trade, he specialized in so-called celebrity portraiture and was active for many years as secretary of the Photographic Society of Vienna.[48]

Luckhardt's essay was followed by a single page listing the officers and board members of the Club of Amateur Photographers in Vienna. These were as follows:

President: Carl Srna

Vice-Presidents: Dr Federico Mallmann, Carl Ulrich

Secretaries: Anton Einsle, Dr Julius Hofmann, Carl Winkelbauer

Treasurer: Friedrich Vellusig

Librarian: Robert Ritter von Stockert

Other board members: Alfred Buschbeck, Oberlieutenant Ludwig David, Fritz Goldschmidt, Carl Hiller, Alfred Freiherr von Liebieg, August Ritter von Loehr, Nathaniel Freiherr von Rothschild

On the next page, two columns listed the ten members of the exhibition jury, along with jury spokesman and technical adviser Fritz Luckhardt. The jurors were as follows:

Heinrich von Angeli painter; professor at the Imperial and Royal Academy of Arts, Vienna [1840-1925]

Johannes Benk Jr. sculptor [1844-1914]

Julius Berger painter; professor at the Imperial and Royal Academy of Arts, Vienna [1850-1902]

Joseph Fux painter; head of education at the Imperial Hofburgtheater, Vienna

Carl Karger painter; professor at the Imperial and Royal School of Art and Industry, Vienna [1848-1913]

Sigmund L'Allemand painter; professor at the Academy of Fine Arts, Vienna [1840-1910]

Franz Rumpler painter; professor at the Academy of Fine Arts, Vienna [1848-1922]

August Schaeffer jury foreman; painter; director of the Imperial Picture Gallery, Vienna [1833-1916]

Emil Schindler painter; honorary member of the Academy of Fine Arts, Vienna [1842-92]

Victor Oskar Tilgner sculptor; professor and honorary member of the Academy of Fine Arts, Vienna [1844-96]

Jury spokesperson and technical adviser: Fritz Luckhardt, photographer [1843-94]

There followed by a list of royal exhibitors and their photographic works, under the heading 'Honorary Guests: *hors concours*'. They can be summarized as follows:

Her Imperial Highness Archduchess Maria Theresa [1855-1944]: 4 works

His Imperial Highness Grand Duke Ferdinand of Tuscany [1835-1908]: 4 works

Her Royal Highness the Princess of Wales [Alexandra of Denmark: 1844-1925]: 2 works

His Royal Highness Prince Henry of Bourbon, Count of Bardi [1851-1905]: 4 works

EXHIBITORS

The following is a list of exhibiting countries broken down by number of works accepted (in descending order) and number of exhibiting photographers:

England: 180 works by 52 photographers; **Austria**: 129 works by 32 photographers, plus an additional 8 works by an unknown number of student photographers; **Germany**: 60 works by 20 photographers; **France**: 43 works by 12 photographers; **Italy**: 43 works by 8 photographers; **United States**: 30 works by 10 photographers, plus an additional 2 works by a German diplomat, Alfons Mumm von Schwarzenstein, who lists Washington, D.C., as his residence; **Scotland**: 12 works by 5 photographers; **Russia**: 12 works by 3 photographers; **Switzerland**: 11 works by 8 photographers; **Hungary**: 11 works by 5 photographers; **Belgium**: 11 works by 4 photographers; **Spain**: 9 works by 3 photographers; **Canada**: 6 works by 2 photographers; **Portugal**: 5 works by 3 photographers; **African countries**: 4 works by 1 photographer; **Czech and Slovak lands**: 4 works by 1 photographer; **Poland**: 2 works by 1 photographer; **Australia**: 1 work by 1 photographer; **Denmark**: 1 work by 1 photographer; **Egypt**: 1 work by 1 photographer

Anton Einsle, *At the Garden Fence*, 1891.
© PhotoSeed Archive

NOTABLE PARTICIPANTS

By and large, almost all of the exhibiting photographers remain unknown today, despite the fact that many exhibited also in the 1888 Salon. The argument might be made that they were 'one-hit wonders', but the truth is that all 174 photographers (with perhaps the exception of the royal exhibitors) were actively committed to their craft and certainly used to participating in competitions. Some names on the list stand out, however:

> **Austria**: Dr Hugo Henneberg (1863-1918; cat. 219): early member of the Brotherhood of the Linked Ring; he later joined with Heinrich Kühn and Hans Watzek in forming the Austrian Trifolium; Baron Nathaniel von Rothschild (1836-1905; cats. 401-11b): early member of the Brotherhood of the Linked Ring, descended from the Austrian branch of the Rothschild banking family.

> **Belgium**: Edmond Sacré (1851-1921; cats. 418, 420-21)

> **Germany**: Wilhelm Dreesen (1840-1926; cats. 148-59): German-Danish photographer

> **Great Britain**: George Davison (1854-1930; cats. 114-31): future founding member of the Brotherhood of the Linked Ring; Alfred Horsley Hinton (1863-1908; cats. 233-37): devoted English landscape photographer, member of the Brotherhood of the Linked Ring and editor of London's *Amateur Photographer* journal; Henry Peach Robinson (1830-1901; cats. 366-79): future founding member of the Brotherhood of the Linked Ring and one of the most important voices in promoting the advancement of pictorial photography worldwide; Frank Meadow Sutcliffe (1853-1941; cats. 506-17): very early member of the Brotherhood of the Linked Ring.

> **Italy**: Vittorio Sella (1859-1943; cats. 472-79)

> **Russia**: Alexis Mazourine (1846-1911; cats. 283-86)

> **Switzerland**: Frédéric Boissonnas (1858-1946; cat. 54)

> **United States**: Alfred Stieglitz (1864-1946; cats. 491-95): a member of the Vienna club by 1890, he went on to found the American Photo-Secession movement in 1902.[49]

NOTES

1 A. Horsley Hinton, 'Pictorial Photography in Austria and Germany', in *Art in Photography: With Selected Examples of European and American Work*, special issue of the *Studio* (1905), p. G1.

2 See *Catalog der internationalen Ausstellung künstlerischer Photographien in Wien* (exh. cat.: Club der Amateur-Photographen in Wien, Vienna, 1891), cats. 233-37.

3 In 1891 the museum was known as the K.K. Österreichisches Museum für Kunst und Industrie (Imperial Royal Austrian Museum of Art and Industry).

4 For background, see 'The World's Photography Focussed' in *Wilson's Photographic Magazine*, ed. Edward L. Wilson, vol. XXVII (4 October 1890), pp. 604-5. It is possible that the exhibition may actually have opened to the public on 30 April, before the official launch.

5 See cats. 11-14.

6 See the 'Mitteilungen des K.K. Oesterreich. Museums für Kunst und Industrie' [Transactions of the Imperial Royal Austrian Museum of Art and Industry], *Jahresbericht des K.K. Oesterr. Museums für Kunst und Industrie*, no. 72 (315) (December 1891), p. 556.

7 *Wiener Abendpost*, 4 May 1891, p. 3, column 1. Visible on the Austrian National Library website: http://anno.onb.ac.at/cgi-content/anno?aid= wrz&datum=18910504&seite=3&zoom=10 (accessed 18 March 2014).

8 'Internationale Ausstellung künstlerischer Photographien in Wien 1891', *Photographische Rundshau*, May 1891, p. 165.

9 'Der Club der Amateur-Photographen in Wien. Ein Rückblick', review in *Photographische Rundschau*, July 1893, p. 224.

10 Manon Hübscher, 'The Vienna Camera Club: Catalyst and Crucible', in Patrick Daum, Phillip Prodger and Françoise Ribemont (eds.), *Impressionist Camera: Pictorial Photography in Europe, 1888-1918* (London: Merrell, 2006), p. 125.

11 Ibid.

12 'Der Club der Amateur-Photographen in Wien', p. 225.

13 Ibid. According to Christian Joschke, in 1888 the *Photographische Rundschau* 'found a publisher in Halle an der Saale in Germany. Wilhelm Knapp was an important scientific publisher whose brother Carl was directly interested in photography. So for five years the journal was written in Vienna by Club members, published in Halle an der Saale, and distributed in Germany and Austria.' See Christian Joschke, 'Amateurism and Cultural Change: Photography in Germany and Austria, 1880-1900', in Daum et al., *Impressionist Camera*, p. 109.

14 Ibid., pp. 225-26.

15 'An International Photographic Exhibition', *The Photographic Times and American Photographer*, 20 April 1888, p. 189.

16 On 28 September 1888 the *Photographic News of London* stated that more than 200 exhibitors would be showing their work in the exhibition.

17 Review, *The Photographic Times*, 21 December 1888, p. 624.

18 'Ein Rundgang durch die wiener internationale Ausstellung von Amateurphotographien', *Photographische Rundschau*, October 1888, p. 340.

19 Ibid., p. 347.

20 Ibid., p. 350.

21 Ibid., p. 346.

22 Ibid., p. 347.

23 Ibid., p. 351.

24 'Der Club der Amateur-Photographen in Wien', p. 226.

25 'Ein Rundgang durch die wiener internationale Ausstellung von Amateurphotographien', *Photographische Rundschau*, October 1888, pp. 352-53.

26 'Der Club der Amateur-Photographen in Wien', p. 226.

27 Tom Beck, *An American Vision: John G. Bullock and the Photo-Secession* (New York: Aperture; Baltimore: University of Maryland Baltimore County, 1989), p. 43. For background, see Gary D. Saretzky, 'Elias Goldensky: Wizard of Photography', in *Pennsylvania History*, vol. 64, no. 2 (spring 1997).

28 Quote by Alfred Stieglitz, cited in Katherine Hoffman, *Stieglitz: A Beginning Light* (New Haven and London: Yale University Press, 2004), p. 96. Known as the *Deutsche Gesellschaft von Freunden der Photographie*, the exhibition was directed by Hermann Wilhelm Vogel and featured 'artistic photography by amateurs from all over the globe', one of the four judging categories in the show.

29 See 'Introduction: The 1891 Vienna International Photographic Exhibition' and 'Amateur-Kunst: 1891 Vienna Exhibition' on *PhotoSeed.com* [website]: http://photoseed.com/collection/group/ amateur-kunst-/ (accessed 18 March 2014).

30 Cat. 318: *Der Dorfschuster*.

31 'The World's Photography Focussed', pp. 604-5.

32 'Der Club der Amateur-Photographen in Wien', p. 227.

33 It is not clear if the 1891 exhibition was housed in more than two galleries, although four were used for the 1888 Salon, including the large hall on the ground floor that showcased scientific photography (now home to the MAK's Baroque and Rococo collection).

34 Observations based on full-page halftone image by Carl Ulrich reproduced in *Photographische Rundschau*, October 1888, p. 343.

35 'Besuch und Benützung des Museums', in the 'Mitteilungen des K.K. Oesterreich. Museums für Kunst und Industrie', *Jahresbericht des K.K. Oesterr. Museums für Kunst und Industrie*, 1892, p. 2.

36 See 'II. Ausstellungen' [Exhibitions], in ibid., p. 4

37 Jacob von Falke, 'Die photographische Ausstellung im Oesterr. Museum', in the 'Mitteilungen des K.K. Oesterreich. Museums für Kunst und Industrie', *Jahresbericht des K.K. Oesterr. Museums für Kunst und Industrie*, no. 66 (309), June 1891, p. 383.

38 Dr. H. W. Vogel: 'Letter from Germany', in *Anthony's Photographic Bulletin*, 25 July 1891, pp. 420-21.

39 Henry Peach Robinson, a fierce advocate of photographic art, had
    been elected president by his peers but declined the role owing to
    physical disability. He was replaced, after an election, by Davison.
    See *Wilson's Photographic Magazine*, 5 September 1891, p. 543.

40 *Anthony's Photographic Bulletin*, 13 August 1892, pp. 466-72.

41 In English, 'Society for Art Duplication'.

42 The Photographic Salon, founded in 1892 by a breakaway group
    from the Royal Photographic Society in London, is also known as
    the Brotherhood of the Linked Ring.

43 Known as the Photo-Secession, this American school was founded
    in 1902 by the photographer and editor Alfred Stieglitz (1864-1946).

44 A. Horsley Hinton, 'Pictorial Photography in Austria and Germany',
    pp. G1-8.

45 A digitized copy can be consulted online, scanned from the original
    in the Joyce F. Menschel Photography Library, which holds the
    library of Alfred Stieglitz; Metropolitan Museum of Art, New York,
    Collection of Alfred Stieglitz, N1300, OCLC number 825778218.

46 K.K. Lehr- und Versuchsanstalt für Photographie und
    Reproductionsverfahren. See cats. 251-58a.

47 'Ein Rundgang durch die wiener internationale Ausstellung von
    Amateurphotographien', *Photographische Rundshau*, October 1888,
    p. 344.

48 Fritz Luckhardt in *Photographische Correspondenz*, no. 413
    (January 1895), p. 65; entire obituary pp. 59-65. His catalogue entry
    reads: 'Fritz Luckhardt, kaiserlicher Rath, K. u. k. Hof-Photograph,
    Secretär a. h. der Photographischen Gesellschaft, herzogl. Sachsen-
    Mainingen'scher Professor, Ritter des kaiserl. österr. Franz Joseph-
    Ordens etc. etc.'

49 The titles of his 1891 works are as follows: *Study, Before the Smithy's,
    Marina, Study in Gray, In the Field.*

Marius de Zayas, caricature of
Alfred Stieglitz on the cover
of *Camera Work* no. 30, 1910.

5

Alfred Stieglitz and 291

Alessandra Mauro

Issue no. 47 of the journal *Camera Work* (July 1914) posed a question to its readers: 'What is 291?' The responses were extremely varied, as were the readers who replied; all were ready to give their account of what was taking place in the gallery on New York's Fifth Avenue that, in the space of just a few years, had revolutionized the way in which photography and art were viewed and appreciated. The magazine's leading light and the director of the gallery were one and the same man: Alfred Stieglitz.

A unique and fascinating character, a photographer, gallery owner, editor, promoter of the arts and patron (though not in a grand, financial sense, since he did not possess the necessary means),[1] Alfred Stieglitz was born in 1864 to a family of German origin in Hoboken, New York State. After studying for a time at the Technische Hochschule in Berlin, in 1863 he abandoned a potential career as a mechanical engineer in order to follow courses on photography and photographic chemistry at the same school. He was attracted by the processes of printing and experiments in colour, and he was fascinated stylistically by the blurred and intense Pictorialist style, much in vogue in Europe at that time. His interest in photography was genuine and profound; not only did he practise photography himself, but he also collaborated with journals such as *Amateur Photographer*, the *Photographische Mitteilungen* and the *Photographische Rundschau*.

Upon returning to New York in 1890, Stieglitz learnt the process of photogravure. Although he was still much in thrall to European Pictorialism, his first snapshots of New York were taken in a direct, even geometric style, more in keeping with the energy of the rapidly expanding city. He became a member of the Society of Amateur Photographers. His ambition to become a true 'cultural agitator' led him to accept the editorship of the journal *American Amateur Photographer* in 1893 and to organize the first photographic salon in the United States. He would, however, soon be forced to offer his resignation: amateur photography was not for him, it turned out, and he often found himself labelling many of the photos that he had asked readers to submit as 'technically perfect' but also 'pictorially rotten'.[2] Besides, as far as he was concerned hobbies did not exist – only passions, among which photography was perhaps the most consuming. In 1921, to mark a retrospective of his work at the Anderson Galleries in New York, he would write a brief introduction to the show, in which he feverishly concluded: 'I was born in Hoboken. I am an American, Photography is my passion. The search of Truth my obsession.' It was this obsession – or, as he wrote in another text, his 'photographic predestination' – that led him to devote himself to Pictorialist photography and to seek a new dimension in his work.

For Stieglitz, the need to create a point of reference and to consider the United States on equal terms with Europe in the debate surrounding contemporary photography (including the still-contentious question of whether photography should be considered an art form) would provide him with the endless drive necessary to conceive new projects, discover fresh inventions and new talents, formulate standpoints and wage heated arguments, all the while refusing to back down.

In 1897 Stieglitz became vice-president of a new society, the Camera Club of New York, formed by the amalgamation of the Society of Amateur Photographers and the dissident New York Camera Club. At the same time, he began to edit its new quarterly journal, *Camera Notes*. As the pages of the journal declared, the primary aim of the Camera Club was to improve Pictorialist photography in America. According to its editor, this would happen through the establishment of a National Academy of Photography and, at the same time, an annual exhibition that would present artists and works of an extremely high standard. Individual photographers would not be rewarded, but their participation in the event would be acknowledged by the presentation of a certificate. In brief, American photography had to discover within itself the means of its own emancipation, to emerge from amateurish beginnings into fully fledged adulthood, as befitted the new nation and its challenges. It had to be ready to engage in dialogue with its European counterparts and to accept, without any sense of embarrassment or inferiority, possible directions suggested by other forms of artistic expression. It was an ambitious project, but also one that Stieglitz knew he could deliver. The *Camera Notes* journal (almost entirely funded by Stieglitz himself) gathered under its aegis important art critics and photographers who were ready to embrace this European

Cover of *Camera Notes*, vol. 1, no. 4, 1898. Graphic design by Thomas A. Sindelar.

Cover of the second issue of *Camera Work*, April 1903. Lettering and graphic design based on ideas by Edward Steichen.

heritage in order to remould it into something truly American – figures who included Gertrude Käsebier, Clarence White, Fred Holland Day and Edward Steichen. Working alongside them, in March 1902 he staged an exhibition entitled *American Pictorial Photography*.

During the early years of the century, Stieglitz began to gather around him a circle of likeminded people capable of embracing his revolutionary ideas. As Sarah Greenough has remarked, these were the years in which Stieglitz created the theoretical and structural framework that would allow him to influence, in a clear and unequivocal way, the artistic debate in his own country.[3] His activity, so crucial to the growth and consolidation of modern American art, went in various directions, leaving no field or means of expression uncovered, from painting to sculpture, from African art to art created by children. In the same way he left no medium untouched, from newspapers to the walls of galleries and museums. At heart, his endeavours underlined his belief that photography could play a role in affirming an authentic, newly expressive social dimension for 20th-century humankind.

The creation of the Photo-Secession group in February 1902 marked a fresh attempt to challenge the conservative photographic style that, in Stieglitz's opinion, had invaded the Camera Club of New York, and at the same time earned for himself the role of undisputed leader of American photography. As a new means of artistic expression, photography needed to gain admittance to the American museums. As well as Edward Steichen, Gertrude

Advertisement for
Collinear lenses. *Camera
Work* no. 2, 1903.

Käsebier and Clarence H. White, the group that formed around Stieglitz included such figures as Frank Eugene, Joseph Keiley and, later, Alvin Langdon Coburn, Anne Brigman and George Seeley. They and Stieglitz wished to create an association for organizing exhibitions in museums and at international fairs that would showcase new photographic developments. Stieglitz also realized that the Photo-Secession needed a focal point, a journal in which the photographers' images could be reproduced, the sharpest reviews published and the most pressing themes debated.

In 1903 *Camera Work* was born. It was highly sophisticated, characterized by elegant graphics, a beautiful design, magnificent photogravure reproductions on Japanese paper, and refined and perceptive essays. Critical contributions were written specifically for the journal, but it also published existing texts by European authors, including Kandinsky's essay 'On the Spiritual in Art'. Everything about *Camera Work* made it a forum of excellence, in which photography could - without prejudice - enter into a dialogue with the other arts. Even the advertisements, which were designed by the editorial staff, blended in with the page design. The journal was published until 1917, and many of its fifty issues were monographs, devoted entirely to an individual photographer.

The next step was almost inevitable: the creation of a meeting point, an suitable exhibition space for Stieglitz and his acolytes. So it was that 'The Little Galleries of the Photo-Secession' were born. It was Edward Steichen, Stieglitz's friend and esteemed colleague, who had urged him to lease the three-room studio at 291 Fifth Avenue, next to the Save New York Committee.[4] At first, Stieglitz was reluctant to commit, thinking of the rent and the onerous responsibility it represented. In addition, he feared not finding enough photographers to fill the gallery's programme. However, Steichen's enthusiasm finally won him over, and in issue 12 of *Camera Work* (November 1905), in a note about the Photo-Secession's imminent, much anticipated exhibition, Stieglitz wrote:

> The Photo-Secession, for the present thus unable to hold the proposed big exhibition, has determined to present in detail some of the work which had already been selected and which would have been embraced therein, and for that purpose has leased rooms at 291 Fifth Avenue, New York City, where will be shown continuous fortnightly exhibitions of from thirty

Alfred Stieglitz or Paul Strand,
Exterior of 291 Fifth Avenue,
before 1913. © Yale Collection
of American Literature, Beinecke
Rare Book and Manuscript Library

to forty prints each. These small but very select shows will consist not only of American pictures never before publicly shown in any city of the country but also of Austrian, German, British, and French photographs, as well as such other art-productions, other than photographic, as the Council of the Photo-Secession will from time to time secure. These rooms will be opened to the public generally without charge, and the exhibitions will commence about November first.

The gallery opened its doors on 25 November 1905. While the original idea had been to establish a gallery that could also operate on a financial basis, receiving a 15 per cent commission on the sale of members' photographs, it gradually became apparent that to Stieglitz the marketability of the works on display was merely an indicator of the American public's appreciation rather than a true priority. Moreover, the gallery was located in a prime position on Fifth Avenue, at a particularly busy point near to shops. Gradually, the space also began to serve as the editorial office for *Camera Work*, and it soon became known - particularly after 1910 - simply by its street number: '291'.

The gallery at 291 was to become a fundamental reference for photography and art, in both America and Europe. At the same time, it marked a turning point in the development of exhibition spaces: it was conceived as a combination between a commercial gallery, a place in which to consider photography and occasionally other forms of artistic expression, and a public institution.[5] It was a magnet: a place where culture was created, where photography was central but not exclusive, and where, above all, one man's unique vision shaped an artistic manifesto through the gallery's exhibition programme. Stieglitz combined a museum director's approach with the calling of a prophet, the pragmatism of a gallerist and the ambition of a cultural promoter. He did not want the limelight for himself and his associates, but aimed to establish a meeting point where, between exhibitions characterized by their substance and international flavour, photography could enter into dialogue with painting, drawing, sculpture, and the latest artistic trends from Europe and the United States.

The first exhibition, inaugurated on 25 November 1905 and on view until 5 January 1906, included thirty-nine images by members of the Photo-Secession.[6] The selection was made after Stieglitz had called a meeting of all his photographer colleagues. A biting review appeared on the pages of the *New York Evening Sun*, accusing the Photo-Secessionists of extreme vanity and of using terms such as 'master' and 'masterpiece' to describe their own creations with excessive self-indulgence.[7] Nonetheless, Stieglitz pressed on with his programme, dedicating an exhibition to French photographers chosen by Robert Demachy, and then putting on a brief, anomalous solo show of illustrations by Herbert G. French for Tennyson's *Idylls of the King* (justified by the generous contribution of a sponsor), and then a photographic dialogue between White and Käsebier (p. 110), which also featured the English trio David Octavius Hill, James Craig Annan and Frederick H. Evans.

In March 1906 Steichen organized a show of sixty-one of his own images, including a series of experiments in colour, that also appeared in the April issue of *Camera Work* right after the exhibition. This is a good illustration of the type of cultural short-cut that Stieglitz favoured - one that appealed to his role of promoter of the arts and great communicator. The year concluded with an exhibition of German and Austrian photographers, but Stieglitz failed to stage two shows that he had already announced. The first was to have been a sort of Salon des Réfusés, grouping together painters who had been rejected by the country's major institutions (a project perhaps too ambitious for the Little Galleries); the second abandoned show would once again have presented work by members of the Photo-Secession.

The cultured and well-informed East Coast public seemed to like the formula that the Little Galleries had adopted, and in the course of its first year nearly 15,000 people visited 291 Fifth Avenue, showing their appreciation for its stylistic choices and also acquiring a substantial number of works. Stieglitz was encouraged by this success. Although Steichen left for Europe in 1906, he continued in his mission, considering it his duty to be in the gallery every day, greeting and educating visitors.

The Little Galleries of the Photo Secession: opening exhibition, November 1905. *Camera Work* no. 14. © Library of Congress, Washington, D.C.

Convinced that his charisma was more important than his artistic talent (in an interview with the critic Paul Rosenfeld, he was to say of himself: 'I'm not sure about being as much an artist as one of the leading spiritual forces of this country'[8]), Stieglitz saw 291 as a place for initiation into art. Although a private undertaking, the gallery appears to have functioned something like a training ground for artistic knowledge and spiritual enrichment. In 1908, in an article that appeared in the *New York Morning Sun*, unsigned but edited by Agnes Ernst, Stieglitz summarized the philosophy of his gallery and his work:

> We are searching for the ultimate truth, for the human being who is simple in every way that he can look at things objectively, with a purely analytic point of view. We are striving for freedom of experience and justice in the fullest sense of the word ...
>
> We believe that if only people are taught to appreciate the beautiful side of their daily existence, to be aware of all the beauty which constantly surrounds them, they must gradually approach this ideal ... And we believe the camera is one of the most effective means of teaching people to distinguish between what is beautiful and what is not. It forces upon them a realization of line and composition and forms in them the habit of looking for the pictorial side of everything.[9]

The way photographs and paintings were displayed followed this basic ideal: everything was designed to allow the visitor a sense of intimate, profound communion with the works and with the nature of the artist who created them. Right from the start, the aim was to make the gallery comfortable and welcoming for art lovers, who would find not only excellent exhibitions there, but also the best publications and international journals to browse.[10]

The gallery walls at 291 were covered with a rough, pale-coloured cloth - a solution that would be adopted twenty-five years later at New York's Museum of Modern Art by Alfred H. Barr, its first director. A floor-length curtain hung from a wooden rail that ran around the walls at waist height; just above the rail was a small shelf that marked off the hanging space above. On a square pedestal at the centre of the gallery there was usually a large copper vase filled with foliage and grasses. The space was lit by diffused lighting. Stieglitz wanted to maintain the rooms' proportions, which in effect meant that only the upper section of the walls could be used for display. Exhibited works were therefore usually hung in a single horizontal line; only rarely was one work placed above another. Occasionally, Stieglitz allowed himself to be guided by the works' formal qualities, arranging them in irregular shapes along the walls. His aim was clear. When displayed in a single line, the works occupied the same space and were treated equally, as objects to be appreciated in their own right. When they were arranged in groups, the viewer was encouraged to discern formal relationships between the various works.

This overall equilibrium was reinforced by type of frame that Stieglitz favoured: thin, squared off, sometimes painted black or white, or decorated by the artists themselves (as was the case with John Marin and Marsden Hartley) but without too much emphasis being placed on the decoration. In this new type of display, the images 'breathed' autonomously and resembled unique creations that deserved attention and special concentration away from possible distractions. As Kristina Wilson has noted, when 291 opened, Stieglitz's method of showing the artworks was a radical departure from the displays common in American museums at the time.[11] The great public collections had inherited the European Salon tradition of hanging works at various heights, perhaps divided up by genre, and packed together on the walls, one next to the other, according to the canvases' various shapes and measurements. At 291, on the other hand, the uniformity of the frames, the space between them and the pale colour of the wall aimed to impose an atmosphere of genteel poverty on the rooms in order to help the visitor set aside his or her preconceptions and remain open to any possible critical impression.

In the years that he worked at 291, Stieglitz honed his understanding of the finer points of installation. He realized that the way in which works were shown should not only highlight an artist's themes and inspiration, but also lead the visitor towards a state of knowledge, convincing him or her of the concept that led the curator (or gallery owner) to present that individual work. If this did not happen, the exhibition risked being 'nothing more than a market-place for the mediocre or the parading ground for the stupid vanities of the small mind'.[12]

The lighting, the arrangement of the images, their sequence, the frames - all helped transform an exhibition into a veritable cognitive and spiritual journey. The installation itself was a complex task, requiring careful planning - a process that was routine but became increasingly effective between one exhibition and the next.

The editorial of issue 14 of *Camera Work* confirmed the great importance of proper display at 291:

> Heretofore, with but two or three exceptions, photographs have not been shown to their best advantage; the crowding of exhibits, the garish, or, still worse, insufficient light, the incongruous color-scheme have certainly not helped in affording the public an opportunity of satisfactorily studying pictorial photographs. With these facts in mind, the Secession Galleries were arranged so as to permit each individual photograph to be shown to the very best advantage. The lighting is so arranged that the visitor is in a soft, diffused light while the pictures receive the direct illumination from a skylight; the artificial lights are used as decorative spots as well as for their usefulness.
>
> One of the larger rooms is kept in dull olive tones, the burlap wall-covering being a warm olive gray; the woodwork and molding similar in general color, but considerably darker. The hangings are of an olive-sepia sateen, and the ceiling and canopy are of a very deep creamy gray. The small room is designed especially to show prints on very light mounts or in white frames. The walls of this room are covered with a bleached natural burlap; the woodwork and molding are pure white; the hangings, a dull ecru. The third room is decorated in gray-blue, dull salmon, and olive-gray. In all the rooms the lamp-shades match the wall-covering.[13]

Stieglitz often spoke of 291 as a kind of laboratory where, in exhibition after exhibition, he staged a continuous experiment for the benefit of visitors, who, stripped of every artistic prejudice, could now appreciate the works fully and thus find the true way to self-expression.

Each exhibition thus became part of his mission as spiritual and artistic guide to the American people. The selections - which looked far beyond Stieglitz's core group of artists and photographers - reflected this goal and the almost initiatory path he intended his public to follow. He showed that it was possible to arouse heated debate, challenge the preconceptions of the orthodox and provoke the establishment solely by organizing exhibitions of modern art.

The first non-photographic exhibition at the Little Galleries was in 1907: a series of drawings by the Symbolist painter Pamela Colman Smith, which took the place of a show dedicated to Holland Day that Stieglitz had been unable to deliver.[14] Although the exhibition appeared to disorientate those who did understand the apparent change in direction, Stieglitz himself appeared to have no doubts about the consistency of his choice. He gradually began to distance himself from the Secessionists and, moreover, to find their circle and requirements suffocating. For his own part, he sought not a close affiliation with the group, but the salvation of Secessionism as a 'spirit' or moral drive that would help people go beyond the conventional, established order, towards a pure and honest form of self-expression - in other words, to be free. Pamela Colman Smith's drawings thus presented an opportunity to demonstrate how the Secession encompassed a broader idea, a moral point of reference free from impediments. In this sense, the acquisition of drawings and photographs could only be an enrichment, and remained true to that guiding principle. In the next ten years of the gallery's existence, Stieglitz was to organize and present many other exhibitions of drawings, paintings and sculpture.

The news of Smith's exhibition took Steichen by surprise. The two men had agreed that it would be Steichen who would be responsible for putting together the gallery's non-photographic programme, and he had already asked Rodin to inaugurate the series with an exhibition of drawings. He was deeply annoyed by Stieglitz's apparently hasty decision to launch it with an almost complete unknown, and he began to distance himself from the running of the gallery and its programme. But, thanks to a generous and enthusiastic review that appeared in the pages of the *New York Sun*, the exhibition proved to be a success, further confirmed by the large number of sales. Many of the Secessionists, however, were angered by Stieglitz's decision, convinced that an exhibition such as Smith's could have been held in any of the city's other gallery spaces. Stieglitz's personality encompassed an undeniable charisma, but also a strong streak of independence, and an unwillingness to appreciate the needs of others or the necessity of active collaboration with colleagues and companions. It was these faults that prompted his eventual rift with Gertrude Käsebier.

The most important debut of 1907 was undoubtedly the great exhibition by the French photographer Adolf de Meyer. Others were to follow; Stieglitz kept apace with developments in the European avant-garde on the walls of the gallery. On 2 January 1908 the Rodin exhibition finally opened. It consisted of fifty-eight drawings and watercolours of nudes - preparatory studies chosen by Stieglitz and Rodin together. In the puritan atmosphere of New York they caused a scandal, provoking a debate - which Stieglitz favoured more than ever - on the appropriateness of displaying works that could be considered either as 'obscene'

Views of the Gertrude Käsebier and Clarence White exhibition at The Little Galleries of the Photo-Secession, April 1906. *Camera Work* no. 14. © Metropolitan Museum of Art, New York

or as unequivocal signs of purity and freedom of expression. Such controversy served to increase the gallery's notoriety. From then on, Stieglitz was always on the frontline in the battle against puritanism, which was an obstacle to the free expression of the new American man. The Rodin exhibition was a great success and was greeted as the most significant cultural event of the year.

That same January in 1908, Stieglitz met Georgia O'Keeffe, the artist who would be his companion for the rest of his life, on a visit to see Rodin's show. The gallery door was always open: many recalled that this was the first thing the visitor noticed when arriving at 291. As with the churches and other places of worship on Fifth Avenue, entry to 291 was also free. In *Our America*, Waldo Frank described 291 as a fascinating temple: 'It is an altar where talk was often loud, heads never bared, but where no lie and no compromise could live.'[15] The priest who officiated at the temple was of course the omnipresent Stieglitz, who, aside from a brief lunch break, was always in the gallery, talking almost continuously and punctuating his speech with eloquent and charismatic silences. The critic Henry McBride commented: 'It is something of a question in our mind whether it is Mr. Stieglitz or the pictures on the wall at the Photo-Secession that constitute the exhibition. The pictures change from time to time in the little rooms, different artists emerge from somewhere to puzzle us, and having succeeded go again into the mist, but Mr. Stieglitz is always in the centre of the stage, continually challenging us, continually worrying us, teasing us, frightening and inflaming us according to our various natures.'[16]

Stieglitz's messianic nature emerged so forcefully that a semi-serious warning appeared in the pages of the *New York Sun*, written by James Huneke, advising readers to visit the gallery at lunchtime, when its director was not there, in order to avoid the seduction of his words: 'Once open the porches of your ears to his tones and ere long you will begin to believe that photography it was that originated Impressionism; that camera and Monet rhyme; that the smeary compound of mush and mezzotint which they have christened the New Photography is one of the fine arts. There's no resisting Stieglitz. He believes what he preaches, a rare virtue nowadays.'[17]

Leaving aside the anecdotes about his verbosity and facility in addressing both public and friends (his lengthy letters were as proverbial as his speeches), for Stieglitz art was the principal means by which the new citizen could be formed: an individual conscious of his own means, his inner, spiritual strengths that might enable a longed-for mystic, moral union between earth and humankind. For Stieglitz, the artistic experience was never an end but a means. It was art that could free the individual from superstition, labels and prejudices.

The gallery's commercial aspect followed this ambition - or at least attempted to. Much has been said about Stieglitz's lack of practicality; if, in part, it was perhaps more of an affectation than a reality, his work at 291 undoubtedly made it very different from any other commercial venture. Playing on the personality that he had carved out for himself, Stieglitz claimed that he could sell anything in his gallery, but that he wished to do so only when he spotted a true, genuine, authentic love for the works he exhibited. People who did not feel the need to own a particular work did not deserve it. Naturally, finances presented a not insignificant problem. Stieglitz was forced to re-examine his plans in February 1908, when he realized that, once the lease on 291 Fifth Avenue expired, he would not be able to renew it without incurring a rent increase he simply could not afford. The arrival of a patron, Paul Burty Haviland, allowed him once more to occupy a space in which he could continue his work as gallerist and editor. The gallery simply changed address, moving next door to number 293 Fifth Avenue. The new gallery, which opened on 1 December 1908, kept its old name ('Somehow 291 sounded more euphonious to me than 293,' he said[18]).

For many artists, 291 became their preferred venue. For practical reasons, it seemed to specialize in exhibiting small- or medium-sized works. On 30 March 1909, it hosted the first exhibition to show the work of young American modernists such as Alfred Maurer and John Marin; these two artists were members of the Society of American Artists in Paris, newly established on Steichen's personal initiative. During 1909-10, there followed an exhibition of drawings by Toulouse-Lautrec, one dedicated to Matisse, and yet another to Rodin. It was these shows that guaranteed 291's success and also resulted in excellent sales. The gallery became a focal point for modernism, not only publicizing new artists but also giving them legitimacy. Photography lay at the heart of this phenomenon. Sarah Greenough remarks that:

> By 1913 Stieglitz and his associates at 291 were fully up to date with the latest advances in modern European art. Through their exhibitions and publications, as well as the discussion that Stieglitz initiated at the gallery, this group of artists, photographers, and critics had not only introduced modern art to the American audience, but they had also formulated a cogent argument for its legitimacy and defense. With the fervor and idealism of young converts, they had established 291 as a revolutionary outpost that was known and admired by artists in both Europe and America for its commitment to a wide-ranging and unfettered examination of new or unconventional ideas about art. As one critic noted in 1912, they had brought 'New York almost abreast of Paris, to say nothing of London, Berlin or Munich, in its level of activity and understanding of new art'. And Stieglitz had succeeded in placing photography at the very center of the evolving discourse on modernism. 291 was, as Herbert Seligmann wrote a few years later, 'a vision' conceived and constructed 'through photography'.[19]

Except for the summer of 1910, when it remained open intermittently while Stieglitz prepared for an exhibition at the Albright Art Gallery in Buffalo, the gallery usually closed between May and November. During the winter and spring, each show was part of a packed, coherent programme that Stieglitz had drawn up. His rejections - like his artistic passions - might vary in the way he attempted to justify them, but were nevertheless occasionally surprising. On one occasion, despite numerous requests, he decided not to even consider works by the young Max Weber, who wished to exhibit at 291 at all costs (and who would subsequently become one of his closest collaborators); Stieglitz merely told him that it was out of the question, even if he had been 'Leonardo da Vinci, Rembrandt, Michelangelo and God himself rolled into one'.[20] Artists had to submit to his will, as well as to the spiritual aura surrounded the gallery. In a letter to the painter Marsden Hartley, Stieglitz recalled the reasons and the context that had led him to decide to show his work: 'When I suggested you should have a show elsewhere you remarked you'd have a show at 291 or nowhere, as you liked the spirit of the place & didn't like the spirit of the other places. I asked you a few questions and then, in spite of myself & my great tiredness and determination not to have any more shows, I gave you a show to <u>help you</u>. And for no other reason. I believed in you & your work, because I felt a spirit I liked - or rather, thought very worthwhile.'[21]

In 1909 there was one exhibition that did not prove a success: a show dedicated to caricatures by Marius de Zayas. It was followed by a solo exhibition of works by Alvin Langdon Coburn, another of Adolf de Meyer, and then a solo show of the photographs Steichen had made of Rodin's statue of Balzac. Between then and the gallery's closure in 1917, there would be only four more exhibitions of photography: Steichen's colour photos (1910), a new solo exhibition by Meyer (1911), a retrospective of Stieglitz's work (1913), and the debut of Paul Strand (in March 1916).

In the pages of *Camera Work* in January 1909, Paul Haviland - who was not only patron, but also a principal collaborator and theorist of the group surrounding 291 and *Camera Work* - announced that, since photography had now been fully recognized as one of the fine arts, the gallery and the journal would be keeping a close eye on the progress of all the arts and the most interesting examples of artistic expression. Within the journal and on the gallery's walls, the debate on the relationship between art and photography became heated: if, with the advent of photography, art no longer needed to be representational - indeed, needed to discover its own path quite separate from photography - then it could be abstract. On the other hand, if photography could not be pictorial, it should not strive to be aesthetically pleasing so much as truthful - or, as Marius de Zayas wrote in *Camera Work* in 1913, it should provide 'the plastic verification of fact'. For two decades, Stieglitz had fought hard to have photography accepted as an art form. As de Zayas's declaration showed, photography had now been consecrated as an independent medium, complete with its own history, nobility and an intrinsic value that, although entirely different, was the equal of any of the established arts. This spirit was the spirit of the celebrated final issue of *Camera Work*, published in 1917. It was marked by Paul Strand's overwhelming photographs and his accompanying essay, which, like a declaration of intent, proclaimed the new vision:

> The existence of a medium, after all, is its absolute justification, if as so many seem to think, it needs one at all, comparison of potentialities is useless and irrelevant. Whether a water-color is inferior to an oil, or whether a drawing, an etching, or a photograph is not as important as either, is inconsequent. To have to despise something in order to respect something else is a sign of impotence. Let us rather accept joyously and with gratitude everything through which the spirit of man seeks to an ever fuller and more intense self-realization.[22]

First and foremost, the exhibitions were demonstrations of what art could reveal and of the search for a new means of expression. This was particularly the case with the shows by Picasso (1911) and Matisse (1912). Curated by de Zayas, Steichen, Haviland and the artist

himself, Picasso's show was a 'demonstration of development', as Haviland remarked in *Camera Work*, giving the American public an opportunity to comprehend what was happening on the other side of the Atlantic. The aim of the Matisse exhibition, however, curated by Steichen and the artist, was to show 'the principal steps of Matisse's evolution as a sculptor', as Haviland wrote in *Camera Work*. Filling the rooms at 291 with their sculptural, volumetric power, Matisse's nudes shocked the establishment and caused a scandal. Stieglitz was not disappointed, however, since this reaction highlighted his self-appointed role as educator of the public.

Towards the end of the 1930s, years after 291 had closed, Stieglitz recalled how his intense activity as a 'revolutionary' had in fact prevented him from completing a series of images he had planned on the city of New York, and reaffirmed the didactic significance of the exhibition he staged:

> But somehow this series [of photographs of New York] that was clearly in my mind never was fully realized. The struggle for true liberation of self and so of others had become more and more conscious within me and before I realized it I was editing magazines, arranging exhibitions (demonstrations), discovering photographers and fighting for them. In short, trying to establish for myself an America in which I could breathe as a free man.[23]

By now a central figure in the world of contemporary art, Stieglitz received many requests to bring to the United States a large exhibition of the best of contemporary European art - in fact, the same Post-Impressionist works that had attracted the attention of the most informed critics in 1910. Despite these requests, and perhaps daunted by the size of the undertaking, Stieglitz refused to take part in what became the International Exhibition of Modern Art, which opened in February 1913 at the 69th Infantry Regiment's Armory in New York. More than a thousand sculptures, paintings and works on paper made it one of the most important art exhibitions in America, which is now known simply as the Armory Show. Although he was not involved directly, Stieglitz used the opportunity to demonstrate how America was not an outpost of modernism but, thanks to the long and careful efforts of his gallery, was in fact a centre of primary importance. He lent works that belonged to 291, openly urged the public to attend the event in a series of interviews and convinced many artists in his circle to participate. As it happened, he acquired a painting by Kandinsky called *The Garden of Love (Improvisation Number 27)* from the Armory Show - one of the artist's most radical and abstract works. That was not all. Running almost in parallel with the Armory Show, he conceived three solo exhibitions focusing on the new modernist aesthetic, featuring work by John Marin, Stieglitz himself and Francis Picabia.

Marin's watercolours showed a New York of skyscrapers that resembled cathedrals, changing perspective, colour and atmosphere as the hours passed - almost like those painted by Monet. The exhibition of Stieglitz's photography opened on 24 February, a week before the launch of the Armory Show, and comprised thirty works taken between 1892 and 1912, including French landscapes, the Tyrol of his travels as a young man, and views of Lake

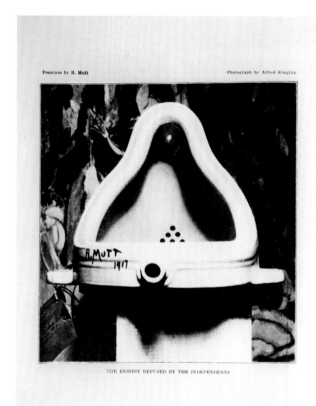

Fountain by R. Mutt — Photograph by Alfred Stieglitz

THE EXHIBIT REFUSED BY THE INDEPENDENTS

THE BLIND MAN

The Richard Mutt Case

They say any artist paying six dollars may exhibit.

Mr. Richard Mutt sent in a fountain. Without discussion this article disappeared and never was exhibited.

What were the grounds for refusing Mr. Mutt's fountain:—

1. Some contended it was immoral, vulgar.

2. Others, it was plagiarism, a plain piece of plumbing.

Now Mr. Mutt's fountain is not immoral, that is absurd, no more than a bath tub is immoral. It is a fixture that you see every day in plumbers' show windows.

Whether Mr. Mutt with his own hands made the fountain or not has no importance. He CHOSE it. He took an ordinary article of life, placed it so that its useful significance disappeared under the new title and point of view—created a new thought for that object.

As for plumbing, that is absurd. The only works of art America has given are her plumbing and her bridges.

"Buddha of the Bathroom"

I suppose monkeys hated to lose their tail. Necessary, useful and an ornament, monkey imagination could not stretch to a tailless existence (and frankly, do you see the biological beauty of our loss of them?), yet now that we are used to it, we get on pretty well without them. But evolution is not pleasing to the monkey race; "there is a death in every change" and we monkeys do not love death as we should. We are like those philosophers whom Dante placed in his Inferno with their heads set the wrong way on their shoulders. We walk forward looking backward, each with more of his predecessors' personality than his own. Our eyes are not ours.

The ideas that our ancestors have joined together let no man put asunder! In La Dissociation des Idées, Remy de Gourmont, quietly analytic, shows how sacred is the marriage of ideas. At least one charming thing about our human institution is that although a man marry he can never be only a husband. Besides being a money-making device and the one man that one woman can sleep with in legal purity without sin he may even be as well some other woman's very personification of her abstract idea. Sin, while to his employees he is nothing but their "Boss," to his children only their "Father," and to himself certainly something more complex.

But with objects and ideas it is different. Recently we have had a chance to observe their meticulous monogamy.

When the jurors of The Society of Independent Artists fairly rushed to remove the bit of sculpture called the Fountain sent in by Richard Mutt, because the object was irrevocably associated in their atavistic minds with a certain natural function of a secretive sort. Yet to any "innocent" eye

Gorge, Stieglitz's summer retreat. Most important, however, were thirteen photos portraying the city of New York, at different times of day and from various viewpoints and perspectives. Since photography had been entirely excluded from the Armory Show, Stieglitz's choice had the air of a challenge; as its instigator himself confirmed, it was designed to test the role of photography as a profoundly modern art form and mode of expression. The idea was to show how modernism had already arrived in the United States and, in a certain sense, had even been created in the New Continent. *The Flatiron* (1902; p. 117) and *The Steerage* (1907) were among the celebrated images included in this one-man show. While Marin's vertical views transmit the intrinsic energy of New York, *The Flatiron*, with its various layers of perspective and soft rendering of atmosphere, highlights the outline of the famous building and crowns it as an unequivocal symbol of a new world and, above all, a new aesthetic. Immediately after the closure of the Armory Show, Stieglitz launched Picabia's exhibition at 291: sixteen works inspired by the impressions the French artist had gained of New York, his memories and his swift mental associations.

Fountain by Marcel Duchamp on exhibit at 291, from the magazine *The Blind Man* no. 2, May 1917. © Philadelphia Museum of Art/ Beatrice Wood Center for the Arts/Scala

The three exhibitions thus formed part of a distinct manifesto with regards to modern art and its celebration. While the Armory Show represented a sort of call to arms, on American soil, of the new art, Stieglitz presented himself as the figure who had inaugurated modernism. This he demonstrated not by boycotting the event, but by supporting it and revealing to all what the new language of the future might be.

So it was in 1917, when Duchamp, under the pseudonym 'R. Mutt', submitted his celebrated urinal, entitled *Fountain*, to the Society of Independent Artists. After it had been rejected, he sent it to 291. Not only did Stieglitz accept it, but he also found a suitable background for the object: Marsden Hartley's painting *The Warriors* (1913). Stieglitz photographed Duchamp's 'ready-made' positioned on a pedestal - the customary method of displaying rare works of art - and submitted the resulting picture to *The Blind Man* magazine (see p. 117).[24]

Freedom from the restrictions imposed by public institutions, the ability to form independent judgments and a constant attention to new trends led Stieglitz to make room for sometimes eccentric forms of artistic expression that had not yet been accepted into the mainstream: 'primitive' art and children's art, for instance. The first exhibition of the latter was held in 1912; it presented a series of drawings, watercolours and pastels by young artists between the ages of 2 and 13. The aim was to highlight 'visual writing' - a spontaneous form of drawing, free from convention, in which great European artists (above all Kandinsky and Klee) searched for the true seed of artistic creativity. Children's poetry also appeared on the pages of *Camera Work*, and again in 1914. In 1915 and the following year, children's work was once again shown on the walls of 291.

In 1909 Max Weber had introduced Stieglitz to African sculpture. Five years later Stieglitz finally mounted an exhibition of African art, announced in the July issue of *Camera Work* under the emblematic title *Statuary in Wood by African Savages: The Root of Modern Art*. The galleries of 291 had already hosted a show by Constantin Brancusi, which caused an uproar, and now the director of the gallery chose to emphasize the works' artistic significance rather than their anthropological interest, writing in the programme that it was the 'first time in the history of exhibitions that Negro statuary will be shown from the point of view of art'. Stieglitz considered the show, which was curated by Marius de Zayas, the Mexican artist and caricaturist, one of the most important ever realized: he kept a number of the exhibits for himself and used them years later in a series of portraits. Two similar exhibitions followed, providing continuity to Stieglitz's understanding of African art as the root of contemporaneity.

Stieglitz's show of African sculpture is one of the few exhibitions at 291 for which photographic documentation exists.[25] The display was revised while the show was already under way, and the images reveal a bold and attractive change in design that Edward Steichen claimed as his own. This can be seen as an example of his facility for design and communication that would later form an integral part of his experience at MoMA. Steichen tells the tale in his autobiography:

Alfred Stieglitz, *Brancusi exhibition at 291*, 1914.
© Museum of Modern Art, New York/Scala/SIAE

Back in New York, I found the Photo-Secession in the doldrums. An exhibition of African sculpture collected by de Zayas was on display. The burlap walls were dust-covered, and there was a dust-covered atmosphere about the whole place. No one came but the few 291'ers. I asked Stieglitz to let me brighten up that fine exhibition, and he agreed. I bought several reams of yellow, orange, and black sheets of paper. I took all the sculptures down and made an abstract geometrical pattern on the walls with the gay-colored papers, then put the sculptures back in place. The whole room came alive, the colored papers serving like a background of jungle drums. We all seemed in somewhat better spirits when Stieglitz said, 'Well, what are you going to do after this?' I told him this was the first time he had ever questioned me as to what I was going to do.

We had a few drawings by Braque and Picasso, and I determined that they would be fine material for the next exhibition. I bought some bolts of cheesecloth, the cheapest I could find, and we covered the dust-darkened burlap walls with it. A lad by the name of Zoler, who

had become a sort of shadow of Stieglitz, helped me pin up the cheesecloth. I took down the denim curtains hiding our storage shelves and sent them out to be dyed black. Then I hung the few Braques and Picassos on the walls and several of the more or less related African sculptures with them. The place looked clean, fresh, and alive again, but I felt something was missing. The exhibition needed a real object, a stone or a piece of wood or something. When I mentioned this, Zoler said he had a big wasp's nest in fine condition. A wasp's nest was perfect, especially in relationship to the Cubism we had on the wall, and it was brought in. The exhibition inspired my friend Charles Sheeler to make a couple of his finest photographs.[26]

Female artists also attracted Stieglitz's attention. He believed that they were capable of expressing the intuitive, spontaneous power he found in primitivism - something that that the pretentious and 'corrupt' art of many male artists failed to do. In addition to representing the female photographers of the Photo-Secession, in 1915 he mounted exhibitions by Marion Beckett and Katharine N. Rhoades, and in 1916 he even staged a show of drawings

Alfred Stieglitz, *Exhibition of African art at 291*, from *Camera Work*, October 1916.

and watercolours by his ten-year-old niece. During the final year of the gallery's activity, 1917, he included works by Georgia O'Keeffe in three different exhibitions. O'Keeffe, his new companion and future muse, was in Stieglitz's eyes one of the most interesting and deeply American artists of her generation. He called her 'great Child' or 'Child of nature', and was to dedicate the gallery's final show to her.

Much had changed since the early days of 291. The overall situation in New York had altered radically; other galleries had appeared, transforming the relationship between collectors and the public. Back in 1915 Stieglitz had already declared in the pages of *Camera Work* that he no longer wanted to exhibit European artists, but wished instead to concentrate on the energy and drive of new American art. So it was that in the last two years of 291's activity, in 1916 and 1917, Stieglitz turned to two American artists, one of whom was the young photographer Paul Strand. The exhibition of Strand's work opened on 13 March 1916 and was accompanied by a selection of photos published in *Camera Work* in October 1916 and June 1917, the journal's final two issues. No trace of a catalogue remains, nor any documentation that might hint at how the works were displayed. Neither do we have a clear idea of which images were included: we know of only five photographs that were definitely shown (and the celebrated *Wall Street* of 1915 was not among them). It was Stieglitz who suggested to Strand that he choose a 'sharper focus' for his images, following which he perfected his style, selecting his subjects more carefully, turning to the city around him and its stream of inhabitants for inspiration. At the same time, he tackled individual architectural elements, creating abstract views of great compositional power, following the example of the great contemporary European artists. This was the 'new photography': pure, direct, yet cultured and informed, full of classical echoes in its robust and formal construction. The choice to showcase Strand's talents arose from Stieglitz's need to demonstrate - particularly to his friends de Zayas and Picabia, who had accused him of exhibiting European artists almost exclusively - how he was still capable of discovering fresh American talent.

A series of photographs showing the layout of Georgia O'Keeffe's solo exhibition of 1917 in effect allows us to 'visit' the show. What comes across most strongly are the abstract, fluid forms that would remain the most recognizable characteristic of her work. Influenced by the theories of Kandinsky and the artists of the European avant-garde, O'Keeffe was trying to capture on canvas a sense of vital cosmic flux, an intense musical rhythm, a movement that echoed the primordial forces of water and wind. Together, the photographs of Paul Strand and the canvases of Georgia O'Keeffe embodied the American expression of the new aesthetic and, as Stieglitz believed, helped to reveal an America that had not yet been discovered in its entirety.

In June 1917, two months after the United States had declared war on Germany, Stieglitz closed 291. The situation had changed: the public seemed indifferent to the gallery's offerings, the war had altered everything and, furthermore, financial problems prevented him from continuing. Stieglitz's photograph *The Last Days of 291* (overleaf) is particularly symbolic: a warrior tired of battle seems no longer to have the strength to impose a new way of seeing art. Or rather, of experiencing it, appreciating it. Instead, as Stieglitz later remarked, he 'sat in the desolate, empty, filthy, rat-holed, ill-smelling little space that originally was part of the 291 ... Or I walked up and down in my overcoat, my cape over the coat, hat on, and still I would be freezing. There wasn't a trace of heat even though there were two radiator openings in the walls. I had nowhere else to go - no working-place, no club, no money. I felt somewhat as Napoleon must have on his retreat from Moscow.'[27]

Stieglitz had been curator of a place that was much more than simply a gallery: it was a unique place of development and creativity, in which the public could encounter the most recent developments in artistic expression. Stieglitz himself had played a central role in the choice of exhibitions, in identifying new talent, in selecting artworks, and in the rarefied way the galleries were arranged.

Thus, in answer to the question 'What is 291?' that appeared in *Camera Work* three years before the gallery closed, the replies were many.[28] The journal published all the sixty-nine responses it received: the reflections of artists, writers and several photographers (surprisingly few, in fact). The anarchic artist Adolf Wolff mentioned the air of freedom, spontaneity and enthusiasm that circulated at 291. Edward Steichen wrote a long essay recalling its most brilliant moments - such as the fundamental role 291 had played with regard to the Armory Show - but also the difficulties of its final years and its bewilderment in the face of recent international events. Man Ray described the rooms at 291, with their warm, neutral colour, continuously presenting new objects, taking even the most attentive visitor by surprise. He also highlighted how one man was at the centre of all this:

> The gray walls of the little gallery are always pregnant. A new development greets me at each visit, I am never disappointed. Sometimes I am pleased, sometimes surprised, sometimes hurt. But I always possess the situation. A personality lives through it all. Each time a different element of it expressed by the same means appears. There is a unity in these succeeding and recurring elements ... A Man, the lover of all through himself, stands in his little gray room. His eyes have no sparks - they burn within. The words he utters come from everywhere and their meaning lies in the future. The Man is inevitable. Everyone moves him and no one moves him. The Man through all expresses himself.

John Marin wrote a poem dedicated to the gallery and, of course, its authoritative 'father': 'The place is guarded, / well guarded it / by He - who jealously guards / its innocence, purity, sincerity / subtly guarded it / so that - it seems - not guarded at all / no tyrant - yet tyrant of tyranny / so shout - we who have felt it / we who are of it / its past - its future / this place / what place? / Oh Hell 291.' Others, such as Hodge Kirnon, the building's elevator man, responded to Stieglitz's question in a heartfelt manner: 'I have found in "291" a spirit which fosters liberty, defines no methods, never pretends to know, never condemns, but always encourages those who feel a just repugnance towards the ideals and standards established by convention.'

After Stieglitz resolved to close 291, he took up his camera once more but soon realized that he could not abandon his activity as a cultural provocateur. Despite no longer having an independent space, he organized several exhibitions at the Anderson Galleries, at 489 Park

Avenue. There, in 1925, he unveiled *Alfred Stieglitz Presents Seven Americans: 159 Paintings, Photographs, and Things Recent and Never Before Publicly Shown, by Arthur G. Dove, Marsden Hartley, John Marin, Charles Demuth, Paul Strand, Georgia O'Keeffe, Alfred Stieglitz*. Although created to celebrate 291's twentieth anniversary, in reality the exhibition bore little resemblance to previous shows, instead emphasizing the common vision of a heterogeneous but compact group of artists who (at least in theory) would give substance to a visual and existential experience that was profoundly American. The show was not the commercial success that had been hoped for.

In December 1925 Stieglitz rented a space in the same building as the Anderson Galleries. Rising from the ashes of 291, but inspired by a new and entirely American relationship with spirituality and artistic creation, the space was christened the 'Intimate Gallery' and was designed to concentrate on the 'Seven Americans' (the artists who participated in the inaugural show) in their role as 'mediators' of American-ness.[29]

His precarious financial situation prevented Stieglitz from continuing in this experiment, however, and in 1929 the Intimate Gallery was forced to close. That same year, Stieglitz nevertheless managed to find new premises from which he could pursue his promotion of selected artists. At 509 Madison Avenue he established An American Place, where, once again, John Marin, Arthur G. Dove and Georgia O'Keeffe were the artists whose works most frequently adorned its walls.[30] But subsequent events - the Wall Street Crash, the beginnings of the Great Depression and, on the contemporary art front, the foundation of the Museum of Modern Art in November 1929 - once more conspired to create challenging conditions.

Alfred Stieglitz (?), view of the *Ansel Adams* exhibition at An American Place, New York, 1936.
© Yale Collection of American Literature, Beinecke Rare Book and Manuscript Library

In 1936 Beaumont Newhall, whom the Museum of Modern Art's director, Alfred Barr, had appointed to organize a large retrospective on the history of photography, invited Stieglitz to preside over the scientific committee. The photographer refused. Newhall made one more attempt when, as head of the photography department, he offered Stieglitz a retrospective. Once again, Stieglitz did his utmost to back out and the project never saw the light of day. An American Place continued its exhibition programme - with all the inevitable ups and downs caused by disastrous financial management - until the week before Stieglitz's death, on 13 July 1946.

Alfred Stieglitz (?), view of the exhibition *Beginnings and Landmarks* at An American Place, New York, 1937. © Yale Collection of American Literature, Beinecke Rare Book and Manuscript Library

NOTES

1   Stieglitz's career was varied. Sarah Greenough notes: 'Throughout his long career, Alfred Stieglitz could be characterized in a number of ways: as an engineer, an amateur photographer, a pictorial photographer, and simply a photographer; as a proponent of the art of photography, an advocate for modernism, and a champion of modern American art. As he affected these transformations, he also reformulated his ideas and reoriented his mission. In his later years when he told the story of his life, he usually presented it as a seamless narrative in which his ideas and activities were inevitable, pre-determined, almost pre-ordained, and that his life and work formed a unified whole, rather than the disjointed and at times uncertain series of events that, in reality, they were.' See 'Alfred Stieglitz, Facilitator, Financier, and Father, Presents Seven Americans', in *Modern Art and America: Alfred Stieglitz and his New York Galleries* (exh. cat., National Gallery of Art, Washington, D.C., 2001), p. 277.

2   See Richard Whelan, *Alfred Stieglitz: A Biography* (New York: Little, Brown, 1995), pp. 107-15.

3   See S. Greenough, 'Alfred Stieglitz, Rebellious Midwife to a Thousand Ideas', in *Modern Art and America*, p. 24.

4   Whelan, p. 211.

5   The artists Stieglitz went on to show at 291 include Matisse (in 1908, 1910 and 1912), Toulouse-Lautrec (1909, 1910), Cézanne, Rousseau, Renoir and Manet (all 1910), Picasso (1911, 1914), Braque (1914), Elie Nadelman (1915), Max Weber (1910, 1911), Stanton MacDonald-Wright (1917, 1932), Alfred H. Maurer (1909), John Marin (1909 and later), Marsden Hartley (1909 and later), Arthur G. Dove (1912 and later) and Georgia O'Keeffe (1916, 1917).

6   Mounted in collaboration with Steichen, the show included works by Clarence H. White, Gertrude Käsebier, Stieglitz, Joseph Keiley, William Dyer, John Kerfoot, William Post, Sarah Sears and Eva Watson-Schütze, among others.

7   Whelan, p. 213.

8   Kristina Wilson, *The Modern Eye: Stieglitz, MoMA, and the Art of the Exhibition, 1925-1934* (New Haven and London: Yale University Press, 2009), p. 29.

9   Cited in Whelan, p. 234.

10 Ulrich Pohlmann has remarked how, in the early 20th century, the way in which photography was displayed changed once it had assumed the status of art and entered commercial galleries such as Stieglitz's 291: 'As a consequence of the reevaluation of the medium as an art form, its manner of display was transformed. Although, at the beginning, prints were intermingled with no regard for their format, subject or creator, photographs were increasingly treated as unique images.' See 'Les premières expositions de la photographie', in *Exposition et médias: Photographie, cinéma, télévision* (Lausanne: L'Âge d'Homme, 2012), p. 61.

11 Wilson, pp. 31-33.

12 Greenough, 'Alfred Stieglitz, Rebellious Midwife', p. 33.

13 Editorial, *Camera Work*, no. 14, April 1906, p. 48.

14 On the meeting between Stieglitz and Pamela Colman Smith, see Whelan, p. 218.

15 Whelan, p. 260.

16 Whelan, p. 262.

17 Ibid.

18 Whelan, p. 243.

19 Greenough, 'Alfred Stieglitz, Rebellious Midwife', p. 41.

20 Whelan, 255.

21 See Whelan, p. 251.

22 *Camera Work*, no. 49-50 (June 1917), p. 4.

23 Alfred Stieglitz, 'Notes made by Stieglitz' (edited by Dorothy Norman), in *Twice a Year. A semi-annual Journal of Literature, The Arts and Civil Liberties*, n.1, Fall-Winter 1938, pp. 97-98.

24 See *New York et l'art moderne: Alfred Stieglitz et son cercle (1905-1930)* (exh. cat., Musée d'Orsay, Paris/RMN, 2004), in particular Francis M. Naumann's essay 'The Blind Man. *Fontaine* de R. Mutt photographiée par Stieglitz', pp. 155-62.

25 These include Steichen's first show, the exhibition of African art already mentioned and an exhibition by Georgia O'Keeffe.

26 Edward Steichen, *A Life in Photography* (New York: Doubleday, 1963), chapter 5, facing plate no. 62.

27 Alfred Stieglitz, quoted in Dorothy Norman, *Alfred Stieglitz: An American Seer* (New York: Aperture, 1960), p. 116.

28 *Camera Work*, no. 47 (July 1914).

29 'It will be in the Intimate Gallery only that the complete evolution and the more important examples of these American workers can be seen and studied. Intimacy and Concentration, we believe, in this instance, will breed a broader appreciation. This may lead to a wider distribution of the work. The Intimate Gallery will be a Direct Point of Contact between Public and Artist. It is the Artists' Room.' Stieglitz is cited in Herbert J. Seligmann, 'A Vision Through Photography', in *America and Alfred Stieglitz: A Collective Portrait*, ed. Waldo Frank et al. (New York: The Literary Guild, 1934), p. 122.

30 Dorothy Norman described the gallery as follows: 'When you enter An American Place the first thing you feel is the quality of light ... The Place itself is divided into well-proportioned rooms of varying sizes, each almost square in shape. There are thresholds without doors, the rooms leading one into the other without barrier. The walls in the different rooms are painted from varying pale luminous grays to white, which reflect the light coming in through large windows, so that with the white ceilings and bare, uncovered light gray painted stone floors, there pervades the space a clear and subtly fluid ever varying glow of light ... A single threshold with door leads out of the larger rooms, separating them from a smaller section.

In this section there is space, small, enclosed, windowless, painted black, with two openings: a small aperture in the wall and a double threshold also without doors, both equipped to be tightly sealed so that no light may enter, none may be reflected. Here, darkness and room are one. At times there are pictures on the walls of the larger rooms, and on shelves in some of the smaller rooms there are books and more pictures, sometimes covered, sometimes visible. The door leading into this specific enclosed space - in simplest terms, space in America, "An American Place" - is open to all.' She also related the story of a visitor whom Stieglitz refused to help, in a mystifying fashion. To the confused bystanders, he explained: 'Something more was at stake than her knowing where she was for the moment. And I am not in business. I am not interested in exhibitions and pictures. I am not a salesman, nor are the pictures here for sale, although under certain circumstances certain pictures may have been acquired. But if people really seek something, really need a thing, and there is something here that they actually seek and need, then they will find it in time. The rest does not interest me.' See Dorothy Norman, 'An American Place', in *America and Alfred Stieglitz*, pp. 126-27.

Exhibition poster for *Film und Foto*,
Stuttgart,1929. © Gift of The Lauder
Foundation, Leonard and Evelyn
Lauder Fund/MoMA/Scala

6

The *Film und Foto* Exhibition of 1929

Francesco Zanot

The historical background to *Film und Foto*

During the 1920s the practice of Pictorialist photography lost its relevance as a form of artistic enquiry, having gradually been reduced to a style employed mostly by hacks and amateur photographers. The impetus for this change came from two directions. In the United States, the so-called 'straight photography' - an objective, realist style, in contrast to the painterly images of Pictorialism - had brought about a revolution. Pioneered by Paul Strand, it rapidly branched off in several directions, from the documentary style of Walker Evans to the formation of Group f/64, led by Ansel Adams, Willard Van Dyke and Edward Weston, whose manifesto declared: 'The Group will show no work at any time that does not conform to its standards of pure photography. Pure photography is defined as possessing no qualities of technique, composition or idea, derivative of any other art form. The production of the "Pictorialist," on the other hand, indicates a devotion to principles of art which are directly related to painting and the graphic arts.'[1]

In Europe, the role of instigating a similar break fell to German photographers, who occupied a position of central importance for the first time, just like the Düsseldorf School of Photography in the final quarter of the 20th century. The 1920s saw the dissemination of the work of three photographers who were conducting their own independent investigations, but who nevertheless shared the common notion of photography as a neutral device for the recording and faithful reproduction of the world around them: these were Karl Blossfeldt, August Sander and Albert Renger-Patzsch. To show things just as they were: this was the basic imperative that governed their work, and that brought them close to the most explosive artistic movement of the time in Germany, the Neue Sachlichkeit ('New

Objectivity'). Although it had not been planned, these three figures thus came to represent the movement's photographic wing. Only Renger-Patzsch, the youngest of the three, actively participated in the debate, declaring on several occasions his interest in using the camera in such a way that would emphasize certain qualities: accuracy (the subject matter described in the smallest detail), its ability to focus on foregrounds and neutral backgrounds, and its democratic aspect, since everything that ended up in front of the lens would be treated in the same way. In 1927 he wrote in the annual publication *Das deutsche Lichtbild*: 'The secret of a good photograph – which, like a work of art, may possess aesthetic qualities – is its realism ... Let us therefore leave art to artists and endeavor to create photography that will last because of its photographic quality, because its uniquely photographic property hasn't been borrowed from another art.'[2]

Shortly after, in 1928 and 1929, several books appeared that set out the basic tenets of this new approach: *Urformen der Kunst* ('Archetypes of Art') by Karl Blossfeldt, a significant work halfway between art and science, including 120 plates of botanical subjects;[3] *Antlitz der Zeit* ('Face of Our Time') by August Sander, a complex investigation of the social structure in Germany presented in the form of a typological inventory;[4] and *Die Welt ist Schön* ('The World is Beautiful') by Albert Renger-Patzsch, a sort of universal atlas in which photography highlights a consistent thread connecting all visible things, from plants to people, buildings and industrial objects.[5]

Albert Renger-Patzsch was not alone in conducting a specific programme aimed at renewing photographic expression in Germany during the 1920s. During the same period László Moholy-Nagy, a Hungarian of Jewish origin, who had moved to Berlin in 1920, developed an innovative approach for which he coined the label 'Neue Sehen' ('New Vision'). He promoted his idea from within the most significant 'laboratory of ideas' of the time, the Bauhaus, where from 1923 he had taught metalwork and run the preliminary course (*Vorkurs*) alongside Josef Albers. According to Moholy-Nagy, the value of photography lay above all in its ability to provide humankind with a type of reality that did not correspond with direct observation: the camera acted as a kind of prosthesis, extending and improving upon what we perceive with our eyes. Oblique horizons, close-up details, high or low viewpoints, movements frozen by rapid shutter speeds: these were some of the recurring motifs with which the New Vision proposed to broaden the common experience of seeing. The aim was to break down barriers between the various contexts in which photography might be used. From the medium's scientific, industrial and purely documentary practice, artists of the New Vision singled out a number of technical applications that they promptly plundered for their own ends. In his *Malerei, Photographie, Film* ('Painting, Photography, Film') – a text produced by Moholy-Nagy and Walter Gropius, and the eighth in a series of books published by the Bauhaus – alongside his own creative experiments and those of numerous colleagues Moholy-Nagy included a similar number of photos of a commercial or professional kind, such as X-rays, magnified images, astronomical photos, sporting snapshots and documentation of battle scenes. The first few lines of the book's introduction serve to outline his vision:

The camera has offered us amazing possibilities, which we are only just learning to exploit. The visual image has been expanded and even the modern lens is no longer tied to the narrow limits of our eye; no manual means of representation (pencil, brush, etc.) is capable of arresting fragments of the world seen like this; it is equally impossible for manual means of creation to fix the quintessence of a movement; nor should we regard the ability of the lens to distort - the view from below, from above, the oblique view - as in any sense merely negative, for it provides an impartial approach, such as our eyes, tied as they are to the laws of association, do not give; and from another point of view: the delicacy of the grey effects produces a sublimated value, the differentiation of which can transcend its own sphere of influence and even benefit colour composition. But when we have enumerated these uses, we are still far from having exhausted the possibilities in the field. We are only beginning to exploit them; for - although photography is already over a hundred years old - it is only in recent years that the course of development has allowed us to see beyond the specific instance and recognise the creative consequences. Our vision has only lately developed sufficiently to grasp these connections.[6]

Despite their similar points of departure, which led both to give the camera a role of primary importance in shaping the image, Albert Renger-Patzsch and László Moholy-Nagy came to widely differing conclusions. The main difference lay in where they focused their attention in terms of principal subject matter. In Renger-Patzsch's case, the photograph attempted to reflect the whole world, beginning with the accumulation of individual elements captured according to a consistent approach. The author vanished (his photographs, essentially, took themselves), leaving the way open for the pure expression of the beauty of everyday items. Moholy-Nagy's interest, on the other hand, shifted from content to means of expression: what drove his search, and that of the New Vision in general, was the process of transforming reality into image, which could be explored in many different ways. While the influence of Renger-Patzsch's minimalist leanings proved to be longer lasting - also because they were more deeply embedded in the German cultural tradition - the doctrine formalized by his Hungarian colleague enjoyed a period of overwhelming and undisputed success between the publication of *Malerei, Photographie, Film* and the end of the decade, when it faded and finally disappeared with the closure of the Bauhaus in 1933.

A series of large group photography exhibitions, more numerous in Germany during the 1920s than in any other country, constitute an ideal reference point for evaluating the expansion of the New Vision. On 15 August 1926 the *Deutsche Photographische Ausstellung*, a sort of survey of the latest and most outstanding innovations in the field, opened in Frankfurt. Although on this occasion creative and scientific images were shown side by side, there was no acknowledgment of a strong connection between them, and it seemed that they were linked only by an earlier conception of photography as something that was hand-produced. More important was the very presence of works by Moholy-Nagy and his colleagues, albeit relegated to a section dedicated to amateurs, and the fact that they were able to win the approval of an extraordinarily wide and varied audience.

This large exhibition was followed by *Foto-Malerei-Architektur* ('Photography-Painting-Architecture'), which opened on 12 February 1928 at the private art school founded by Johannes Itten in Berlin, and by *Neue Wege der Photographie* ('New Paths in Photography'), organized by the celebrated painter and typographer Walter Dexel, on view from 25 March until 6 May 1928 at the Kunstverein in Jena. Both exhibition titles took their inspiration from Moholy-Nagy - the former from his book *Malerei, Fotographie, Film*, first published in 1925 (and already reprinted in a revised edition in 1927), and the latter from an article of the same title that had appeared a few months earlier in the magazine *Photographische Rundschau und Mitteilungen*. In both shows not only were works of art exhibited together with several examples of so-called 'professional' photography, but a relationship was established between them. Whereas images that had arisen in different contexts had previously been shown together, with the primary aim of highlighting the numerous possibilities offered by the medium, in these later exhibitions the gap between photography's various functions was narrowed: the use of common materials and shared stylistic choices were emphasized. The professional photographs were no longer generic examples demonstrating a variety of technical and commercial applications, but images that were significant on account of their individual qualities. At the same time, fine art photographs no longer stood out from all the others but assumed the same formal characteristics as the images produced outside the art system. In his book *Avant-Garde Photography in Germany*, Van Deren Coke remarked: 'The 1928 Jena show truly marked the beginning of a wider acceptance not only of the new vision but also of new concepts in the art of *exhibiting*. Creative photographic works were shown alongside photographs used for industrial, technological, and scientific purposes. Thus, industrial and advertising photographs took on a less functional aspect when seen within the context of formalism as an aesthetic concern for its own sake.'[7]

The new order dictated by this change in perspective had already been perfectly illustrated by the poster for *Neue Wege der Photographie*: the names of the participating artists (Hugo Erfurth, Lotte Errell, László Moholy-Nagy, Lucia Moholy, Walter Peterhans, Hannah Reeck, Albert Renger-Patzsch and Umbo) were at the top, while a list of the various types of photograph to be found in the exhibition (portraits, aerial views, scientific photographs, photomontage, advertising images, etc.) appeared at the bottom. Art, in other words, was separate from other forms of photography, but only in conjunction with those other forms was it possible to represent the complexity of a technology so convincing that it had altered man's relationship with the world.

A third exhibition, *Fotografie der Gegenwart* ('Contemporary Photography'), opened on 20 January 1929 at the Folkwang Museum in Essen. Organized by Kurt Wilhelm Kästner, it included the screening of several films and was conceived as a travelling exhibition (it subsequently went to Hanover, Berlin, Dresden, Magdeburg and London). Although they did not originate within the movement itself, in terms of scope these two characteristics of the exhibition - the use of film, and the show's peripatetic nature - were excellent illustrations of the New Vision's ambitions.

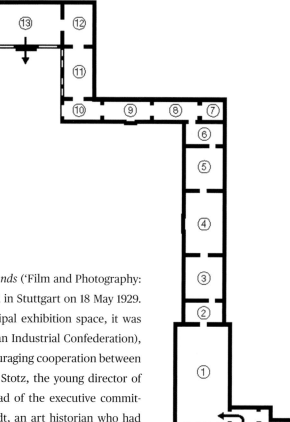

Film und Foto: The exhibition

Film und Foto: Internationale Ausstellung des Deutscher Werkbunds ('Film and Photography: International Exhibition of the Deutscher Werkbund') opened in Stuttgart on 18 May 1929. Located in the Städtischen Ausstellungshallen, a new municipal exhibition space, it was promoted and organized by the Deutscher Werkbund (German Industrial Confederation), an association founded in 1907 in Munich with the aim of encouraging cooperation between art, technology and industry. It was the brainchild of Gustaf Stotz, the young director of the Württenburg branch of the Deutscher Werkbund. As head of the executive committee, he invited three colleagues to join him: Hans Hildebrandt, an art historian who had once described himself as an expert in 'problems situated at the limits of, and intersection between, the visual arts and architecture';[8] Bernhard Pankok, professor of architecture at the Gewerbeschule in Stuttgart; and Jan Tschichold, a graphic designer specialized in book design and the theorist behind *Die neue Typographie* ('The New Typography'), published the year before. None of them had any particular expertise in the field of photography, but the task they set themselves was not so much selecting the works to be exhibited as establishing guidelines for the exhibition and the way in which it should be arranged. Indeed, they generally left the responsibility of filling it with images to a carefully selected group of specialists.

FiFo (as it was soon to be christened) was the first major international exhibition to explore the field of photography as a whole without reference to any hierarchies of use or function. Rather, it considered photographic images first and foremost as fundamental tools of communication in contemporary society, irrespective of their scientific value or artistic qualities. The exhibition was designed in such a way that visitors were taken from an introductory space through a series of thirteen rooms arranged in linear fashion following a double 'L' plan. Each room was dedicated to a specific theme, be it the work of an individual artist, a technical process, a photographic genre or, most often, the work of a particular country. Thus, in addition to the first room, which offered a broad introduction to the history and language of photography, there were rooms devoted exclusively to

Floor plan for *Film und Foto*, Städtischen Ausstellungshallen, Stuttgart, 1929.

photomontage, photographic propaganda, scientific photography and advertising. Among the individual photographers who were represented, there was a personal show by László Moholy-Nagy and a small room featuring images by the married couple Sasha and Cami Stone. Sections devoted to individual countries were given over to artists or academics, and in some cases officially labelled as collaborative efforts. The figures who were named explicitly include László Moholy-Nagy (Germany), Edward Weston and Edward Steichen (United States), El Lissitzky (Soviet Union), Piet Zwart (Netherlands), and Friedrich Traugott Gubler and Sigfried Giedion (Switzerland). Man Ray and Christian Zervos were unofficial curators of the French gallery, whereas Great Britain, Austria and Czechoslovakia participated in a minor role only. The result was a selection of over 1,000 photographs (the catalogue listed 991 works, but some would have been series) accredited to more than 180 different authors, including individual and professional artists, groups, archives and other sources.

Responsibility for the first, introductory section (p. 136) was assigned to Moholy-Nagy. Occupying by far the largest gallery in the exhibition, it began by outlining the history of photography and relied exclusively on works drawn from the collection of Erich Stenger. According to Beaumont Newhall, curator of photography at MoMA, Stenger's archive had represented 'the largest [collection] in private hands anywhere in the world'.[9] (It was subsequently acquired by Agfa-Gevaert, the Belgian film manufacturer.) There is no surviving list detailing exactly what this section included, but it was here that the foundations for considering photography as an autonomous means of expression were established. There were examples of the various supports used over the course of history, from daguerreotypes to salted papers, from ferrotypes to albumen, but their progression was not interpreted in an evolutionary sense. Indeed, the display showed a certain reverence for the earliest examples of Daguerre's technique, which was capable of providing an image that was sharper and more detailed even than the works of the Neue Sachlichkeit then on view. A panel hanging in the room stated: 'Daguerre could not retouch nor make copies. His photographs possess a strong documentary urgency. With Talbot's paper negatives, the grain of the paper surely makes itself felt, and this is the root of painterly photography. Because they also have a painterly sensibility, the creative intensity of Hill's photographic portraits may be mistaken for a traditional painterly aesthetic. In reality, their appearance stems from the insufficiencies of the photographic process.'[10]

Following the historical introduction, Moholy-Nagy illustrated the principles of the New Vision by means of a significant and highly effective display. This movement, being founded on respect for the objectivity of the photographic medium and its intermediate position between art and science, was perfectly in tune with the rationalist and functionalist outlook of the Deutscher Werkbund. Images that were extremely varied in terms of content and provenance were shown side by side; the logic was that any photograph could be 'read' beyond the purpose for which it was taken, thus influencing the viewer's perception of the world. In 1978, in a long essay devoted to *Film und Foto*, Newhall wrote: 'Moholy-Nagy was a pioneer in the recognition of what I choose to call the *found photograph*. Just as Marcel

Duchamp transformed a utilitarian bottle-rack into a piece of sculpture by selecting it and isolating it and exhibiting it, so did Moholy-Nagy elevate a news photograph taken by nobody-knows-whom to aesthetic consideration by creating for it a new context in an exhibition, or within the covers of a book.'[11]

Photographs of various kinds - zoological, astronomical, botanical, aerial, medical, forensic, industrial, journalistic - were exhibited in rows, on purpose-built structures that hung on the gallery walls. To give an idea of the arrangement, the image of a dirigible in flight (which came from the Luftschiffbau Zeppelin company in Friedrichshafen) shared the same space as photographs of a young gorilla by Hedda Walther, a murder victim in the middle of a street in Württemberg (sourced from the city's police headquarters) and the sky above the Archenhold Observatory in Treptower Park, Berlin. With the exception of some enlargements positioned at the edges of the partition walls, which also acted as graphic elements emphasizing the articulation of the space (a life-size X-ray of a male skeleton, realized on the island of Java by Dr Denis Mulder, hung beside the door that lead into the next

Room 4 of *Film und Foto*: El Lissitzky's selection of Soviet films and photographs. The exhibition also included machines designed by the director Sergei Eisenstein, on which the films could be watched.

gallery, for example), all the prints in this section were of the same relatively small size and unframed, mounted on simple white card. Photographers' names were not displayed alongside. The works were hung in three parallel rows, and the overall effect was something like a typical 17th-century picture gallery, with its standardized, geometrical arrangement. Any hierarchy of images was thus avoided; instead, the hanging invited the formation of hitherto unimagined connections. It was a perfect demonstration of photography's vitality and unitary essence.

Of the various sections that represented individual nations, those dedicated to Germany and the Soviet Union were evidently the most important: the former for the great quantity of pieces on show, and the latter for the complexity of its layout. In addition to several works by its curator, Moholy-Nagy, the German gallery featured some of the most significant artistic and cultural movements of the first half of the century: Neue Sachlichkeit, Dadaism and Bauhaus. By drawing attention to the critical role Germany played in the early 20th-century art scene, this collection of works also highlighted the particular interest in photography shown by German artists. In each of the three movements mentioned above, the use of photography assumed a different form: in the case of the Neue Sachlichkeit it

Room 1 of *Film und Foto*, curated by Moholy-Nagy and dedicated to the many genres and techniques of photography.

constituted an autonomous means of expression; it was dissected and combined with other idioms by the Dadaists; and within the Bauhaus it was used for recording architecture and other manufactured products - but in fact everyone employed this medium for a characteristic that corresponded closely to the rigour of the teutonic tradition: clarity.

Albert Renger-Patzsch was particularly well represented in the German section, with twenty or so prints, alongside works by Willi Baumeister, Karl Blossfeldt, Hugo Erfurth, Franz Fiedler, Lucia Moholy, Yva, and Bauhaus teachers including Herbert Bayer, Max Burchartz, Walter Peterhans and Umbo.

The whole of the fifth room was dedicated to the work of Moholy-Nagy and contained no fewer than ninety-seven images. It was a sort of homage to the principal promoter behind the idea of *FiFo* itself, examining his work as a photographer from the early experiments right up to images taken just before the exhibition. It began with a series of photograms - images taken without the use of a camera by placing objects directly onto light-sensitive paper, in a process very similar to the 19th-century 'photogenic drawings' of William Henry Fox Talbot - before arriving at more recent works in which the Hungarian-born photographer challenged the conventions of photography, choosing viewpoints that were unusually high, low, close or oblique.

A separate room was also reserved for photos by the husband-and-wife team of Sasha and Cami Stone. He was of Russian nationality (having been born in St Petersburg to Jewish parents), and Cami was Belgian. They had met in Berlin, and it was there that, in the 1920s, they had begun to experiment, borrowing elements of Dadaism, Constructivism, Bauhaus and De Stijl in accordance with the practice of the magazine *G*, to which they contributed along with Hans Richter (the publication's founder), Ludwig Mies van der Rohe, El Lissitzky and Walter Benjamin. The second room of *Film und Foto* - one of the smallest in the whole exhibition - presented a selection of approximately forty works from their studio and focused in particular on portraits, both of celebrities and ordinary people. This was but a part of their studio's eclectic output, which also included architecture (Sasha Stone's book *Berlin in Bildern* ['Berlin in Pictures'] was published in Leipzig that very same year, 1929), nudes, reportage and advertising. Members of the Berlin Dadaist group were the most conspicuous contributors to the section on photomontage, which was dominated by the presence of numerous collages created by John Heartfield for the covers of books and magazines, but also included works by Raoul Hausmann, Wieland Herzfelde, Hannah Höch, George Grosz and others. In addition to the wall-mounted photographs, in the middle of the room were cases containing various publications in which photomontages were reproduced (overleaf), highlighting the effectiveness of this technique when applied to mass communication. Photomontage was the preferred medium for political posters and pamphlets, but it was also used for advertising; the slogan *Benütze Foto als Waffe* ('Use photography as a weapon') that towered in block letters above the entrance to the room could well have referred to both. Displayed nearby was a large poster designed by Heartfield to support the German Communist Party during the 1928 elections, showing an open hand and the words

'The Hand Has 5 Fingers, With 5 You Grab the Enemy!' Any opportunity could be useful for winning the viewer over to one's own side.

The fourth room of *Film und Foto* was dedicated to the Soviet Union. It did not consist merely of works displayed on the walls, but encompassed an entire layout designed expressly by El Lissitzky, the artist, designer, typographer, architect and critic who was already a pioneer of the Constructivist and Suprematist avant-gardes in his own country. His design was not dissimilar to the one he had presented the previous year at *Pressa*, a huge exhibition on the international press held in Cologne, in which a series of pavilions were ranged along a two-mile stretch of the Rhine. In this instance, too, the images exhibited belonged exclusively to the category of journalistic photography – in other words, they avoided any claim to artistic value, but aimed to record various aspects of people's daily lives, from factory work to the transformation of agriculture, from traditional ways of life to new urban settlements.

Determining this approach were the guidelines that had been formulated by LEF (*Levi Front Iskusstv*, or 'Left Front of the Arts'), an association of intellectuals founded in Moscow in 1922 by Vladimir Mayakovsky to combine artistic practice with revolutionary commitment.

Above: **Room 3 of *Film und Foto*: the display cases contained books that featured the technique of photomontage.**

Opposite: **John Heartfield, *The Hand Has 5 Fingers, With 5 You Grab the Enemy!*, poster, 1928.** © Photo Scala, Florence/ BPK, Bildagentur für Kunst, Kultur und Geschichte, Berlin

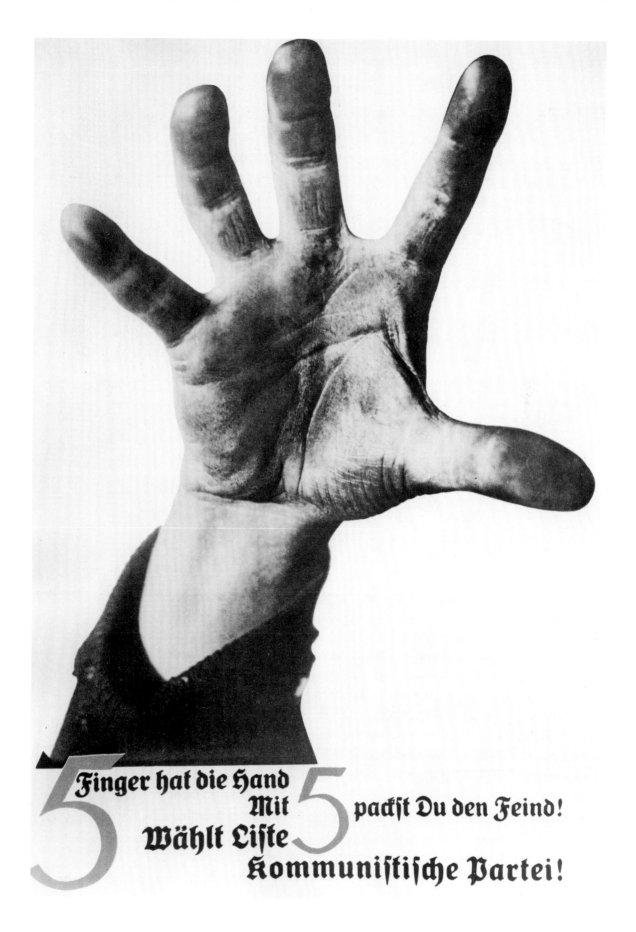

5 Finger hat die Hand
Mit 5 packst Du den Feind!
Wählt Liste 5
Kommunistische Partei!

According to LEF, anything produced had to be useful and devoid of individualist content. In the case of photography, this objective took two identifiable forms: the activity of the Oktyabr group, which formed around the figure of Aleksandr Rodchenko in 1928, and that of the Russian Association of Proletarian Photo-Reporters (ROPF), founded in 1931. Although the ROPF was officially established after *FiFo* had closed, both of these associations were fully represented, showing images by Alexander Rodchenko, Gustav Klutsis, Boris Ignatovich and Dmitry Debabov for the former group, and Max Alpert, Semyon Osipovich Fridlyand and Arkady Shaikhet for the latter. The fundamental differences between them can be rapidly summarized: whereas Oktyabr's members imposed a formal structure on their images that was specifically photographic and supposedly uncorrupted by bourgeois culture - echoing the writer Viktor Shklovsky's notion of 'defamiliarization' through the use of unusual viewpoints (Rodchenko also spoke of the 'revolution of perception') - the rules of the ROPF rejected any form of representation that could not be readily understood by all.

El Lissitzky positioned images by these photographers within a modular structure in light-coloured wood that allowed the prints to be hung at different levels, from floor to ceiling (p. 135). This arrangement underlined the boldness of certain perspectives, producing an overall effect reminiscent of the geometric structure of a Suprematist work, and fully immersing the public in an appropriately avant-garde context. His vision for the Soviet gallery was completed by the provision of ingenious devices, designed by Sergei Eisenstein, that allowed viewers to watch film clips. The exhibition was thus transformed into a vast apparatus celebrating post-revolutionary Soviet culture.

For the American section, located in the sixth room, Edward Weston chose the photographers he considered most representative of the field of so-called 'straight photography' - including not only those involved in investigations like his own, but also photographers who were more distant in terms of both geographical origin and subject matter. About twenty of his own photographs were also on display - all of them taken after 1922, the year of his definitive break with Pictorialism. There were portraits, nudes, details of factories and nature photographs, testifying to the medium's ability to describe any subject in the same way. Weston's portrait of his friend Manuel Hernández Galván, the Mexican senator and general, constitutes one of the high points of the entire show: taken at the precise moment when the subject fired his revolver, only the subject's face is framed, perfectly expressing the simultaneous narrowing and broadening of the human viewpoint that photography can achieve. Although the general's overall pose is lost for ever, it is possible to make out details in his face that would scarcely have been visible to the naked eye. Among the future members of Group f/64 shown alongside Weston were his son, Brett, and Imogen Cunningham. Older photographers, who in this case assumed the role of 'founding fathers', included Charles Sheeler, who showed some industrial photographs that inevitably impressed the German public, and Edward Steichen, whose photographic experiments were flanked by six fashion photos lent by *Vogue* magazine. The future of American photography was represented by a diverse group of authors: Berenice Abbott, for example, with a series portraying figures

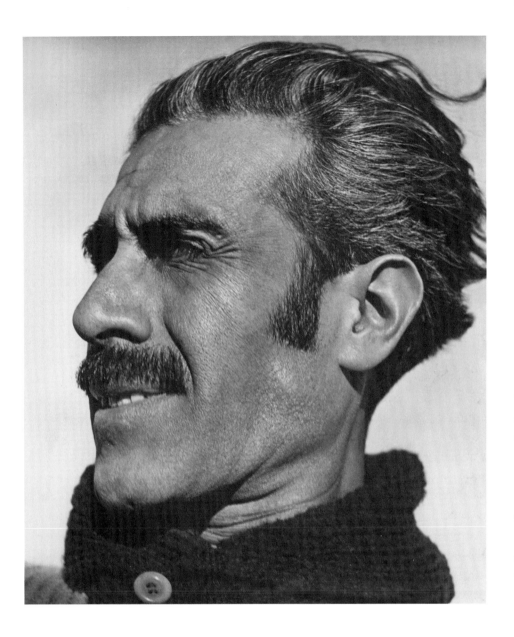

from the art and literary world that predated her more famous studies of New York architecture, began in 1929; Paul Outerbridge, who showed some sophisticated still lifes; and Ralph Steiner, former pioneer of the 'documentary style' in the United States, with his photographs of buildings, cars and electric circuits.

The French section included the only photographer in the whole exhibition who was no longer alive (with the exception, of course, of the introductory room). This was Eugène Atget, who was represented by five images of Parisian streets, perennially deserted except for the mannequins occasionally visible in shop windows (the famous photograph of the corset-maker's shop on the Boulevard de Strasbourg was included). Man Ray, who curated this room together with the publisher Christian Zervos, had recognized Atget as a precursor of Surrealism in 1926, when four of his images were published in *La Révolution Surréaliste*.

Edward Weston, *Manuel Hernández Galván, Shooting,* **1924.** Edward Weston Archive/Gift of the Heirs of Edward Weston. © 1981 Center for Creative Photography, Arizona Board of Regents

Numerous works by Man Ray himself were exhibited close by, including examples of the technique he had invented in 1921 and christened 'rayograph' (with a nod to his own name). This process was very similar to the one Moholy-Nagy adopted for his photograms – in which an object was positioned between a light source and the light-sensitive paper – but whereas Moholy-Nagy focused attention on the formal effects, Man Ray preferred to chose items on the basis of their evocative power: machinery, scissors, magnifying glasses, thermometers, light bulbs and so on. The French gallery was one of the most diverse in the whole of *FiFo*, just as the photographers it brought together were of different origins – a testament to the vivacity of the cultural scene in France and its extraordinary capacity to welcome artists from elsewhere. As well as the two selectors, Man Ray (an American) and Christian Zervos (whose origins were Greek), other contributors included Florence Henri (born in New York), André Kertész (Hungarian), Germaine Krull (born in Poland, she had also lived in Germany, France, the Netherlands, Brazil, Congo, India and Thailand) and Eli Lotar (who was of Romanian origin).

Organized by Friedrich Traugott Gubler, the director of the local Werkbund, in collaboration with Sigfried Giedion, an art historian and architecture critic, the small Swiss section provided an opportunity to view the country's excellence in the field of graphic design, including a selection of photographic posters created by Walter Cyliax, Ernst Keller and Walter Wäch. By contrast, the Dutch focused mainly on advertising, highlighting material by the section's designer and curator, Piet Zwart, produced for the cable company Nederlandse Kabelfabriek, and also including Paul Schuitema's sophisticated creations and his campaigns for Van Berkel Patent, a well-known company that produced weighing machines and

View of the *Film und Foto* section dedicated to Russia, Martin-Gropius-Bau, Berlin, 1929.

food slicers. Zwart himself admitted the lack of photographic experimentation in his own country in an article published on 9 July 1929 in the newspaper *Het Vaderland*: 'And the Netherlands? We only submitted a small contribution: it could not have been otherwise, given the anaemic nature of photographic practice in our country. It is typical that, despite the repeated reminders placed in the press about the preparation for this exhibition by the compiler of the Dutch contribution, not one professional photographer came forward, with the result that the compiler had to fall back on avant-gardists he himself knew.'[12]

Film und Foto concluded with a final gallery dedicated entirely to 'Photography and Advertising', prefiguring the importance of the medium in communications throughout the rest of the century.

But this was not all. As its title proclaimed, the event was enriched by the inclusion of a full cinematic programme, organized by Hans Richter (also the founder of *G* magazine). Stuttgart's central cinema, the Königsbau-Lichtspiele, was given over to screenings. Here, between 13 and 16 June, it was possible to view some of the most significant films produced over the previous decade throughout the world, with a particular emphasis once more on Germany and the Soviet Union. The most popular films included *The Cabinet of Dr Caligari* (1920) by Robert Wiene; *Varieté* (1925) by Ewald André Dupont; *Battleship Potemkin* (1925) and *October* (1928) by Sergei Eisenstein; *The Adventures of Prince Achmed* (1926; this was the first feature-length animation ever made) by Lotte Reininger; *Arsenal* (1928) by Alexander Dovzhenko; *The Passion of Joan of Arc* (1928) by Carl Dreyer; *The Circus* (1928) by Charlie Chaplin; and *The Man with the Movie Camera* (1929), directed by Dziga Vertov. There were also numerous experimental works, such as *Entr'acte* (1924) by René Clair; *Symphonie Diagonale* (1924) by Viking Eggeling; *Berlin, Symphony of a Great City* (1927) by Walter Ruttmann; *L'Étoile de mer* (1928) by Man Ray; *Lev Tolstoy* (1928) by Esfir Shub; and *The Bridge* (1928), *Breaking* (1929) and *Rain* (1929) by Joris Ivens. The choice of films highlighted the strong relationship between photography and cinema during the 1920s, as linguistic and formal tricks (phrases such as *bottom-up* and *top-down*; ways of framing, slanting horizons, double exposures, fade-outs, etc.) developed in one practice and were absorbed by the other. Together, these media provided a new vision of the world filtered through the lens.

FOCUS

FILM UND FOTO: ITS PUBLICATIONS AND ITINERARY

The catalogue for *Film und Foto* consisted of a small booklet (measuring approximately 21 × 14.5 cm, or 8¼ × 5¾ in.) containing seven brief texts, a list of exhibited works (described in general terms and undated) and twenty-one illustrations. After a brief introduction by Peter Bruckmann, the president of the Deutscher Werkbund, there followed essays by Edward Weston (writing about American photography), Vitaly Zhemchuzhny (Russian photography), Hans Richter (the latest experiments in film), and Olga Davydovna Kameneva and Mikhail Kaufman (both on Russian cinema). The catalogue's most significant text, however, was a brief summary of the plan behind *FiFo*'s creation, contributed by Gustaf Stotz, the director. He wrote:

> The development of photographic equipment, the invention of cinematography, and the perfection of technical image reproduction have created a specialized field that is unusually broad and world-encompassing in its range and influence. This development came so surprisingly that oddly enough, up until now, no one anywhere has tried to deal with this area in its entirety, to clarify the domain it affects, or to demonstrate its developmental possibilities through its best and newest accomplishments.
>
> The Stuttgart exhibition, engaged in by the Deutscher Werkbund at my suggestion, ventures the first attempt. It could not involve simply giving a cross-section of photographic production and its working methods, but rather it was important first of all to emphasize what is actually the working scope of photography: that which can be created only through photographic methods that are essential and belong exclusively to it. Consequently, the question of so-called artistic photography moved to the background ...
>
> The exhibition's intention had to do from the start with obtaining, as completely as possible, works by the personalities who were the first to recognize photography as our most up-to-date means of production, and worked with it accordingly.[13]

This declaration signalled a radical stance. Firstly, the debate surrounding the medium's artistic value, which had inspired numerous photographic shows in the past, was no longer current. Photography's worth was now taken for granted. As a result, the discussion had now moved onto a different level, namely the possibility of considering photography as a whole, without reference to hierarchies or divisions. Secondly, Stotz excluded the introduction of any works of a Pictorialist nature, thus demonstrating that *FiFo* was not merely an opportunity to bring together the disparate photographic practices of the early 20th century, but was founded on a precise theoretical and aesthetic programme corresponding to the dictates of the New Vision.

However, the catalogue was not the only publication to accompany *Film und Foto*. The great interest surrounding the Stuttgart exhibition, which was apparent even while it was still under preparation, resulted in two other books that can be considered as unofficial catalogues. The first publication was announced in *Die Form*, the official newspaper of the Deutscher

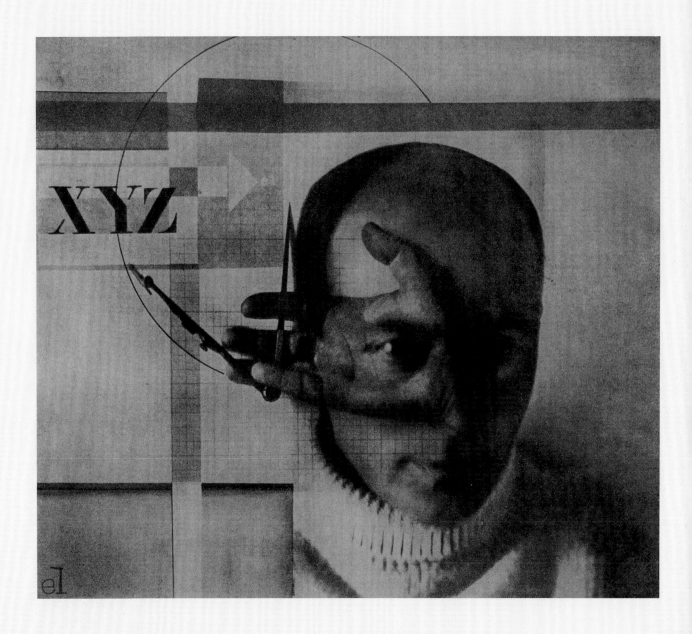

Werkbund between 1925 to 1934, on the very day the exhibition opened. Entitled *Es kommt der neue Fotograf!* ('Here comes the new photographer!'), it was edited by Werner Gräff, a member of Deutscher Werkbund, for the Berlin publisher Hermann Reckendorf. Over 128 pages long, it tackled the theme of the new photography principally from a technical point of view. It was structured like a sort of manual and drew on approximately 150 images to illustrate various technical processes. The chapters were divided up by theme, covering the close-up, photomontage, the photogram and advertising images, among other topics, and the book concluded with a didactic section on cameras.

Self-portrait of El Lissitzky for the cover of *Foto-Auge*, 1929.
© Private collection/Scala

By contrast, *Foto-Auge... Oeil et photo... Photo-Eye* adopted a more speculative approach. Published in Stuttgart by the Akademischer Verlag Fritz Wedekind, it contained a selection of seventy-six images by forty different photographers, only three of which were not included on the official exhibition list. Its editors were Jan Tschichold, who was responsible mainly for creating a design that was simple yet powerful (the cover featured El Lissitzky's celebrated self-portrait of 1924, reminding viewers that the modern artist was expected to know how to align eye, hand and camera), and the art critic Franz Roh, whose essay (translated into three languages, as can be inferred from the book's title) played a key role in securing the acknowledgment of photography as a medium in its own right with communicative value.

The success of *Film und Foto* was enormous and immediate: approximately 10,000 people visited between 18 May and mid-June. After it had closed on 7 July, the exhibition toured to many other cities: Berlin, Munich, Zurich, Basel, Gdansk, Vienna, Zagreb and, in reduced form, Tokyo and Osaka, where it concluded its travels in 1931. It was now the era of the Great Depression, but this did not dampen enthusiasm for photography, which would, after all, play a significant part in relaunching cultural creativity and the economy worldwide.

NOTES

1 Mary Street Alinder, Therese Thau Heyman and Naomi Rosenblum, *Seeing Straight: The f/64 Revolution in Photography* (Baltimore: University of Washington Press, 1992), p. 20.

2 *Das Deutsche Lichtbild* (Berlin: Robert & Bruno Schultz, 1927), p. 18, cited in Van Deren Coke, *Avant-Garde Photography in Germany 1919-1939* (New York: Pantheon Books, 1982), p. 13.

3 Karl Blossfeldt, *Urformen der Kunst* (Berlin: Ernst Wasmuth AG, 1928).

4 August Sander, *Antlitz der Zeit: 60 fotos Deutscher Menschen* (Munich: Transmare Verlag & Kurt Wolff, 1929).

5 Albert Renger-Patzsch, *Die Welt ist Schön* (Munich: Kurt Wolff, 1928).

6 László Moholy-Nagy, *Bauhausbücher 8: Malerei, Fotographie, Film* (Munich: Albert Langen, 1925); published in English as *Painting, Photography, Film*, trans. Janet Seligman (Cambridge, Mass.: MIT Press, 1967), p. 7.

7 Van Deren Coke, p. 11.

8 See Spyros Papapetros, 'An Ornamented Inventory of Microcosmic Shifts: Notes on Hans Hildebrandt's Book Project *Der Schmuck* (1936-1937)', in *Getty Research Journal*, no. 1 (2009), p. 89.

9 Editorial published on the death of Erich Stenger in *Image: Journal of Photography and Motion Pictures of the International Museum of Photography at George Eastman House*, no. 57 (1958).

10 See Friedrich Matthies-Masuren, 'Zur Werkbundausstellung Film und Foto in Stuttgart', in *Photographische Chronik*, 11 June 1929, reprinted in Bruce Altschuler (ed.), *Salon to Biennal: Exhibitions That Made Art History*, vol. 1: *1863-1959* (London: Phaidon, 2008), p. 230.

11 Beaumont Newhall, 'Photo Eye of the 1920s: The Deutsche [*sic*] Werkbund Exhibition of 1929', in David Mellor (ed.), *Germany: The New Photography 1927-33* (London: Arts Council of Great Britain, 1978), pp. 77-86. See also Jorge Ribalta (ed.), *Public Photographic Spaces: Exhibitions of Propaganda, from* Pressa *to* The Family of Man, *1928-55*, (exh. cat.: Museu d'Art Contemporani de Barcelona, 2009), pp. 117-34.

12 Piet Zwart, 'De Fifo te Stuttgart', in *Het Vaderland*, 9 July 1929, reprinted in Altschuler, p. 233.

13 Gustaf Stotz, in *Film und Foto: Internationale Ausstellung des Deutscher Werkbunds* (exh. cat., Stuttgart, 1929), pp. 11-12, reprinted in Altschuler, p. 226.

Wayne Miller, *The Family*
of Man, **New York, 1955.**
© Wayne Miller/Magnum Photos

Photography at MoMA: Four Landmark Exhibitions

Alessia Tagliaventi

Photography 1839-1937

On 13 March 1937 a press release from the Museum of Modern Art, New York (MoMA), announced: 'The aim of the Museum of Modern Art's first photographic exhibition is to show how photography since 1839 has become an increasingly vital method of visually interpreting man and his affairs. It is the hope of the Museum and of the Advisory Council that this exhibition will enable visitors to understand the principles which have governed photography since the earliest days and that it will demonstrate the capabilities of the camera as a medium of expression'.[1] Four days later, on 17 March, the Museum of Modern Art inaugurated *Photography 1839-1937*, the exhibition that would mark the beginning of the museum's systematic and consistent commitment to photography.

Alfred H. Barr, the museum's first director, had always been convinced that any museum of modern art should not only concentrate on painting and the traditional arts, but also cover architecture, design and photography. In *Looking at Photographs*, John Szarkowski - who later headed the photography department - writes: 'In 1929, when the acquisition of a painting by Cézanne was still considered adventurous, the proposition that photography deserved serious critical study would have been simply unintelligible to the leaders of most art museums. Alfred H. Barr, Jr., who became the founding Director of The Museum of Modern Art in that year, believed that the visual arts were so intimately interdependent that one medium could not be properly studied in isolation. It was his conception that a genuinely modern museum must pay serious attention to architecture, film, industrial design, and photography, as well as to painting, sculpture, drawing, and traditional prints. He is reported to have once said that his chief interest was in contemporary things before they became respectable.'[2] In fact, MoMA started to collect photographs in the spring of 1930, only a year after its inception, when it acquired an image by Walker Evans entitled *Lehmbruck: Head of a Man*; this became the twenty-third work to enter the museum's collections.

In the following years, the collection grew around a nucleus that consisted essentially of a group of West Coast photographers whose works had been offered to the museum by Albert Bender, a collector and patron of the arts based in San Francisco, at the suggestion of Ansel Adams. These images included many prints by Adams himself, as well as works by Edward Weston, Imogen Cunningham and other contemporary Californian photographers. In addition, the Farm Security Administration donated a selection of works by Walker Evans, Dorothea Lange, Arthur Rothstein and other members of its photographic department; and the museum benefited from 104 prints by Man Ray, gifted by the collector James Thrall Soby.

In 1932 MoMA staged *Murals by American Painters and Photographers*: the museum's first exhibition in which photography played a primary role.[3] Four years later, in the spring of 1936, as the 100th anniversary of the medium's invention approached, Alfred Barr invited Beaumont Newhall, an art historian and the museum's librarian at the time, to curate a historical exhibition on photography. This would be the first major photography show to be held at MoMA.

Since neither the curator nor the museum had yet made names for themselves in the photographic world, it was decided to nominate an international advisory board that was to serve as sponsor and thus compensate for the institution's lack of standing. The first person Beaumont Newhall invited to become a member of the committee was Alfred Stieglitz, the patron saint of artistic photography in America. Yet Stieglitz scornfully turned down the invitation: he had an extremely negative view of the exhibition and of Newhall as curator, maintaining that MoMA's exhibition programme was too commercial and reliant on economic and political factors. In a letter to a friend, Stieglitz wrote: 'I have nothing against the Museum of Modern Art except one thing and that is that the politics and the social set-up come before all else. It may have to be that way in order to run an institution. But I refuse to believe it … Of course there is always a well-meaning "the best we could do under the circumstances," etc. etc. The reason for not supporting [Newhall] was that I realized that the spirit of what he was doing was absolutely contrary to all I have given my life to.'[4] Stieglitz also refused Newhall's offer to dedicate the exhibition and its catalogue to him, in recognition of the pioneering work he had carried out on photography's behalf over the years, as well as the invitation to exhibit many of his images in the show. He allowed only the use of material that had already been published; his work was thus represented solely by photogravures taken from *Camera Work*.

The second person Newhall invited to join the committee was Edward Steichen, who immediately accepted. The other members were C. E. Kenneth Mees, director of research

View of the exhibition
Photography 1839–1937,
New York, 1937. © Museum of
Modern Art, New York/Scala

at the Eastman Kodak Company in Rochester, New York; Douglas A. Spencer, president of the Royal Photographic Society of London; Charles Peignot, publisher and editor of *Arts et métiers graphiques* in Paris; László Moholy-Nagy, artist and former teacher at the Bauhaus in Dessau; Paul Rotha, director of productions at the Strand Film Company in London; and Alexey Brodovitch, art director of *Harper's Bazaar*. In his search for images for *Photography 1839-1937*, Newhall travelled to Europe, spending six weeks in Paris and London, but not visiting Berlin because of the political situation there. This meant that significant German photographers such as Albert Renger-Patzsch and August Sander were not represented, and the majority of images were by French, English and American photographers. Newhall's exhibition was not explicitly concerned with the old issue of photography's status among the arts, but went further in fully affirming its position, for example by highlighting the photography of the European avant-garde.

The type of radical and extensive survey that Europeans had been able to see for over a decade, especially in Germany, now appeared in America for the first time. In terms of organization, Newhall's exhibition in fact followed the series of major exhibitions held in Germany between 1925 and the early 1930s, placing the camera at the centre of the technological aesthetic that marked the post-war years. Newhall conceived his exhibition with a fundamentally didactic purpose in mind, seeing it as a lesson on the evolution and specialization of photographic techniques. This was a great novelty compared to the usual practice of American art museums. In fact, in this first exhibition, rather than defining a photographic aesthetic in a strict and exclusive sense, Newhall chose to place at its core a history of the medium's technological development, selecting a great variety of images ranging from the earliest daguerreotypes to the latest X-ray images. The works also derived from a wide range of sources, both 'high' and 'low': rare prints were displayed alongside photographs from magazines, advertising, anonymous and scientific images, and even film stills.

Entrance to the exhibition
Photography 1839–1937,
New York, 1937.
© Museum of Modern Art,
New York/Scala

Reviewers were surprised by this inclusive selection, and it aroused a certain amount of criticism. Lewis Mumford, for example, writing in the *New Yorker*, declared: 'What is lacking in the present exhibition is a weighing and an assessment of photography in terms of pure aesthetic merit - such an evaluation as should distinguish a show in an art museum from one that might be held, say, in the Museum of Science and Industry. In shifting this function onto the spectator, the Museum seems to me to be adding unfairly to his burden and at the same time reducing its own sphere of influence.'[5] At the same time, however, as Christopher Phillips affirmed in 'The Judgment Seat of Photography', it did not escape the most sophisticated critics that, in reality, the display reflected the concept expressed by Newhall in the exhibition catalogue, which outlined photography's history 'primarily as a succession of technical innovations - independent, for all intents and purposes, of developments in the neighbouring graphic arts or painting - that were to be assessed, above all for their aesthetic consequences'.[6]

The exhibition consisted of 841 images arranged over all four floors of the museum - and was thus on a scale entirely unusual for the time. The photos were often grouped together on large panels with mounts, and, in the majority of cases, transparent plastic was used instead of glass. At the entrance to the exhibition, visitors were met by a life-size photograph of a man with a 35mm camera in his hand (opposite). Mounted on a wooden frame, the image was suspended from the ceiling. Its style and tone evoked the 'New Vision' aesthetic, but was also reminiscent of advertising posters. This photograph of an everyday middle-class man holding the latest camera could be seen as a reference to, and celebration of, the growing practice of amateur photography at that time. It was placed beside an enlargement of a mid-19th century engraving showing a daguerreotypist with his photographic equipment. The posters at the exhibition's entrance were designed by the Swiss graphic designer Herbert Matter, who was noted for his pioneering use of photomontage and for his innovative and experimental designs.

In the corner of the first gallery, next to the entrance and opposite the information desk, a large camera obscura had been set up. It projected the upside-down image of the receptionist; visitors could go inside in order to grasp the fundamental principle of how a photographic image was created. They were then ready to make their way through the exhibition and to follow the progress of photographic technology. Having emerged from the camera obscura, visitors arrived in a dimly lit room where daguerreotypes were exhibited in wall cases.

Apparatus of various kinds could also be found throughout the four floors of the museum - particularly items connected to the major techniques that had developed since 1835 (these included several tools used by William Henry Fox Talbot), such as equipment for developing daguerreotypes. The images and their accompanying objects were grouped according to technique (daguerreotypes, calotypes, collodion, gelatin silver bromide, etc.) and contemporary application (press photography, infrared, X-rays, astronomical and 'creative' photography). In other words, Newhall considered that a thorough understanding of

One of the rooms at the exhibition
Photography 1839–1937, New
York, 1937. © Museum of Modern
Art, New York/Scala

technological progress was indispensible if visitors wished to grasp the development of the medium itself. Within each sequence photographers followed each other in simple alphabetical order.

The abundant display of different materials and techniques might in some ways have reflected Newhall's great interest in the ideas of Moholy-Nagy and his New Vision. Christopher Phillips maintained that 'Newhall's Exhibition ... clearly seems guided more by Moholy-Nagy's expansive notion of *fotokunst* than by Stieglitz's *kunstphotographie*.'[7] Indeed, Moholy-Nagy was one of Newhall's principal advisers during the exhibition's preparation stage. But in reality Newhall's conception of the installation was rather different from Moholy-Nagy's usual approach, which combined historical and contemporary works within the same space. Instead, Newhall organized the images according to strict chronological order, leading visitors through the sequence of rooms and a series of technological innovations, and finally presenting them with a collection of contemporary works and 'non-creative' photography.

In addition, the installation included several 'atmosphere rooms': rooms arranged in such a way as to evoke the atmosphere of a particular historical period, together with features associated with the various techniques. The exhibition began, in fact, with a room devoted to the daguerreotype, where the walls were painted in 'Morocco-leather' brown, and the display cases were lit from inside and lined with red velvet. In the next room, which was dedicated to the calotype, the walls were painted dark blue, while light blue was used for the cornices. In the section devoted to contemporary French photography, the walls were painted greenish-grey, while the photographs were framed and mounted in series under glass plate. This method of conceiving the display resulted in a sort of aestheticization, especially of the 19th-century photography. At the same time, however, through the didactic and interactive elements - more commonly found in scientific exhibitions than artistic ones - Newhall illustrated and explained the various technical processes that lay at the heart of the story of photography. The exhibition thus preserved a strongly didactic focus.

The final part of the exhibition route presented sections entitled 'Press Photography, Scientific Photography, Moving Pictures'. The images here were arranged in groups, mounted on card or exhibited in light boxes. They included a picture that appeared in the *New York Daily Graphic* on 4 March 1880: the first direct reproduction of a photograph to be featured in a daily newspaper. There was no single section devoted to photomontages or photography books. As Newhall wrote in the catalogue: 'An exhibition covering so broad a field must necessarily be limited. Certain omissions have been deliberate. Book illustration and the photomechanical reproductive process demand an exhibition in themselves. The development of the photo-montage ... and layout, while dependent on photography, has an independent esthetic character.'[8] Similarly, the narrative and serial aspects of photography were virtually ignored in favour of the singularity and originality of the photographic print. Likewise, there was no true investigation of political or social context (Lewis Hine, for example, was not represented in the show).

However, in his first written history of photography, conceived as an introduction to the catalogue, Newhall identified two principal interpretations or traditions that, in his view, ran through the entire history of the medium: the concepts of detail and of fidelity of tonal value. For him, these were photography's most important intrinsic traits. As he wrote in a new preface the following year, his aim in organizing the exhibition as he did was to construct 'a foundation by which the significance of photography as an aesthetic medium can be more fully grasped'.[9] This focus on its formal aspects - on what Newhall called the 'relationship between technique and visualization' - represented the first signs of a formalist aesthetic in MoMA and a recognition that the photographic image was something of cultural value. In other words, Newhall inscribed photography within the history of art, establishing a canon and a historical approach based on the notion of the print as a form of personal expression, and on the medium's ability to produce proper compositions with proper attention to detail.

The catalogue for *Photography 1839-1937*, published by the Museum of Modern Art itself, was chosen by the American Institute of Graphic Arts as one of the fifty 'best printed' books of the year. It contained Beaumont Newhall's lengthy introductory essay on the history of photography, which was re-edited in 1938 and published under the title *Photography: A Short Critical History*. This work subsequently became the celebrated *The History of Photography*, which was reprinted numerous times over the years and is still available today. It soon became a canonical text and established itself as the core narrative of the medium's history, having served to broaden a debate that was practically non-existent in the United States before Newhall's exhibition.

In conclusion, Newhall's installation seemed to express a dual conception of photography as simultaneously an aesthetic practice and a series of technological innovations that had shaped, and continued to shape, modern culture. Of all MoMA's photographic exhibitions, *Photography 1839-1937* undoubtedly presented the most varied treatment of the medium and the widest demonstration of its potential as a means of expression. After it had closed in New York, the exhibition travelled throughout the United States and was shown in Philadelphia, Boston, San Francisco, Milwaukee, Cleveland, Buffalo, Manchester (New Hampshire), Andover and Springfield (Massachussetts). *Photography 1839-1937* met with great public and critical acclaim, and the artists it featured went on to become some of the best-known figures in photography's history. On 29 March 1937 *Time* magazine called it 'the most exhaustive photography exhibition ever realized in the United States'. On 19 March, the *New York Herald Tribune* published an emotional account of the visual experience of visiting the show:

> Mounting from one floor to the next, one comes up through this short hundred years of achievement, from the first fading but magic successes of Daguerre, Talbot, and Bayard, to the marvels of the natural-color photography of today. One sees the camera as the technically triumphant instrument of exact depiction, as a sensitive medium of artistic record, as a device creating new imaginative worlds out of its own limitations and possibilities, going on to exploit

Exhibits on display at
Photography 1839–1937,
New York, 1937.
© Museum of Modern Art,
New York/Scala

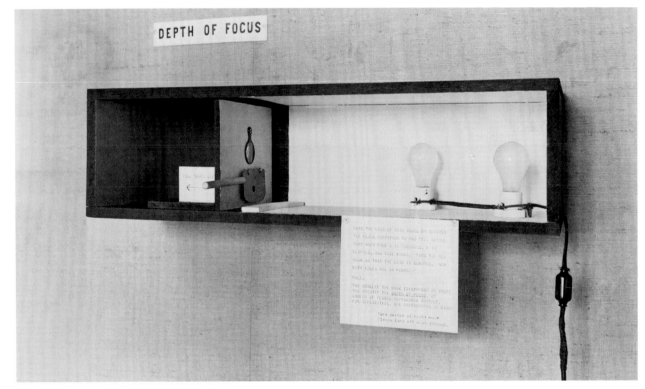

DEPTH OF FOCUS

its deliberate distortions of light and form for their own sake until finally even the camera itself disappears, leaving the abstract 'shadowgraphs' of Man Ray and others. Simultaneously, one sees it reaching out to report the whole of experience, developing motion, penetrating to the structure of the atom and of the giant star cluster. One sees it spreading in another sense, first to books, then to current magazines and newspapers and advertisements and its own pictorial theaters, until it makes the daily world of the modern man a pictorial world to a degree beyond anything in human experience.[10]

The exhibition thus succeeded in expressing the powerful notion that photography, by virtue of its versatility and technical characteristics, was capable of bringing art to ordinary people without clinging to a curatorial canon reserved for the convenience of experts. In this sense, as Christine Y. Hahn has remarked, the curator almost performed the role of an archivist: 'one who gathers, but leaves the choice and creation of meaning to the viewer'.[11]

In reality, situating an exhibit within an art museum always implies an act of judgment, just as the selection process defines an aesthetic and thus means taking sides in a sphere where various aesthetic viewpoints compete. Right from the outset Beaumont Newhall was aware of this, to the extent that, years later, he would write in his autobiography: 'When I began to make my selection of photographs for the 1937 retrospective exhibition, I treated soft-focus work as an aberration that should be eliminated. And I found a strong affirmation of straight photography in the magnificent nineteenth-century work of Nadar, the Brady school, Hill, and Adamson, among others, and in the twentieth-century work of Eugène Atget, Alfred Stieglitz, and later Ansel Adams, Paul Strand, and Edward Weston.'[12] Nonetheless, this was the precise model on which, three years later, the first department of photography in the entire history of museums was founded. 'The message of my historical survey,' Newhall wrote, 'and of my catalogue, and of all the work I have done for the museum, was simply this: photography is a fine art, on a par with painting, sculpture, prints, architecture, and cinema. My 1937 exhibition and catalogue, and the foundation of the department of Photography, changed the way in which people viewed the medium. It persuaded people to look at and collect photographs and the galleries to exhibit them.'[13]

One of the rooms at the exhibition
Photography 1839–1937, **New
York, 1937.** © Museum of Modern
Art, New York/Scala

FOCUS

MOMA'S DEPARTMENT OF PHOTOGRAPHY

ALESSIA TAGLIAVENTI

For over half a century, through its influential exhibitions and publications, the Department of Photography at MoMA has helped shape our general 'horizon of expectancy' with regard to photography. Beginning in 1940, its history represents a fascinating journey through the artistic and curatorial practices that characterized Western culture and photography in the post-war years. It was within this context that the dominant aesthetics in the rich and varied world of photography were decided – but not without conflict. What happened during that period helped shaped the photographic landscape and still, whether we like it or not, serves as a model today.

However, the history of photography at MoMA – like all histories – is neither linear nor uniform, but the result of cultural battles and compromises that reflect the mood of the time. On the one hand, MoMA's photography department played a vital role in bestowing on photography what Walter Benjamin referred to as the 'aura' of traditional art (a genre that, according to him, photography itself might be capable of overthrowing); but at the same time it has increasingly highlighted what Benjamin viewed as the consequence of the technical reproducibility of images, namely their political and social function.

The creative minds behind the new department were undoubtedly Beaumont Newhall and Ansel Adams, who benefited from the vital support of Alfred H. Barr, the museum's director, and David H. McAlpin, a banker, lawyer and generous patron of the arts. In his introduction to *Making a Photograph*, published in 1935, Adams had spoken of the inadequacy of institutions then involved with photography and expressed the need for a place that would enable it to be studied seriously: 'What is required above all else is a number of centralized institutions which combine competent instruction in theory and practice with library and Museum features. Repositories of the most significant photography, past and contemporary, are sorely needed. The understanding of photography as a form of art implies much more than a knowledge of physics and chemistry and a superficial education in the aspects of painting and other media. It is necessary to study photography itself – to interpret the medium in its own terms and within its own limitations.'[14]

Ansel Adams was ahead of the times and, before it had occurred to anyone else, had not only identified a gap that needed to be filled, but also set out a plan to do so. Three years later, Beaumont Newhall discovered in Adams a natural ally and, in a letter dated 14 February 1938, wrote: 'We are considering setting up an ambitious photographic section to the museum, to collect and exhibit photographs, and to publish monographs and picture books – all in the cause of what we consider to be the most creative aspect of photography. I remember being impressed by the lines in the foreword your book about the need of such a project. As we shall have to raise a substantial sum of money to make the project really worth while, and as we want to make the project fit into the needs of the outstanding photographers of the country, I should appreciate very much an expansion of the foreword to *Making Photographs*, in the form of a letter.'[15]

Adams not only promoted the founding of a department devoted to photography within MoMA, but worked side by side with Newhall in suggesting ways in which this goal could be achieved. The first step was to set up a committee that would guarantee adequate support, and that would possess the necessary authority and prestige to present the project to MoMA's board of trustees. The plans envisaged the creation of a substantial collection of historical and contemporary photography, a library and a study room, along with an extensive exhibition, lecture and conference programme. In addition, Adams himself would act as an intermediary with David McAlpin - one of MoMA's great benefactors, particularly in the advancement of photography as 'fine art', who immediately set aside $1,000 towards the creation of a department. Finally, on 17 September 1940 the museum's board of trustees approved Newhall's proposal and appointed him curator. The other members of the committee were David H. McAlpin, president; Ansel Adams, vice-president; John E. Abbott, executive vice-president of the museum; Alfred H. Barr, Jr., director of the museum; Dr Walter Clark, assistant to the director, Research Laboratory, Eastman Kodak Company; Archibald MacLeish, poet and librarian at the Library of Congress; Laurance S. Rockefeller, director; and James Thrall Soby, collector and art critic.

So it was that the first photography department in museum history was born. At the time it was established, MoMA's collection already consisted of 700 prints. The new department's first declared objective was to fight for the full recognition of photography as an art form. In a letter dated 21 March 1941, Newhall wrote to Adams: 'Our job, as I see it, is to stress originality, quality and - if one can use the word - "character" in photography. We shall present photography as one of the arts - not as a broad and universal method of communication, without regard to quality, but with stress on universality and quantity.'[16]

Newhall's objectives were clear from the start, having been revealed in the *Photography 1839-1937* exhibition. From the beginning, the new department of photography intended to adhere to the path mapped out by Alfred Stieglitz. In 'The New Department of Photography', which appeared in the *Bulletin of the Museum of Modern Art*, David H. McAlpin proclaimed this affiliation, remarking: 'Photography is deeply indebted to Alfred Stieglitz - for his courageous pioneering and experimentation, for his struggle to have it recognized as a medium of artistic expression, for his impact on more than a generation of workers and his uncompromising demands on them to achieve the finest quality of craftsmanship and perception, and for his influence on the taste and discernment of the public. He more than anyone else has summed up with the camera his experiences and feelings about life. At the inception of this Department, we are happy to acknowledge his outstanding contributions to Photography.'[17] Newhall and Adams - disciples of Stieglitz in the struggle to gain recognition for photography as a form of artistic expression - adopted aesthetic quality as their only benchmark. The museum's task was to raise photographers' artistic standards, and to educate the public and increase its ability to make aesthetic judgments. In order to achieve this, the department was to show only the best photographs, both past and present. In other words, it was to become both a guide and focal point for debate regarding the aesthetics of photography.

The first exhibition presented by the new department was *Sixty Photographs: A Survey of Camera Esthetic*. Newhall and Adams worked together on the organization of the show and on selecting the images. The exhibition opened on 31 December 1940, running until 12 January 1941. Its aim, as stated in the *Bulletin*, was to introduce the new department through a visual survey of photography's various aesthetics: 'The sixty photographs indicate various individual approaches to the medium. These represent, without regard to chronology, a range of vision from objective, almost literal, interpretation of fact to abstract creation of form by the camera-less shadowgraph.'[18] It would present the fundamental characteristics of photographic imagery, from David Octavius Hill to the works of the present day, considering the images for their intrinsic aesthetic qualities and removing them entirely from any historical or artistic context. Supporting this approach was the fact that, according to the original floor plan for the exhibition, the photographs were to be displayed without any titles, dates or other information, so that the viewer could concentrate on looking without being distracted or influenced in his or her judgment by historical or social considerations. Instead, it was planned that the catalogue would provide all the necessary information. In the exhibition's final design, however, it was decided that a few essential details should be displayed alongside the photographs. Each of the sixty photos on display had been chosen as a standalone work, but once they were presented together they offered, in the words of the curator, the 'clear evidence of an understanding of the qualities, limitations, and possibilities of photography'.[19]

Sixty Photographs occupied only a single gallery on the museum's top floor, Newhall on this occasion distancing himself from the experimentation and grandeur of *Photography 1839-1937*. It consisted of sixty black-and-white photographs in white mounts, positioned at eye level in the neutrally painted galleries. The works were thus presented in the same way as paintings and had the same status conferred upon them: that of objects worthy of official admiration. The exhibition won Stieglitz's approval, and there was a reasonable stream of visitors, but it did not match the numbers for *Photography 1839-1937*. It was also received in a lukewarm manner by the press. In a letter, Newhall informed Adams that Stieglitz had visited the exhibition on its opening day, commenting: 'Mistakes, yes; not the way I would have done it, but sincere and fine ... You have a lot to fight for. So long as you do the things you believe in, so long as you can please yourself, all will be well. You'll be criticized. Correct only the misstatements, the falsifications.'[20]

As far as the critics were concerned, Stieglitz was right. In 'The Judgment Seat of Photography', Christopher Phillips describes how, during Beaumont Newhall's time there, the majority of the press spoke out angrily against the Department of Photography's modernist aesthetic regime, describing it as 'snobbish', 'pontifical' and shrouded in 'esoteric fogs'. The press, still unaccustomed to discussing matters of photography, sided almost unanimously with the wider public of amateurs.

The same sentiments, however, also began to spread within the management of the museum itself. Opposition to the vision promoted by Newhall and Adams came not only from important writers and critics such as Tom Maloney (then editor of *Camera Craft Magazine* and

U.S. Camera Books), but also the influential figure of Edward Steichen, who maintained that MoMA should treat photography as a wider cultural phenomenon and an important means of communication rather than a language for personal expression.

Within the department the conflict between the conception of photography as an art and the notion of photography as a modernist idiom and technology intensified during the 1940s. The debate itself highlighted perfectly the significant philosophical and critical issues raised by the introduction of photography into museums.

THE MUSEUM GOES TO WAR

The year 1939 proved to be a significant one for MoMA. With much celebration, its new site, which it still occupies today, was opened on 10 May, designed by the modernist architects Philip. L. Goodwin and Edward Durell Stone. In addition, 1939 was the museum's 10th anniversary, which was marked by a series of important exhibitions, increasing its international reputation. History, however, was about to disrupt proceedings. The first exhibition held in the new building had not yet drawn to a close when, on 1 September, World War II broke out. The United States did not officially enter the war until 7 December 1941, following the attack on Pearl Harbor. The intervening years marked not only a period of great activity for the museum, but also a fresh opportunity to construct and affirm its own cultural role and identity in American society.

In June 1941 the Central Press News Service issued a story that appeared in many newspapers: 'The latest and strangest recruit in Uncle Sam's defense line-up is - the museum!' The article quoted the chairman of MoMA's board of trustees, John Hay Whitney, who defined the museum as 'a weapon for national defense'.[21] In his history of MoMA, *Good Old Modern*, Russell Lynes writes: 'In a sense the Museum was a minor war industry and, like other such enterprises, entered into contracts with the procurement bureaus of the federal government. Its product was a cultural one, to be sure. It executed thirty-eight contracts with the Office of the Coordinator of Inter-American Affairs, the Library of Congress, the Office of War Information, "and other agencies" before the war was over, and the contracts added up to $1,590,234.'[22] In addition, there had always been numerous close links between MoMA and the US government. 'I learnt my politics at the Museum of Modern Art', Nelson Rockefeller was to declare. Elected as chairman of the board of trustees in 1939, he would dominate it in one way or another until 1958, the year he was elected governor of New York. This scion of the well-known family was not the only museum official to have a political career. John Hay Whitney worked for the Office of Strategic Services during the war; René d'Harnoncourt came to the museum as the representative of a federal agency when, in 1941, he organized the exhibition *Indian Art of the United States*; and Thomas W. Braden, MoMA's executive secretary in 1948 and 1949, subsequently worked for the CIA between 1952 and 1954.[23] Strong links to politics were only to be expected in an institution of the Museum of Modern Art's calibre.

What is interesting, however, is the fact that, during World War II and the critical years of the Cold War, MoMA established an exhibition programme in which the ideological dimension of the museum became more explicit through a series of shows conceived with the intention of persuading, encouraging and stimulating patriotism. During World War II, for instance, there were twenty-nine exhibitions centred around the theme of war.

The conflict was to bring about many changes. Nelson Rockefeller resigned as chairman at the beginning of 1941, when he became the 'Government's Coordinator of Inter-American Affairs'. John Hay Whitney was elected in his place, only to resign shortly afterwards to join the Air Force, being replaced by Stephen C. Clark, then president of the board of trustees.

Beaumont Newhall was also called up in 1942, leaving the running of the newly created Department of Photography to his wife, Nancy, who was appointed as acting curator.

In short, in times of war even art had to serve its country. Encouraged by Edward Steichen, the conviction within the museum itself that photography could carry out the task of persuasion better than any other form of expression increasingly gained ground. In order to do so effectively, however, it had to break loose from strict modernist aesthetic practices and allow the photograph to speak directly to the hearts and minds of the public. Furthermore, accusations of snobbishness directed at the department on account of Newhall's attempt to define photography by adopting the same criteria as for the other arts meant that influential people on the board of trustees began to urge that greater attention be paid to the tastes and needs of the general public. In September 1941, without consulting Nancy Newhall, David McAlpin invited Steichen to curate a major photographic exhibition on the theme of national defence. *Road to Victory* was to represent 'one of the most powerful propaganda efforts yet attempted', according to the exhibition's press release.

Road to Victory

Road to Victory, which opened on 21 May 1942, attracted over 80,000 visitors to MoMA – an average of 800 people a day. After it closed, the exhibition toured the country, and a reduced version even travelled beyond the United States. Its impact on the public was enormous, and it met with almost unanimous critical acclaim. Edward Allen Jewell wrote in the *New York Times*: 'The supreme war contribution ... was the magnificent "Road to Victory" at the Museum of Modern Art ... Composed of striking photographs, many of them enlarged to full mural dimensions, this veritable portrait of America was created by Lieut. Comdr. Edward Steichen and Carl Sandburg, working in collaboration. Their achievement, heroic in stature, I have already characterized as the season's most moving experience.'[24]

    Road to Victory in fact represented a decisive moment in the history of MoMA's photography department, inaugurating a different approach towards the function of photographic evidence. The exhibition – devised in September 1941, before the attack on Pearl Harbor – was to form part of the series relating to the theme of national defence. Initially to have been entitled *Panorama of Defense*, or *Arsenal of Democracy*, it was only after the United States officially entered the war that its title became *Road to Victory*. Steichen spent six months selecting the images, viewing some 50,000 photographs, the majority originating from the archives of governmental departments and agencies, including the Army, the Navy, the Department of Agriculture, and so on. Over one-third of the 134 images finally

Above: **Entrance to the exhibition** *Road to Victory*; **the first room was devoted to the conquest of the West. New York, 1942.** © Museum of Modern Art, New York/Scala

Opposite: **Herbert Bayer, diagram illustrating the 'field of vision'.**

chosen came from the archives of the Farm Security Administration. 'The ones chosen to form the exhibition,' Steichen reported, 'not only tell today's story of this country and its citizens, but attest the remarkable excellence of the art of photography.'[25]

Like MoMA's board of trustees, Steichen believed that the times called not only for an epic portrait of the nation, but also and above all for a narrative that would reinvigorate the powerful myth of America, its land and its people. American citizens should feel part of the national, collective effort of a country at war. Both a reaction and an emotional response were required and, to provoke them, Steichen brought documentary photography into play. In addition, to help design the installation he called upon Herbert Bayer, the Austrian-born graphic designer and artist who had studied at the Bauhaus prior to emigrating to the United States in 1938. Bayer's approach to exhibition design was

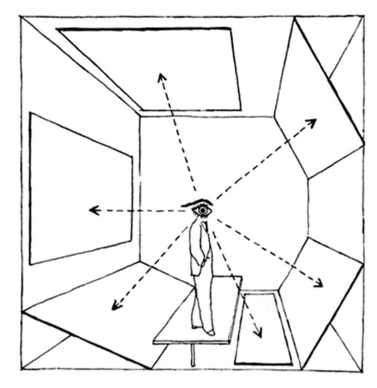

exemplified by his theory of the 'field of vision' and the desire to create a dynamic visual space around the spectator rather than the static space of traditional types of display, which were founded on balance and symmetry. According to Bayer's concept, which he borrowed from the European avant-garde of the 1920s, the installation should constitute a veritable experience for spectators, exposing them to multiple perspectives.

What made *Road to Victory* more than just a propagandist exhibition - one of many that were springing up in American museums at the time - was the very grandeur and complexity of its design. The photographs were arranged like statements that, once combined, would form an articulated argument. The exhibition plan was based on the notion of a dramatic sequence in which every image, every wall, every word would be positioned not only to achieve the best visual effect, but also the most effective emotional and psychological responses. This concern was combined with careful consideration of how best to guide the visitor through the show, both physically and visually. In order to free up space for the construction of this spectacular installation, the internal walls of MoMA's second floor were taken down, thus creating a large, open area. In addition, as Bayer himself explained, the exhibition space was expanded visually by the use of a white-painted floor, which seemed to widen the spectator's angle of vision.

The theme of the United States at war was recounted through images that were often reproduced on a huge scale, many of them measuring 90 × 120 cm (35 × 47 in.); and the climax of the whole exhibition was its photo-mural finale, which stretched across 12 m (39 feet). Used to help articulate the exhibition space, these enlargements were not only

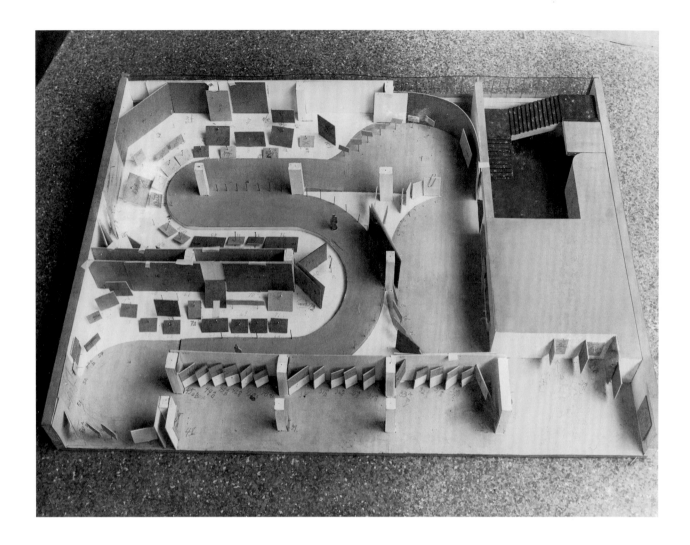

positioned at angles on the wall, but in some cases were simply propped against it. The larger images were installed without frames or mounts and were accompanied by texts by the poet Carl Sandburg, Steichen's brother-in-law. This exhibition was their first collaboration - a particular narrative model that would achieve its ultimate expression in *The Family of Man* exhibition. Photography was used as the illustration of a thesis - as a summary of Sandburg's texts, which expressed an idealized vision of American history and the nation's soul. Steichen, for this part, made use of documentary photography, removing it entirely from its original context. Many of the images sourced from the Farm Security Administration, for example, were cropped, and all the captions were replaced by Sandburg's words of mystical inspiration; and their realism was much diluted by the installation's universalizing narrative. As the art historian Mary Anne Staniszewski observed in *The Power of Display*,

Maquette for the exhibition
***Road to Victory*.**
© Museum of Modern Art,
New York/Scala

the exhibition was organized almost as if it were an attempt to construct a national folktale: the story was linear, the message clear, and the tone both sentimental and militaristic at the same time.[26] 'Each room is a chapter, each photograph is a sentence,' opined Monroe Wheeler in the museum's press release.[27]

The tale opened with a meaningful prologue. At the exhibition entrance, visitors were met by a wooden statue of a great American eagle soaring against the backdrop of a wall spangled with forty-eight stars, one for each state. The text on the wall panel cited Roosevelt's famous doctrine of the 'Four Freedoms': freedom of speech, freedom of worship, freedom from want and freedom from fear. Only then could the epic national story begin.

In the beginning there was the grandeur of a virgin land. Upon entering the exhibition, the visitor found himself standing before a huge panorama of Bryce Canyon, Utah, measuring 4×5 m (13×16 ft). Beside it were panels bearing images of buffalo and close-up portraits of Native Americans. Sandburg's words began to spell out the chapters of a glorious adventure, beginning with a simplistic account (to say the least) of the relationship between the new conquerors and the American Indians: 'In the beginning was virgin land and America was promises – and the buffalo by thousands pawed the Great Plains – and the Red Man gave over to an endless tide of white men in endless numbers with a land hunger and no end to the land they wanted – over the eastern seaboard through the Appalachians ...' This marked the start of the visit along a strict, prescribed route, leading via a series of ramps and walkways from one vision to the next, from one chapter to another. The sequence of panels continued with images of rural America: cornfields, grazing sheep, noble-looking farm hands. These were followed by others showing simple, healthy small-town family life, and then industrial America, the power of a great nation at work, recounted through images of ambitious government projects. On one hand, the immense potential of the land, on the other, the great strength of its people: here was 'the Arsenal of democracy at work'.

At this point, the visitor was about to encounter the first climax of the exhibition. After passing a mural showing a meeting of the isolationist group America First, with its caption 'It can't happen to us', the spectator rounded a corner to find two large images placed at 90 degrees to each other, filling his field of vision entirely (p. 170). On the right was an image of an explosion at Pearl Harbor, an official US Navy photograph; below it, a smaller image showing two Japanese diplomats. On the left was the portrait of an old Texan farmer taken by Dorothea Lange. The images were arranged in such a way that it seemed as if the Texan farmer were gazing, solemn and indignant, at the explosion and at the two politicians. The text beside the images read: 'War – they asked for it – now, by the living God, they'll get it.'

In the 'chapter' that followed, a platform several centimetres off the floor provided the visitor with a more dramatic view, from a slightly raised position, of a sequence of images showing weapons, military formations and battles. The panels gradually increased in size before reaching the installation's climax: a gigantic curved mural (p. 173), measuring 4×12 m (13×39 ft), featuring rows of marching men as far as the eye could see. Alongside it were images showing mothers and fathers from all over America.

This was the conclusion of the story. The exhibition's message was contained within, and conveyed by, the route the visitor had followed. The entire show had been carefully planned so as to conduct the spectator through a series of emotions that would climax in a surge of patriotism: from the myth of America as an immense, uninhabited, promised land, conquered by brave pioneers, to a modern nation fighting a war in which one should feel proud to participate. It was this sense of belonging to a glorious community that MoMA was seeking to evoke, according to Monroe Wheeler: 'Our purpose in preparing this exhibition was to enable every American to see himself as a vital and indispensable element of victory.'[28] Christopher Phillips wrote: 'Unity-in-diversity was to become one of the overriding themes of American wartime rhetoric, and *Road to Victory* evidenced its earliest and most compelling expression in photographic form.'[29]

In a brief essay written for an American magazine and published in 1939, Bayer summed up his ideas about the exhibition's design: 'The modern exhibition should not

Road to Victory: the space dedicated to Pearl Harbour.
© Museum of Modern Art, New York/Scala

retain its distance from the spectator, it should be brought close to him, penetrate, and leave an impression on him, should explain, demonstrate, and even persuade and lead him to a planned reaction. Therefore we may say that exhibition design runs parallel with the psychology of advertising.'[30] Once on American soil, Bayer had simplified the Bauhaus's complex theories on exhibition design in the name of wider public success. Ambiguity, which constituted one of the avant-garde's principal challenges to the traditional view, had been replaced by a clear and effective control of the spectator's gaze, movements and reactions. Public success was swift. *Road to Victory* received an endless stream of visitors and was almost universally admired by critics.

Writing in *PM* magazine, Ralph Steiner commented: 'The photographs are displayed by Bayer as photographs have never been displayed before. They don't sit quietly against the wall. They jut out from the walls and up from the floors to assault your vision.'[31] On 24 May 1942 Edward Allen Jewell wrote in the *New York Times*: 'It would not at all amaze me to see people, even people who have thought themselves very worldly, nonchalant or hard-boiled, leave this exhibition with brimming eyes.'[32] In the pages of *Photo Notes*, the photography critic Elizabeth McCausland carefully highlighted evidence that 'Here art has been made a weapon of unmistakeable intent and power.'[33] The occasional polemical voice was heard in isolation, and mostly ignored by the press. MoMA's archives contain a letter addressed to the *Herald Tribune* in May 1942 and subsequently copied to the museum. Part of the letter reads: 'Cripes, Commander, you're feeding American complacency! We can't sight-see and wait our way to victory … Give us the boys sweating and toiling in the Carolinas on maneuvers. Give us PT boats … give us helmsmen on tankers, depth charges, MacArthur, blood, bombs, bandages, citizens in line for ration cards, farewell kisses of mothers and sweethearts, parades, war bond selling, air raid wardens and incendiaries, plane spotters freezing on mountain tops. Give us hell! This is war, isn't it?'[34]

The purpose of *Road to Victory*, however, was not so much to show the true face of war as to reignite the myth of American power and to awaken its faith in a glorious future. In June 1942 Wheeler concluded his note on the exhibition thus: 'There has been no minimizing of the gravity of war, but few people will see this exhibition without feeling that they are part of the power of America, and that if that power is exerted to the utmost our freedom shall endure.'[35] Admittedly, at the time a sterile and patriotic image of the war was the only one that would have been available. Film and photographs of the conflict's horrors would not have got past the government censors. It was not until September 1943 that the first images of American dead appeared on the pages of *Life*. As it happened, the layout of magazines such as *Life* and *Look*, and the way they combined images and text, helped ensure that *Road to Victory* fitted within the visual panorama of the time and would not have been entirely unfamiliar to the public. A visitor to the exhibition might have had the feeling of walking inside a gigantic three-dimensional photo essay.

Among the few critical voices were those of Ansel Adams and Beaumont and Nancy Newhall, who hated the exhibition, considering it to be totally inappropriate for MoMA.

Steichen's promotion of photography as a language of mass media and spectacle could not have been further from the modernist aesthetic conveyed by *Sixty Photographs*.

In the meantime, Steichen had been appointed director of the Naval Aviation Photographic Unit in 1945, and the same year had organized another exhibition at MoMA. *Power in the Pacific*, produced in collaboration with the US Navy, used images by photographers from the Navy, the Marines and the Coast Guards. Steichen was discharged with honour in 1946, with the rank of captain. The tension between the two concepts of photography personified by Newhall and Steichen intensified within the department upon Newhall's return from military service. The decisions that the museum's board of trustees took at this point were dictated not so much by aesthetics as by pragmatic, financial considerations. The museum - and the Department of Photography within it - was constantly in need of substantial funds, which were vital for maintaining the role it had created for itself and for developing it further.

John Szarkowski recalls that, at the end of 1945, Tom Maloney - the editor of *U.S. Camera*, an 'external consultant' for MoMA and a great admirer of Steichen - wrote a memorandum to the museum in which he stated that he would be able to raise $100,000 from the photographic industry for the support and development of its photographic programme on the condition that Steichen headed that programme.[36] Maloney's proposal was discussed at length but opposed by those who supported the work that Beaumont Newhall had carried out. Change was already in the air, however. The widespread popular and critical success of the spectacular exhibitions organized by Steichen led Newhall to realize that, as far as photography was concerned, the museum's position was starting to diverge from his own. In April 1947 he resigned from his post at MoMA, as did Ansel Adams, who declared that any kind of collaboration with Steichen would be impossible.

So it was that Captain Edward Steichen, the celebrated photographer, became the Department of Photography's new director; he was now 67 years old. In the press release announcing his appointment, Rockefeller wrote: 'Steichen, the young man who was so instrumental in bringing modern art to America, joins with the Museum of Modern Art to bring to as wide a public as possible the best work being done throughout the world, and to employ it creatively as a means of interpretation in major Museum exhibitions where photography is not the theme but the medium through which great achievement and great moments are graphically represented.'[37]

The large-format mural that
concluded the visitors' route
through *Road to Victory*.
© Museum of Modern Art,
New York/Scala

Cover of the catalogue for
The Family of Man, 1955.
© Museum of Modern Art,
New York/Scala

The Family of Man

The Family of Man opened to the public on 26 January 1955. Despite the bitter New York weather, a long line of people waited outside the museum for the doors to open. *The Family of Man* was to beat nearly all records for the number of visitors to a MoMA exhibition, with the exception of the *Italian Masters* show in 1940. After it had closed in New York, five different versions of the exhibition went on tour, not only in the United States but in over sixty countries, under the aegis of the United States Information Agency (USIA), where they were seen by over 9 million people.

In his autobiography, *A Life in Photography* (1963), Steichen claimed that, despite their widespread popularity and critical acclaim, he considered the exhibitions he had organized previously on the theme of war to be a failure: 'I had failed to accomplish my mission. I had not incited people into taking open and united action against war itself ... What was wrong? I came to the conclusion that I had been working from a negative approach, that what was needed was a positive statement on what a wonderful thing life was, how marvelous people were, and, above all, how alike people were in all parts of the world. The real need was for an expression of the oneness of the world we lived in.'[38] In other words, looking at life might be the best deterrent to the senselessness of war. For Steichen, this expression was *The Family of Man*.

It could be said, therefore, that Steichen viewed his wartime exhibitions as unfinished exercises leading up to the completeness of what he regarded as perhaps the masterpiece of his life. '*The Family of Man* was the most important undertaking of my career,' he wrote.[39] According to various accounts, he appeared to have been mulling over the idea for some time - perhaps since the moment in 1938 when he visited the International Photographic Exhibition at Grand Central Station, New York, a major exhibition of 3,000 images organized by Willard Morgan. Steichen had been particularly impressed by the pictures taken by photographers of the Farm Security Administration, which revealed a hidden side of contemporary America. In the article he wrote on the 1938 show for *U.S. Camera*, Steichen expressed his conviction that the photography could be a force for change: 'If you are the kind of rugged individualist who likes to say, "Am I my brother's keeper?" don't look at these pictures - they may change your mind.'[40] It made an enormous impact on him, and he was particularly struck by the exhibition's ability to highlight the relationship between individual circumstances and universal values. The International Photographic Exhibition was also significant for a different reason: it marked the beginning of his friendship with Dorothea Lange, who was to play a significant role in the conceptual framework of *The Family of Man*.

In a letter to Lange dated August 1952 - that is to say, five years after he had been appointed head of MoMA's photography department - Steichen explained the project he had in mind: 'The stress would be on the universal through the particular with an emphasis on fundamental periodless forces in human relations,' he wrote, adding: 'I hope this will be the realization of the dream I had when I took over this job.'[41] In his autobiography, Steichen

recounts how one day, reading Carl Sandburg's biography of Lincoln, he had come across a speech in which the great man used the expression 'family of man'. This is where inspiration for the exhibition's theme came from.

The Family of Man's aesthetic should therefore be viewed in the light of its relationship to the documentary photography of the 1930s. It is likely that Steichen was also influenced by a series of reportages, entitled 'People are people, the world over', published in 1948 by the *Ladies' Home Journal*, whose picture editor was John Morris. Morris's idea had been to illustrate everyday life across the world from a sociological and anthropological point of view. Morris recounted how Steichen had initially asked for his assistance in organizing the exhibition and, when he declined, then turned to Wayne Miller, who had worked for *Life* and had been one of the photographers in Steichen's Naval Aviation unit.[42] Dorothea Lange and Miller proved to be invaluable in the creation of *The Family of Man*, as well as being the two best-represented photographers in the show.

The preparation process for the exhibition was long and tormented. Discussions started within the museum in 1950. The $100,000 promised by Tom Maloney in his 1945

Wayne Miller, *Edward Steichen with the maquette for The Family of Man.*
© Wayne Miller/Magnum Photos

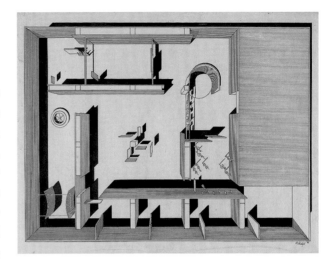

memorandum never materialized, and so under Steichen's leadership the Department of Photography continued its precarious financial existence. In July 1949, writing to Nelson Rockefeller, the museum's president, René d'Harnoncourt, now the museum's director, outlined a proposal for new fund-raising strategies: 'For example, a series of exhibitions of quality but on popular subjects that would be organized by us and shown all over the country. In such a venture we could use Steichen's talent for dramatization. Here is a sample idea: Self-portrait of America, an exhibition of photographs on American life by American photographers, including both professionals and amateurs from all groups that make up this country.'[43] However, Steichen fought from the start against the idea of confining the exhibition to a national context, wishing instead to give it an international flavour, with the main objective being to celebrate the dignity of humankind. Various attempts over a five-year period to find a sponsor for the exhibition failed. In the end, Nelson Rockefeller himself guaranteed to cover the costs, which amounted to $100,000.

Thus in 1952 Steichen began to prepare *The Family of Man* as part of the programme celebrating MoMA's 25th anniversary. The same year, accompanied by Robert Frank in the role of interpreter, he travelled to eleven different European countries in search of material. A letter explaining the project and requesting the submission of images was sent to magazines, associations and individual photographers; Steichen reused the letter, almost in its entirety, as the introduction for the exhibition and its catalogue.

In the summer of 1953, Wayne Miller moved with his family to New York to devote himself entirely to the exhibition. All the preparatory work - the selection of images, the editing and the creation of the installation - took place in a loft that the museum had rented for the purpose on 52nd Street. Miller would later claim that he probably looked through more than two million images, which came in folders from *Life* and other archives. In the end, the most significant group of photographs in *The Family of Man* were from the archives of Magnum (sixty images), followed by those from *Life*: many of the pictures Steichen chose were in fact from well-known reportages already published by the magazine.

The selection process was long and complicated. Steichen immediately realized that his exhibition should not be merely a collection of the best photographs on social issues. Twenty years later, Wayne Miller was to recall: 'We didn't take the best pictures, that wasn't the criterion. The decision point was "what says it best." As we all know you don't know what a white is, until you put a black against it ... so we worked on this in fact almost like music. It had to have peaks, it had to build up and drop down, and build up higher and drop down a little bit ... So it was the [relative] positions that created electricity, as well as individual photographs.'[44] Steichen was aiming for 500 images that would speak with one voice. Probably for this reason, as Szarkowski has suggested, the message had to be a simple one.[45] *The Family of Man* sacrificed parts for the benefit of the whole; normally, as Szarkowski

Floor plan of *The Family of Man*.

noted, this is what artists do, not curators. Steichen himself remarked in his autobiography: 'The creation of this kind of exhibition is more like the production of a play or novel, even a philosophical essay, than it is like planning an exhibition of pictures of individual works of art. Therefore it must have an intrinsic aim that gives it an element of the universal and an over-all unity.'[46]

It was assumed that, for an exhibition of this size, the selection of images and the design of the installation would need run in parallel, each being closely connected to the other. Once the photos had been reduced in number from 10,000 to 1,000, Steichen decided that Wayne Miller should choose the images relating to man and his work; his wife, Joan Miller, was to select images of women and children; and he decided to make the selection of photos relating to broader themes himself. In the run-up to the opening, Steichen decided to include two additional pictures at the last minute: one showed the destructive power of the nuclear bomb; the other, taken by Eugene Harris, was a portrait of a Peruvian

First room of *The Family of Man*.
© Museum of Modern Art,
New York/Scala

flute player - a symbolic image that made reference to music as another universal and non-verbal language. Eventually there was a total of 503 photographs by 273 photographers from 68 different countries. Right from the beginning it was decided not to reveal the authors' identities. Steichen's team assigned a number to every image that arrived in the loft and kept index cards for each photographer, to be consulted only if an address were needed to return a print or to request a negative.

For the exhibition design, Steichen called on Paul Rudolph, a young architect who was dean of the Yale School of Architecture. The installation's underlying concept broadly followed that of the successful *Road to Victory*. The exhibition space was greatly enlarged and occupied the entire second floor of the museum. Rudolph showed that he was inspired by Herbert Bayer's theories on display, and by techniques that exploited peripheral vision, three-dimensional collage and daring perspectives, all of which were designed to have an overwhelming effect on the spectator. The images, which ranged from 20 × 24 cm (7⅞ × 9½ in.) to 3 × 3.6 m (9 ft 10 in. × 11 ft 10 in.) in size, were all exhibited without frames, and often mounted on Masonite panels cut flush and painted black around the edges. The installation was characterized by the use of transparent materials, light supporting structures and dramatic lighting. As in *Road to Victory*, different methods of display were adopted: the photos were attached to beams or mounted on panels of transparent plastic, hung directly from the ceiling or laid horizontally on the floor. In some cases, enlargements were hung from above on chains that could be moved or swung by the visitor: one example was a panel showing, on one side, a young couple on a swing, and on the other a different swing supporting a lively old couple. Forty years later, Rudolph would write: 'Exhibition design can deal very much with storytelling, unlike architecture. I was fascinated with the idea of the psychology of space and what could be manipulated in purely architectural terms, by this I mean space and light, vistas, space, color, and sequence.'[47] In this way, the total effect of *The Family of Man* could be compared to a cinematic experience. The exhibition was also the result, however, of a continuous collision of ideas between the young architect and the older Steichen, as Rudolph recounted: 'I thought some of [Steichen's] ideas were incredibly corny and still do. We had real battles.'[48]

As in *Road to Victory*, another important element in *The Family of Man*'s narrative was the text. This time Carl Sandburg provided only the prologue to the exhibition, which nevertheless was hugely important. Greeting visitors at the entrance, it aimed to reinforce the story of the universal human condition - the theme on which the exhibition was founded. It did so in biblical tones that would give the visitor the sensation of participating in a ritual:

> There is only one man in the world
> and his name is All Men.
> There is only one woman in the world
> and her name is All Women.
> There is only one child in the world
> and the child's name is All Children.

The quotations at the beginning of each thematic section served the same purpose. Steichen had asked the writer Dorothy Norman to explore world literature and find phrases that would confer on the images an aura of timelessness and profundity. Aside from the photos themselves, these quotations gave the exhibition a fundamentally Christian tone, with a strong Old Testament flavour.

The exhibition was divided thematically into thirty-seven sections, each opening with a quotation; Rudolph's design created a narrative flow that linked the various themes and guided the visitor along a prescribed path. The exhibition entrance was already a strong declaration of intent. One wall was entirely covered by a large black-and-white photograph showing a crowd of people - the first of a series of crowd images distributed along the exhibition route with the aim of enveloping the spectator and making him or her feel part of a universal community. As in *Road to Victory*, the objective was to create an environment that would provoke an inevitable emotional response, as Steichen confirmed: 'The people in the audience looked at the pictures, and the people in the pictures looked back at them. They recognized each other.'[49]

After reading Sandburg's introductory text and entering the installation proper, visitors found themselves standing in front of a spectacular image of a canyon, just as in *Road to Victory*. Here, too, the show was introduced through the magnificence of nature, this time a Chinese landscape appropriate to the exhibition's international perspective. Whereas in *Road to Victory* the opening panorama had been accompanied by faces of Native American Indians, here was the portrait of a young Peruvian flute-player. Steichen ascribed to this image a symbolic power, something approaching a musical harmony, and he situated it at various points throughout the exhibition, as well as using it for publicity material and the cover of the catalogue (p. 174).

After the grand image of the canyon, a transparent wall offered a panoramic view of the galleries and the path that would lead the visitor through the great universal themes on which Steichen had constructed his view of humanity. First and foremost was a gallery on the theme of love, which was divided into sections portraying love and marriage before reaching a climax in one of the first significant points in the whole installation: 'birth'. This key moment of creation was narrated within a sort of diaphanous circular temple - a raised platform surrounded by a flimsy, pure-white curtain, lit from above by fluorescent light (opposite). The visitor could enter this intimate space and gaze at images of pregnant young women, women in labour and newborn infants.

Leaving the 'temple of birth', visitors immediately found themselves at the very heart of the exhibition: here, suspended from the ceiling and overlooking the centre of the gallery, were enlargements of photos of families from across the globe. Here was the great 'family of man'. The text proclaimed: 'With all beings and all things we shall be as relatives - Sioux Indian.' Here, Steichen assembled images of the family as a timeless universal social structure, but they were clearly modelled on Western middle-class values. A square platform filled with white pebbles had been created beneath the panels, visually emphasizing their

centrality. The visitor had to walk around this feature in order to admire the images on both sides of each panel. On the walls of this room, photographs illustrating work (agricultural, office, housework) were displayed.

At this point, the linear narrative that had led the visitor to the meaningful core of the exhibition through a sequence of themes – nature, love, marriage, birth, children, the family unit – began to branch out into sections that were less linear in arrangement but still characterized by themes of a universal nature: food, music, play, education and human relationships. The ways in which the images were displayed were extremely varied and changed according to theme: they were suspended from the ceiling, placed on the floor, hung at eye level, blown up to huge, emphatic proportions (Ansel Adams's image of Mount Williamson, for example) or arranged in dynamic juxtapositions, as in the section devoted to dance and music. The area devoted to play included an interesting and evocative idea. This consisted of photographs of children, from twelve different countries across the world, playing 'ring-a-ring-o'-roses', which was presented as a universal game. The photos were mounted on two circular bases whose form and structure recalled a roundabout.

As Mary Anne Staniszewski has remarked: 'The show had a tempo that worked to engender a kind of emotional roller-coaster ride.'[50] While the section devoted to music and play was designed to evoke vitality and light-heartedness, the devices used in spaces given over to more serious issues were very different. From the area devoted to play, the visitor headed towards smaller spaces housing the more reflective part of *The Family of Man*. The theme of death, at the entrance to a narrow corridor, introduced a series of topics such as

The space dedicated to the theme of 'Birth' in *The Family of Man*.
© Museum of Modern Art, New York/Scala

loneliness, suffering, compassion, religion, famine, man's inhumanity to man, and justice. At the end of this section the spectator was confronted with a wall on which nine portraits of people of different ages and origins were exhibited. Situated in the middle of the wall, at eye level, was a mirror. Looking into it, visitors could see themselves as members of the 'family of man'. Rudolph remembered finding this feature rather corny and excessive: 'Really, if you didn't understand by that time in the exhibition that "The Family of Man" was you, I think it was unnecessary.'[51] Even Steichen and Millar evidently came to the same opinion, since the mirror was removed within the show's first fortnight.

Following the portrait section, the visitor was faced with the image of a dead soldier, a quotation from Sophocles beside it: 'Who is the slayer, who the victim? Speak.' This is how Steichen prepared the public for one of the most significant and spectacular images in the entire exhibition: a backlit photograph, measuring 2×3 m (6 ft 6 in. $\times$ 9 ft 10 in.), depicting the explosion of a nuclear bomb. It was the only image in colour and the only one to have an entire room to itself. The image was fairly well known, having been widely publicized by the media: the hydrogen bomb, immensely more powerful than the one that had destroyed Hiroshima, had in fact only just been tested. Emerging from a narrow space, having seen hundreds of black-and-white photographs, visitors suddenly experienced a kind of visual assault. They could not fail to be struck by this polychromatic reality and its relevance to contemporary life.

Above and opposite: **Exhibition views of *The Family of Man.*** © Museum of Modern Art, New York/Scala

Like a modern-day Pied Piper, the curator went to great lengths to guide the public through this meaningful world of images. After the shock of the huge image of a nuclear explosion, immediately he had to refocus visitors' attention on the concept of family in order to dispel fears and doubts concerning the future. The exhibition itinerary now continued towards brighter and more spacious galleries, where spectators found themselves standing before portraits of couples accompanied by a quotation from Ovid: 'We two form a multitude.' Rounding the corner, the public realized that these images were mounted on an enormous photomural showing the United Nations Assembly. Fears about war and the future were thus overcome in the reassuring and optimistic vision of an international community united in building a lasting peace. This, in other words, was the political representation of the family of man.

There was more to come. To bring about a real conclusion to the show, it had to return to the beginning: to nature rather than history, and to the concept of rebirth. Fears needed to be dispelled entirely. As Rudolph related: 'How to end the show was a difficult thing. You couldn't end it with the atom bomb. It was about the idea of childhood and was a rebirth. It was done in pinks, warm colour. It was light'.[52] It was here that W. Eugene Smith's intense and allegorical image entitled *The Walk to Paradise Garden* was placed, showing his two children pictured from behind as they stroll from darkness towards a radiant light. The photograph was accompanied by a quotation by the French poet Saint-John Perse: 'A world to be born under your feet.'

On the whole, the press's reaction was ecstatic. As Mary Anne Staniszewski recounts, some critics even compared the 'gargantuan' exhibition to the wonders of the world for having evoked 'the sensation of walking in the Grand Canyon or in the Carlsbad Caverns or in something equally monumental'.[53] The exhibition received wide coverage in the national press, something that had never occurred previously. Furthermore, it was an enormous hit with the public. In the first fortnight over 35,000 people visited the show. Each day a long queue of people formed outside the museum, waiting for the doors to open, as if they were going to the theatre. The catalogue also enjoyed surprising and enduring success. It was published by Jerry Mason, editor of the small publishing house Maco (founded barely two years earlier), and initially appeared in two editions: a paperback version costing $1, and a deluxe hardback that cost $10. It became an immediate bestseller: by 1961, over 1 million copies had already been sold. The journalist Bob Considine even prophesied that the catalogue would become 'as much a part of the family library as the Bible'.[54]

The reasons for such an enthusiastic reception were varied. The design of *The Family of Man*, like that of *Road to Victory*, reworked the innovative approach favoured by the international avant-garde of the 1920s and 1930s in a language capable of reflecting the 'common sense' of the American public. Provocations were tamed and utilized to express a dominant ideology - reassuring because it was familiar, yet at the same time moving. In other words, the 'family of man' depicted here shared the same values and aspirations as a middle-class American family of the 1950s.

On the other hand, for this very reason the exhibition also attracted strong criticism from both the photographic community and various commentators who highlighted its ideological aspects. One of the earliest and most lucid attacks, published by *Commentary* in October 1955, came from Hilton Kramer, under the title 'Exhibiting *The Family of Man*: The World's Most Talked About Photographs'.[55] Kramer severely criticized the treatment meted out to photography, which was not employed for its artistic value but as something to be shaped for propaganda purposes. Above all, Kramer raised the issue of propagandized ideology and unearthed what, from his point of view, seemed to be significant political dangers:

> [It is] a self-congratulatory means for obscuring under a blanket of ideology which takes for granted the essential goodness, innocence, and moral superiority of the international 'little man,' 'the man in the street,' the abstract, disembodied hero of a world-view which regards itself as superior to mere politics. 'The Family of Man' is thus a reassertion in visual terms of all that has been discredited in progressive ideology.

Another analysis - one of the most quoted and most influential for later evaluations of the exhibition's legacy - was proffered by Roland Barthes who saw the exhibition in Paris in 1956 and included a critique in his book *Mythologies*, considering it the bearer of one of the myths of modern times that needed to be destroyed: the notion of a single planetary community, a mystification from which progressive humanism had to escape. He concluded:

> This myth of the human 'condition' rests on a very old mystification, which always consists in placing Nature at the bottom of History. Any classic humanism postulates that in scratching the history of men a little, the relativity of their institutions or the diversity of their skins ... one very quickly reaches the solid rock of a universal human nature. Progressive humanism, on the contrary, must always remember to reverse the terms of this very old imposture, constantly to scour nature, its 'laws' and its 'limits' in order to discover History there, and at last to establish Nature itself as historical.[56]

According to Barthes, postulating the existence of a human essence meant introducing God into the exhibition:

> The pietistic intention is underlined by the quotations which accompany each chapter of the exhibition: these quotations often are "primitive" proverbs or verses from the Old Testament. They all define an eternal wisdom, a class of assertions which escape History.[57]

Eliminating the burden of history from such themes as family, birth, work and death in some way removed from humankind the value of its own actions in the world. This was the precisely the strategy adopted by every type of mythology: to neutralize any dissatisfaction with the status quo by creating an illusion of timelessness. Barthes concluded his essay: 'So that I rather fear that the final justification of all this Adamism is to give to the immobility of the world the alibi of a "wisdom" and a "lyricism" which only make the gestures of man look eternal the better to defuse them.'

In the years that followed, critics also attempted to analyse the great cultural phenomenon of *The Family of Man* by placing it within its historical context. To understand the implications of the exhibition's message from a historical point of view, the observer needs to consider the situation in the United States during the first half of the 1950s. During this period, the dangers and fears of the Cold War were being exploited and manipulated by politicians such as Joseph McCarthy to create a climate of internal suspicion and to build an image of the world divided into 'us' and 'them'. Steichen's intention to reassert the notion of humankind's oneness - expressed clearly from the moment planning began - could also be seen as a loaded statement in the dark years of McCarthyism. In fact, in December 1954 the US Senate, with its Democrat majority, decided to condemn McCarthy for 'acting contrary to senatorial ethics'. *The Family of Man* opened barely a month later.

The fears of the American public began to evaporate, and in the event Steichen's sentimental ideology coincided perfectly with what the public wanted to see and hear at that time: the myth of the 'American dream'. Commenting on the exhibition's success, the painter and photographer Ben Shahn wrote:

> Let us also note that it is not at all surprising that the public turns to the Steichen show with such undivided enthusiasm. The reason is, I am sure, that the public is impatient for some exercise of its faculties; it is hungry for thinking, for feeling, for real experience; it is eager for some new philosophical outlook, for new kinds of truth; it wants contact with live minds; it wants to feel compassion; it wants to grow emotionally and intellectually; it wants to live.[58]

The Korean War had finished only two years earlier, and barely ten had passed since the traumas of World War II. Steichen was well aware of the contradictions of his time and of the notion of the so-called 'family of man'; but, as he remarked several months after the exhibition had opened, it was meant to be 'an act of faith - an antidote to the horror we have been fed for years on a daily basis'.[59] That *The Family of Man* was a perfect cultural vehicle for the 'American way' is highlighted by the fact that the exhibition's impressive world tour, which took in over sixty countries, was made possible by a government agency, the United States Information Agency (USIA). Established by Eisenhower in 1953, the USIA was dedicated to public diplomacy - a sort of cultured cousin of the CIA - and its main task was to keep other countries informed about American society, culture and politics. The exhibition thus became a sort of manifesto for American cultural politics during the Cold War; it was even shown in Moscow in 1959 as part of the American National Exhibition, during which Khrushchev and Nixon held their famous impromptu debate.

It is also important to bear in mind that the ideological simplifications of *The Family of Man*, and its reduction of humanity to a single socially and historically defined model,

coincided with the development of the concept of mass culture in the media. The conception of the exhibition was an apotheosis of the philosophy and visual language of *Life*, by this point familiar to Western audiences. Legibility was Steichen's main objective. When an anonymous but very strong image entitled *Death Slump at Mississippi*, showing the corpse of a lynched black man chained to a tree, attracted a great deal of attention, Steichen decided to remove it from the exhibition on the basis that the emphasis should be on the overall effect of the images rather than on any individual photograph. Miller explained the reasons for its removal: 'Steichen and I found that spectators were hesitating in front of that photograph. It became a disruption to the overall theme of the exhibition. We wanted the photographs to work together. Although it was a very, very important photograph ... We observed the traffic flow ... We wanted this exhibition to flow ... and the photograph was a stumbling block. People stumbled. It was a fantastic picture. It just didn't work there ... We were dealing with a piece of music and this was a discordant note.'[60] Neither this image nor that of the atomic bomb was included in the catalogue.

The effectiveness of the photographs, therefore, derived from their physical presence and the way they were arranged rather than the artistic or historical value of individual images. They were manipulated in form in order to comply with the overriding linear narrative that had been created: negatives in different formats were enlarged to a standard size, and the original captions and authors' subjectivity were suppressed. Despite the fact that numerous images by the great photographers of the day were featured (including Robert Doisneau, Ernst Haas, Werner Bischof, Robert Capa, Henri Cartier-Bresson, Elliott Erwitt,

George Rodger, Manuel Álvarez Bravo, Robert Frank, Irving Penn, Bill Brandt, Russell Lee and W. Eugene Smith), the authorship and artistic quality of individual photographs took second place to the overall display. In fact, this was one of the photographic world's main criticisms of the exhibition. However, a MoMA press release stated: 'This criticism was offset by Mr. Steichen himself, in his statement that *The Family of Man* was not intended as a photographic display but as a graphic presentation of an idea.'[61]

For John Szarkowski, '*The Family of Man* was, in other words, not a gathering together of a number of discrete, more-or-less successful works of art, but was itself a work of art. The beauty or quality of its component parts was not quite to the point, except as they served their role as threads in a grand tapestry.'[62] Far from being a 'pictorial' exhibition of photographs, the installation recalled Walter Benjamin's notion of the 'decline' of the aura attached to original artworks, instead appealing directly to a mass public with a precise objective. Mary Anne Staniszewski writes that, at the time of the exhibition: 'Steichen, Bayer, Rudolph, and their colleagues did not consider the gallery a neutral container for aestheticized images and objects. Like the objects and images exhibited, the installations were viewed as creations that manifested agendas and ideas and involved politics, history, capitalism, commerce, the commonplace, and, of course, aesthetics.'[63]

Steichen hoped to construct a timeless and universal visual narrative - and in fact the exhibition has attracted audiences even in more recent times. Since 1994 it has been installed as a permanent exhibit at Château de Clervaux in Luxembourg, becoming one of its main tourist attractions. In 2003 it was added to UNESCO's Memory of the World Register.

Above and opposite: **Wayne Miller, visitors at *The Family of Man*, MoMA, New York, 1955.**
© Wayne Miller/Magnum Photos

FOCUS

THE REIGN OF
JOHN SZARKOWSKI

In his fifteen years as director of the Department of Photography at MoMA, Steichen organized a total of forty-four exhibitions. When he resigned from his post in 1961, at the age of 83, he nominated his own successor: John Szarkowski. At that point just 36 years old, Szarkowski had acquired a promising reputation as both a photographer and a writer, and had published two books on photography: *The Idea of Louis Sullivan* (1956) and *The Face of Minnesota* (1958).

Despite having been selected personally by Steichen, Szarkowski immediately showed that he was not his disciple. He later admitted: 'I admired Mr. Steichen tremendously, not only as a photographer, but also as an enormously important historical personage in the history of the medium, and for his work here at MoMA. But I had a different sense of what the museum was for. I think I took the risk of allowing photography to be itself and show itself without being couched in the rubric of philosophical or moral positions. And I think I was able to take a less hortatory position than Mr. Steichen took - to put it bluntly.'[64]

Both of Szarkowski's predecessors had, in different ways, been enormously important for the development and affirmation of photographic language. With no signs of trepidation, Szarkowski assumed their legacy, significantly broadening its achievements. As he himself confirmed, Steichen and Beaumont Newhall, 'consciously or otherwise, felt more compelled than I to be advocates for photography, whereas I - largely because of their work - could assume a more analytic, less apostolic attitude'.[65] This difference in attitude was crucial: Szarkowski's more analytical approach to the language of photography was the foundation on which he began to build a new aesthetic - one that, whether you agreed with it or not, would influence entire generations of photographers and shape our conception of the photographic representation of reality.

In Szarkowski's twenty years as director of photography at MoMA, the medium undeniably achieved the full status of an independent art form, valued for its contemporary viewpoint. In the 1960s and 1970s the number of photographic exhibitions in the museum increased considerably. During the 1940s, an average of five exhibitions a year were held. By the 1960s this number had risen to eight annual exhibitions, reaching a peak of ten between 1970 and 1976. Under Szarkowski's leadership, MoMA staged no fewer than 160 photographic exhibitions in all. A similar, if not greater, increase was apparent in the museum's collection of photographs. In 1958, under Steichen's directorship, the collection consisted of 5,800 prints. In 1964, only two years after Szarkowski took over, the collection numbered 7,000 images, reaching 20,000 by 1979.

Right from the start, Szarkowski declared that he wanted to place greater emphasis on monographic exhibitions and on those that would reveal the formal possibilities of the medium rather than dwelling on the philosophical ends towards which photography could be directed. Five years after his appointment he confirmed his position: 'The history of photography has been less a journey than a growth. Its movement has not been linear and consecutive, but centrifugal - photography, and our understanding of it, has spread from a center: it has, by

infusion, penetrated our consciousness. Like an organism, photography was born whole. It is in our progressive discovery of it that its history lies.'[66]

Steichen and Newhall's differences had not so much concerned photographic style, or which photographers should be promoted or considered great masters, but lay principally in curatorial style and their interpretation of the role of photography. The same divergence would separate Szarkowski from his predecessor. In the exhibition that marked his debut - *Five Unrelated Photographers*, which opened in 1963 - his distance from Steichen's aesthetic model was obvious. The heavily articulated and hyperactive installations disappeared, to be replaced by the typical exhibition model of the white cube: elegant rituality; neutral, austere hues; and spatial conventions that allowed the works to be positioned at eye level and at a specific distance from one another. The earlier mural-like enlargements were resized to conventional proportions, and the eccentric assemblages of images of differing formats made way for an orderly display of prints, all with the same dimensions. Exhibition devices characteristic of Beaumont Newhall's time reappeared: white mounts, wooden frames and protective glass.

Elliott Erwitt, *John Szarkowski*, New York, 1988. © Elliott Erwitt/ Magnum Photos

The repercussions of this approach were felt well beyond the walls of MoMA, throughout an increasingly wide network of galleries, collectors and critics specializing in photography. Szarkowski's appointment marked an important watershed. From this moment onwards, photography at MoMA was no longer shown in a wide variety of display styles but according to a set of well-established rules. Just as with contemporary painting and sculpture, nothing was to distract the visitor's attention from the photographic artwork or interfere with their quest for a more intense and contemplative visual experience. As Mary Anne Staniszewski has remarked: 'Since 1970, the photo department's installation methods, with rare exception, have consistently worked to establish exclusively formalist and aestheticized exhibition conventions.'[67] Szarkowski's main concern was to free photography from the effects of mass culture and to redefine the aesthetic nature of the medium in order to set it squarely on an independent path. Reviewing the new director's first major exhibition, *The Photographer and the American Landscape*, in 1963, Minor White wrote: 'I was grateful to Mr. Szarkowski for materializing an exhibition on a subject that is not modern, art or in fashion; to the Museum for offering the show to the public in a setting that allowed and encouraged the pictures to speak for themselves.'[68]

Despite this apparent independence, it is possible to trace a direct line between the aesthetic approaches of Beaumont Newhall and Szarkowski, for whom the documentary aesthetic of Walker Evans was always a cornerstone, a compass with which to draw a map of the 'main tradition'. In his introduction to the catalogue for the *Walker Evans* exhibition in 1971, Szarkowski set out his aesthetic preferences:

> The photographer must define his subject with an educated awareness of what it is and
> what it means; he must describe it with such simplicity and sureness that the result
> seems an unchallengeable fact, not merely the record of the photographer's opinion;
> yet the picture itself should possess a taut athletic grace, an inherent structure, that
> gives it a life in metaphor ... Evans at his best convinces us that we are seeing the dry
> bones of fact, presented without comment, almost without thought. His lesser pictures
> make it clear that the best ones had deceived us: what we had accepted as simple facts
> were precise descriptions of very personal perceptions.[69]

In Szarkowski's view, the curator's task was to identify and highlight an important thread in the development of photographic expression, which he referred to as a 'usable' tradition:

> It has a certain life and that life has a certain lifeline and certain pictures at certain
> times have about them a vigour and a vitality that has persuaded other photographers
> that there was something in that work that they could use, they could borrow from,
> they could steal and expand, use to their own advantages. And that's tradition, that's
> what I'm interested in. In this job that's all I'm interested in, tradition. By which I don't
> mean old pictures, I mean that line which makes the job as a curator rather similar to
> the job of a taxonomist in a natural history museum.[70]

This tradition, embodied in the work of 'primitives' such as Mathew Brady and Timothy O'Sullivan, was waiting to be acknowledged and appropriated by younger, more informed artists including Walker Evans, Robert Adams and Lee Friedlander, among others.

Szarkowski dominated any serious discussion of American photography at the time. The debate that enlivened the photographic scene in the 1970s revolved in particular around the dual concepts of formalism and humanism: was photography something 'symbolic', principally concerned with the formal properties of the image? Or was it concerned with the 'objective world' and the shared vision of the photographer? In this and other debates, Szarkowski gradually assumed the role of aesthetic guide and authoritative voice for the new generation, recommending the works of masters such as Atget, Brady, O'Sullivan, Sander and Frances Benjamin Johnston - in addition, of course, to Walker Evans. His preference was for that type of photography, preferably in black and white, that examined the so-called social landscape, and his curatorial work emphasized a rigorous formalism.

The formalist theme surfaced explicitly for the first time in the exhibition *The Photographer's Eye* (1964), in which Szarkowski presented a selection of images - some by famous photographers and some anonymous - that, in his opinion, incorporated some of the specific visual characteristics intrinsic to photography. Taken over a period of 125 years, for a variety of reasons, by men who had different objectives and varying degrees of skill, the show's 156 duotone images had very little in common other than that they shared a visual language: in other words, they were unmistakeably photographs.

In his introduction to the catalogue, Szarkowski set out a genuine theory of photography, a series of formal paradigms through which to practise and analyse this language, its grammar and its syntax. He clarified the way in which a photographer might succeed in communicating his own specific way of seeing, and identified five fundamental moments into which the gaze is divided: 'The Thing Itself', 'The Detail', 'The Frame', 'Time' and 'Vantage Point'. The book immediately became a bestseller and one of the basic texts used to teach the photography courses that had rapidly sprung up in American universities. The intense activity within MoMA's photography department - in terms of not merely exhibitions, but also publishing - during Szarkowski's time as director demonstrates his firmly held belief in the important educational role that the museum and its exhibitions had to play: 'I think there is more good photography being done in this country than anywhere in the world ... I think it's absolutely astonishing the amount of good work that's being done here. Now why is that true? I think, in fact, it has something to do with knowledge, something to do with understanding, something to do with the receptiveness to the achievements and the ideas of the important photography of the past ... So I think what we do does have a pedagogical role. But first I think it has to do with pleasure.'[71]

Szarkowski's aim was not only to educate the public, new collectors and gallery owners, but also to awaken photographers to the creative possibilities of their medium and to encourage them to adopt rigorous and precise qualitative standards. Criticism levelled at the Department of Photography during this time accused it of having shown and promoted a

particular taste rather than providing a broad overview of contemporary work. According to Szarkowski's detractors, his excessively formalistic conception of photography tended to favour photographers whose work seemed to be about photography itself rather than the wider world, thereby excluding a great number of works and offering a distorted image of the achievements of photography at the time. Be that as it may, the young photographers who did succeed in attracting his attention and entering his magic circle went on to achieve international fame and a place in photography's history.

Room from the exhibition
The Photographer's Eye, **MoMA,**
New York, 1964. © Museum of
Modern Art, New York/Scala

New Documents

The press release for *New Documents*, which opened on 28 February 1967, presented Diane Arbus, Lee Friedlander and Garry Winogrand as the 'three leading representatives of a new generation of documentary photographers'. They were all under 40 years of age and, despite the fact that each had already received at least one grant from the Guggenheim Foundation, none had yet achieved public fame. Szarkowski's aims in mounting this exhibition were ambitious: to reconfigure the public conception of documentary photography, to reshape its acceptance as a documentary record, and to suggest to the new generation an approach that was well suited to narrating an increasingly complex reality. *New Documents* thus constituted a watershed in the development of contemporary photography.

To introduce the show, Szarkowski wrote: 'In the past decade, this new generation of photographers has redirected the technique and aesthetic of documentary photography to more personal ends. Their aim has been not to reform life, but to know it, not to persuade but to understand. Their work betrays a sympathy - almost an affection - for the imperfections and the frailties of society. They like the real world, in spite of its terrors, as the source of all wonder and fascination and value - no less precious for being irrational.'[72] The approach adopted by these three young photographers differed radically from the traditional documentary photography of the 1930s and 1940s, which was seen as an instrument of social reform. For Szarkowski, 'What unites these three photographers is not style or sensibility; each has a distinct personal sense of the use of photography and the meanings of the world. What is held in common is the belief that the world is worth looking at, and the courage to look at it without theorizing.'[73]

This new vision also presupposed a new formal concept. Attention to the seemingly banal or eccentric aspects of everyday life materialized in compositions that were often asymmetrical, unbalanced, fragmented, highly contrasted and sometimes chaotic, particularly when compared to earlier traditions. This body of work required the viewer to accept formalist techniques that up to that point had been regarded as unconventional. As many critics observed, numerous images in the exhibition may have resembled anonymous snapshots entirely devoid of stylistic concerns, yet Szarkowski highlighted how the criteria that had inspired Walker Evans were still at work here - merely transformed into a more contemporary guise. Diane Arbus, Lee Friedlander and Garry Winogrand might thus be considered the heirs of the glorious documentary tradition, and the founders of a new generation who reshaped 'the documentary tradition based on the artists' own fascination with the snapshot, the most personal, reticent, and ambiguous of documents. These photographers have attempted to preserve the persuasiveness and mystery of these humble and intuitive camera records, while adding a sense of intention and visual logic.'[74]

In accordance with the 'usable' tradition that Szarkowski held so dear, the exhibition was designed to highlight a new relationship between photographer and subject, and a practice of photography that was more personal and subjective. It was not the first time that

Szarkowski had shown work by these three figures: Winogrand had been introduced to the public in 1963, in *Five Unrelated Photographers*, and again in 1965, in *Recent Acquisitions: Photography*, alongside Diane Arbus; and Friedlander had featured in *Photographs for Collectors* (1963) and in *The Photographer's Eye* (1964). *New Documents*, however, was the first show to display a wide selection of their work, confirming a similarity of vision and intent.

The exhibition, opened on 28 February 1967, was staged on the ground floor of the museum. Visitors were greeted by thirty-two images by Diane Arbus, which occupied a whole gallery, while work by Winogrand and Friedlander hung on the walls of a larger adjacent space. In a 1972 interview with Doon Arbus, the photographer's daughter, Szarkowski explained that the exhibition's layout was partly in response to differences in format, style and subject inherent in Arbus's work. It was this exhibition that introduced Diane Arbus to the world. Her images - extremely transgressive both in form and content - captured the attention of the public and the critics. Shot in black and white, exaggerated by the use of flash, portraits of dwarves, transvestites, nudists and people who were marginalized or part of a tasteless middle class followed in succession.

The selected prints were of different dimensions, the largest measuring 40×50 cm (15¾ × 19¾ in.). The majority were square and framed in thin plastic boxes almost the same size as the prints, giving the impression that they were attached directly to the wall. In a panel of text accompanying the show, Szarkowski reminded viewers: 'The portraits of Diane Arbus show that all of us - the most ordinary and the most exotic of us - are on closer scrutiny remarkable. The honesty of her vision is of an order belonging only to those of a truly generous spirit.' Despite many positive reviews in the press, the public was very shocked by Arbus's work. Terrified that it might be misunderstood, and that she would be considered simply as 'the photographer of freaks', Arbus went to the exhibition nearly every day to listen to the visitors' reactions.

The photographs of Winogrand and Friedlander had been taken with a 35mm Leica camera and were rectangular in format. In the *New York Times* on 5 March 1967, Jacob Deschin wrote: 'Mr. Winogrand and Mr. Friedlander complement each other. The former moves in rhythm with human activity, to capture groupings and motion that almost have the equality of a frame from a movie film. They have a mood of climax, of a moment stopped at the peak of a situation. They also have the feeling of a snapshot.'[75] The black-and-white prints showed the public the development of street photography in the mid-1960s: they constituted an urban landscape that was familiar yet at the same time alienating and mysterious, marked by fragmented reflections, the superimposition of signs and bodies, and by an opacity and an ambiguity that were difficult to fathom. The camera captured and cropped fragments of reality and the debris of everyday life, all within seemingly casual shots.

Szarkowski's view of this body of work was apparent from one of the introductory wall panels: 'Lee Friedlander, standing at a greater emotional distance from his subjects, reconstructs our world in precise and elegant metaphors, showing its people in and through their most valued environments: their homes and offices and shops and pageant grounds. Garry

Winogrand's jokes, like those of Rabelais, are no less serious for being funny, and, in the best sense, vulgar. His taste for life, being stronger than his regard for art, makes him equal even to the task of confronting the comedy of his own time. These three photographers would prefer that their pictures be regarded not as art, but as life. This is not quite possible, for a picture is, after all, only a picture. But these pictures might well change our sense of what life is like.'[76] The three photographers on display clearly had different styles and different ways of approaching their work but, in Szarkowski's mind, they shared a radical sensibility that redefined what was worth looking at, what should be considered important: 'In one sense, we could regard it as a group of three little one-man shows. But it was three one-man shows that also had some degree, I think, of coherent meaning in regard to what was new in the mid-sixties, what was new and vital and most original in the mid-sixties.'[77]

Owing to Szarkowski's intuition and his influence as curator, the three photographers who featured in *New Documents* went on to become dominant figures on the photographic scene in the later 1960s - creators of a visual vocabulary that would influence future generations. In 1984, speaking about *New Documents* in an interview with Andy Grundberg for *Afterimage*, Szarkowski declared: 'That work was so marvelously free, free of any kind of

Opening of the exhibition *New Documents*, MoMA, 28 February 1967. © Museum of Modern Art, New York/Scala

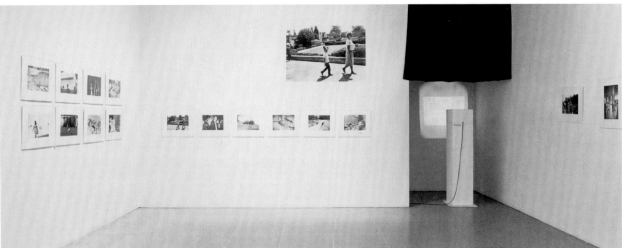

sobering responsibilities. I don't in any way mean to suggest that it was irresponsible. What it was responsible *to* was an absolutely passionate and extremely intelligent and knowledgeable desire to try to find a way to explain one's sense of the world in a photograph and let any chip fall where it may. It was free in that sense. But it was the '60s, too ... The thing that made the world of Winogrand, Friedlander, and Arbus possible, that made it so wonderful, like absolutely the first breath of spring air coming through this smoggy city, was that what had come to be called the documentary tradition had gotten so leaden, tired, boring, dutiful, automatic, Pavlovian ... So, in part, I think people liked the photographers in "New Documents" as a reaction against all that claptrap. When somebody asked Friedlander what he was concerned about, he said "I'm concerned about supporting my family, and making a good picture." ... But he didn't mean that he wasn't concerned about the world; he meant that he wasn't going to lean on that tired old crutch anymore. That nobody was going to

Above: **Room dedicated to Diane Arbus.**

Below: **Room dedicated to Winogrand and Friedlander.**
© Museum of Modern Art, New York/Scala

make him defend his work to the tune of the old gypsy violin accompaniment. Well they washed the slate clean.'[78]

Over the years, one of the main criticisms aimed at Szarkowski was that, under his direction, the Department of Photography at MoMA had ignored social issues and not given wide enough coverage to reportage and photojournalism. In Szarkowski's view, photography was incapable of capturing the enormous scope of some of the news stories and events of the day, for example the Vietnam War. 'Photography's direct report of … recent matters of historical importance seems similarly opaque and superficial, he once said'[79] - the reason why, in his opinion, the most dedicated photographers had acknowledged the inadequacy of the medium and directed the camera towards a more 'personal' approach. In this sense, the concept of *From the Picture Press*, which opened in 1973, was exemplary. Assisted by Diane Arbus and Carole Kismaric, Szarkowski selected a series of photographs from the archives of the *Daily News* for a survey of the formal and iconographic characteristics of newspaper and magazine images. The aim was to show the narrative weakness inherent in the photograph itself, which could not relate an event alone but at most provide a vague impression of the scene. Removed from their original context, shorn of their captions and organized according to broad categories such as 'disasters', 'rituals' and so on, the images revealed the existence of surprising analogies in formal consistency (according to Szarkowski), despite their very different themes: 'As images, the photographs are shockingly direct, and at the same time, mysteriously elliptical and fragmentary, reproducing the texture and flavor of experience without explaining its meaning.'[80] As he had suggested earlier in *The Photographer's Eye*, the photographs should be read not as stories but as symbols.

Abstract photography and conceptual work, for which many artists (Robert Smithson, Richard Long, Richard Prince and Cindy Sherman, for instance) had begun to use photography, were relegated to the wings. During the same period MoMA also entirely overlooked the work of photographers such as Jeff Wall, Sherrie Levine, Louise Lawler and Robert Mapplethorpe, as well as many other technically sophisticated artists whose creativity went beyond the observation of real life towards more directorial methods of composing photographs. It is ironic that someone who had fought so hard for photography to be recognized as an art form should have shown total disinterest in the first generation of image-makers who did not consider themselves photographers but as artists who used photography.

Responding to accusations of formalism and bias, Szarkowski said: 'I can't think of one exhibition that we've ever done that could be thought of as having been designed to demonstrate any such thing … It came to me once, a while ago, that if you are trying to write a sentence as precisely and accurately as you can, there are not really two ways of saying the same thing. You can say similar things … That's true in pictures, too: you can't say the same thing in two different ways. So, if you change the form, you change the meaning, too.'[81] Despite the criticism, Szarkowski stuck steadfastly to his curatorial line, remaining firmly at the helm of the photography department throughout the 1980s and becoming one of the most influential figures in the history of contemporary photography.

NOTES

1 Beaumont Newhall, *Focus: Memoirs of a Life in Photography* (Boston, Mass.: Little, Brown, 1993, p. 47.

2 John Szarkowski, *Looking at Photographs: 100 Pictures from the Collection of the Museum of Modern Art* (New York: MoMA/New York Graphic Society, 1973), p. 9.

3 See Olivier Lugon, 'Entre l'affiche et le monument, le photomural dans les années 1930', in *Exposition et médias: Photographie, cinéma, télévision* (Lausanne: L'Âge d'Homme, 2012).

4 Cited in Russell Lynes, *Good Old Modern* (New York: Atheneum, 1973), pp. 156-57.

5 Lewis Mumford, 'The Art Galleries', *New Yorker*, 3 April 1937, p. 40.

6 Christopher Phillips, 'The Judgment Seat of Photography', in *October*, vol. 22 (Cambridge, Mass.: MIT Press, 1982), p. 34.

7 Phillips, pp. 32-33.

8 Beaumont Newhall, *Photography 1839-1937* (exh. cat., Museum of Modern Art, New York, 1937), p. 8.

9 Beaumont Newhall, *Photography: A Short Critical History* (New York: Museum of Modern Art, 1938), p. 9.

10 *New York Herald Tribune*, 19 March 1937.

11 Christine Y. Hahn, 'Exhibition as Archive: Beaumont Newhall, *Photography 1839-1937*, and the Museum of Modern Art', in *Visual Resources: An International Journal of Documentation*, vol. 18, no. 2 (2002), pp. 145-52.

12 Newhall, *Focus*, p. 46.

13 Ibid.

14 Ansel Adams, *Making a Photograph* (London and New York: Studio Publications, 1935), p. 14.

15 Museum of Modern Art Archives: Newhall II.I.

16 Museum of Modern Art Archives: Newhall II.2.

17 'The New Department of Photography', *Bulletin of the Museum of Modern Art*, p. 2.

18 Ibid., p. 5.

19 Ibid.

20 Newhall, *Focus*, p. 66.

21 Eva Cockcroft, 'Abstract Expressionism, Weapon of the Cold War', *Artforum*, vol. 15 (June 1974), pp. 39-41.

22 Lynes, *Good Old Modern*, pp. 233-38.

23 Cockcroft, 'Abstract Expressionism'.

24 Edward Allen Jewell, 'Portrait of the Spirit of a Nation', *New York Times*, 7 June 1942 (Museum of Modern Art Archives, Reg 182).

25 Ibid.

26 Mary Anne Staniszewski, *The Power of Display: A History of Exhibition Installations at the Museum of Modern Art* (Cambridge, Mass.: MIT Press, 1998).

27 Monroe Wheeler, 'A note on the exhibition', *Bulletin of the Museum of Modern Art*, vol. 9 (June 1942), pp. 18-20.

28 Monroe Wheeler, 'Two famous Americans arrange *Road to Victory* exhibition at Museum of Modern Art', Museum of Modern Art Archives: CUR 182.

29 Christopher Phillips, 'Steichen's Road to Victory', *Exposure*, vol. 18, no. 2 (1981), p. 40.

30 Herbert Bayer, 'Fundamentals of Exhibition Design', *PM*, vol. 6, no. 2 (December 1939/January 1940).

31 Ralph Steiner, *PM*, 31 May 1942; Edward Steichen Archive, Museum of Modern Art.

32 Jewell, 'Portrait of the Spirit of a Nation'.

33 Elizabeth McCausland, 'Photographs Illustrate our Road to Victory', *Photo Notes*, June 1942.

34 Museum of Modern Art Archives: REG 182.

35 Wheeler, 'A note on the exhibition'.

36 John Szarkowski, 'The Family of Man', in *The Museum of Modern Art at Mid-century at Home and Abroad* (New York: Museum of Modern Art, 1994), p. 20.

37 1947 press release; Edward Steichen Archive, Museum of Modern Art.

38 Edward Steichen, *Steichen: A Life in Photography* (New York: Harmony Books/Museum of Modern Art, 1985), chapter 13.

39 Ibid.

40 Edward Steichen, 'The F.S.A. Photographers', *U.S. Camera Annual*, 1939, p. 44.

41 Letter to Dorothea Lange, dated 25 August 1952. Department of Photography files, Museum of Modern Art, New York.

42 See Gabriel Bauret, 'John G. Morris. 1948, dans le *Ladies' Home Journal*', in *The Family of Man: Témoignages et documents* (Luxembourg: Artevents, 1994), pp. 37-43.

43 René d'Harnoncourt to Nelson Rockefeller, 7 July 1950. Museum of Modern Art Archives: René d'Harnoncourt Papers, AAA: 2930; 441.

44 Wayne Miller interviewed by Margaret Mitchell, incomplete transcript in Department of Photography files, Museum of Modern Art.

45 Szarkowski, 'The Family of Man'.

46 'The Museum of Modern Art and "The Family of Man"', in *Steichen: A Life in Photography*, chapter 13.

47 Quoted in Staniszewski, p. 238.

48 Ibid., p. 240.

49 *Steichen: A Life in Photography*.

50 Staniszewski, p. 244.

51 Ibid., p. 244.

52 Cited in ibid., p. 249.

53 Arthur Goldsmith, Jr., 'The Family of Man', *Popular Photography*, vol. 36 (May 1955), p. 88.

54 Hilton Kramer, 'Exhibiting *The Family of Man*', *Commentary*, vol. 20, no. 4 (October 1955), p. 364.

55 Ibid.

56 Roland Barthes, 'The Great Family of Man', in *Mythologies* [1957], trans. Annette Lavers (New York: Hill and Wang, 1972), pp. 100-102.

57 Ibid.

58 Quoted in *The American Artist*, May 1955.

59 Edward Steichen, cited in Eric J. Sandeen, *Picturing an Exhibition: The Family of Man and 1950s America* (Albuquerque: University of New Mexico Press, 1995), p. 57.

60 Quoted in Staniszewski, p. 251.

61 Museum of Modern Art Archives.

62 Szarkowski, 'The Family of Man', p. 14.

63 Quoted in Staniszewski, p. 258.

64 Museum of Modern Art Archives.

65 John Szarkowski interviewed by Mark Durden, 'Eyes Wide Open: Interview with John Szarkowski', *Art in America*, vol. 94, no. 5 (2006), pp. 83-88.

66 John Szarkowski, introduction to *The Photographer's Eye* (exh. cat., Museum of Modern Art, New York, 1966).

67 Staniszewski, p. 110.

68 Quoted in Maren Strange, 'Photography and the Institution: Szarkowski at the Modern', *The Massachusetts Review*, vol. 19, no. 4 (1978), p. 694.

69 Ibid., p. 18

70 Strange, p. 697.

71 Andy Grundberg, 'An Interview with John Szarkowski', *Afterimage*, vol. 12, no. 3 (October 1984), pp. 12-13.

72 Wall label introducing the *New Documents* exhibition (28 February-7 May 1967); Museum of Modern Art Archives.

73 Ibid.

74 Wall label introducing the *Photography: New Acquisitions* exhibition (16 April-5 July 1970); Museum of Modern Art Archives.

75 Jacob Deschin, *New York Times*, 5 March 1967; Museum of Modern Art Archives.

76 Wall label introducing *New Documents*; Museum of Modern Art Archives.

77 Strange, p. 700.

78 Grundberg, 'An interview with John Szarkowski', p. 13.

79 John Szarkowski interviewed by Diana Loercher, 'Photography as Personal Art', *Christian Science Monitor*, 14 September 1978.

80 John Szarkowski, *From the Picture Press* (exh. cat., Museum of Modern Art, New York, 1973), p. 6.

81 Strange, pp. 694-95.

View of the exhibition *Irving Penn*,
9 October–8 December 1986,
Palais de Tokyo, Paris. © CNP

8

The Image-Maker:
Robert Delpire and the
Centre National de la Photographie, Paris

Michel Frizot

The 1980s witnessed a photography boom in France, and the number of photographic exhibitions soared. This expansion was unquestionably due to political circumstances (in particular the election of François Mitterand in 1981), as well as a shift in the general perception of photography and a sudden increase in suitable venues. Interest in the medium had started to grow during the 1970s, at a level that was both institutional and personal, nourished by the reputation of individual photographers (Lartigue and Cartier-Bresson, for instance), an awareness of the historical value of images and of the abundance of national collections, the role played by photography in the press, fashion and advertising, and also the acceptance of photography by avant-garde art movements. This upswing was accompanied by initiatives on the part of the Ministry of Culture (a distinctive feature of French governments since 1959) and in particular the minister himself, Michel Guy, who in 1975 announced the creation of a national institution - the Fondation Nationale de la Photographie - which opened in Lyon in 1978.

The Rencontres Internationales de la Photographie in Arles (from 1970); the foundation of the Galerie du Château d'Eau in Toulouse (1974) and the Galerie Agathe Gaillard in Paris (1975); exhibitions of vintage photographs by the Société Française de Photographie (1976) and the Bibliothèque Nationale (1980, at the Petit-Palais);[1] the opening of the Centre Pompidou (1977), which led to some debate over the role of photography; the creation of the Musée d'Orsay, including a photography department (1978); the introduction of university courses - all of these demonstrated a change of attitude. Previously, it was thought that this ubiquitous medium was of social and media interest, but had little artistic value. Other concrete signs of a turnaround were Jacques Henri Lartigue's donation of all his works to the French state (1979) and the establishment of a photographic heritage unit (1980). These developments were reinforced by changes in cultural policy when the left came into power in 1981. When Jack Lang became Minister of Culture, there were two particularly striking events: the founding of the École Nationale Supérieure de la Photographie in Arles and of the Centre National de la Photographie (CNP) in Paris, both in 1982.

Robert Delpire

The CNP owed its originality to two factors: its subsidy, received from the Ministry of Culture, and the personality of its director, Robert Delpire, who was appointed by the minister. Its constitution was very general, not to say permissive: the aim was to foster 'expressive photography' (others called it 'creative photography') among the 'wider public' (as opposed to aficionados), and to support creativity, principally among young photographers. As a result, the CNP chose to devote itself to exhibitions (on the basis that suitable premises would be found), publications (mainly the Photo Poche series and exhibition catalogues), audio-visual productions (such as *Une minute pour une image* and *Contacts*) and, to a lesser degree, educational projects. It goes without saying that this clear direction - and all the achievements that followed - owed a great deal to the personal involvement of the director, Robert Delpire. Since he had no background in government administration, photography, education or museums, he was considered a 'private' rather than public figure (which was one criticism levelled at him), viewed more as a publisher or gallery owner.

It may be useful at this point to trace the highlights of Delpire's artistic career, which had no small influence on the spirit of the CNP.[2] Born in 1926, he studied medicine, but in 1950 he became publisher of the magazine *Neuf* - an organ of the Maison de la Médicine - in which he included photographs.[3] (The fifth issue was devoted to Brassaï, and the eighth to Robert Frank.) He went on to publish photography books: the Neuf series, which was followed by the Huit (pocket format) and Dix (large format) series,[4] made him perhaps the most forward-thinking publisher of the 1950s. His next venture, the *Encyclopédie essentielle*, was a series of twenty-four titles dealing with documentary themes and using innovative illustrations (the most famous was the fifth volume in the series, *The Americans* by Robert Frank). These publications were strikingly original in terms of layout, graphics, printing quality, jackets and, in short, their whole mode of presentation, thanks to Delpire's choice of 'technical directors' - graphic designers whose style was already highly individual (Pierre Faucheux, who worked on *Neuf*, for instance, or Jacques Monory on the *Encyclopédie essentielle*) - and perhaps also a distinctive Swiss influence. During the 1960s Delpire worked in advertising, eventually running a large agency that most notably handled projects for Citroën. His interest lay in typography, designing logos and the production of booklets, brochures, invitations and posters - which often featured illustrations by well-known graphic artists as well as photographs by André Martin, William Klein and others. Delpire returned

View of the rotunda of the Palais de Tokyo during the exhibition *Le temps d'un mouvement*, April–June 1987, Paris. © CNP

to photography books in the 1970s, publishing *Gypsies* by Josef Koudelka (1975), the Nouvel Observateur/Delpire series (six titles, 1976-78), and the first two titles in the Photo Poche series, published under the aegis of the Fondation Nationale de la Photographie in 1982.

However, the man who took on the running of the Centre National de la Photographie without a clear remit was known within the Parisian exhibition world mostly as the curator and designer of *Citroën, Arts graphiques et publicité* at the Musée des Arts Décoratifs in 1965; the first major Lartigue exhibition at the same museum in 1975; a large-scale Cartier-Bresson retrospective, featuring 300 photographs, at the Musée d'Art Moderne in 1980;[5] and also as the director of the Delpire Gallery at 13 Rue de l'Abbaye (from 1963), where photography had been exhibited since 1973 (his most 'personal' activity, which he ceased when he started at CNP). It should perhaps be emphasized that Delpire had already introduced a very personal style into the exhibitions he curated; aside from their typography and graphic design, they were immediately recognizable by the unusual scale of their photographic enlargements. The Lartigue exhibition, for instance, consisted of sepia-toned enlargements attached to plywood panels that were sometimes several metres long; the original prints, which measured no more than 10 to 15 cm (4 to 6 in.), were not displayed.

Photography at the Palais de Tokyo

The Centre National de la Photographie spent the first few months of its existence working out its policies and plans, despite having no premises of its own[6] and no likelihood of acquiring

any in the immediate future. Its earliest exhibitions were thus on subjects that allowed collaboration with existing photographic institutions, as well as exploring emerging trends. These projects were always dependent on finding a location that was suited to Delpire's style. *Moins Trente*, the first in a series of biennial exhibitions of works by photographers under the age of thirty, selected by means of a competition, took place in April and May of 1983 at the Société Française d'Architecture on the Rue du Cherche-Midi; *Photo Génie*, featuring civil-engineering photographs from the collections of the École des Ponts-et-Chaussées, was presented at the École Nationale Supérieure des Beaux-Arts (September-October 1983); a selection of vintage photographs from the Georges Sirot collection at the Bibliothèque Nationale was shown in its Mansart gallery (the first time it had displayed original prints alongside modern enlargements; September-November 1983); and *Paris de Jean Mounicq* was exhibited at the Musée Carnavalet (November-December 1983). However, these shows, which broke away from the strait-laced conventions observed by the ministry and the more established institutions, attracted little attention to the CNP.

It was not until March 1984 that the CNP took over its new and permanent premises: some rooms in the east wing of the Palais de Tokyo. Donated by the ministry, this space had formerly been used by the Musée National d'Art Moderne, which had transferred to the Centre Pompidou in 1976. The location undoubtedly offered the CNP its big chance.[7] At the time there was no such thing as contemporary art photography, which has since accustomed us to large formats, and so-called 'vintage prints' were in a format much smaller than the exhibition prints used by the great photographers. These rooms, therefore, might have seemed unsuitable and completely out of proportion, but they measured up to Delpire's unusual vision and proved themselves to be a good fit for photography's new world order.

Visitors entered the premises from the Avenue du Président Wilson via a monumental doorway and then crossed a very large hall, which had belonged to the museum. They then descended a flight of stairs and emerged onto a landing, like a kind of balcony, that overlooked a rotunda with eight columns and other adjoining areas, one of which was rectangular. From the landing, which offered an overall view of the largest exhibition space, they descended once more via two symmetrical flights of stairs. The majestic solemnity of the space was striking: its dimensions, its loftiness, the beauty of the first, all-embracing view and the grandiose circular ceiling had all been created with great architectural restraint and without any decoration, solely for the purpose of presenting artworks in large quantities. The Palais had originally been built for the International Exhibition of 1937. The CNP occupied the rotunda and adjoining areas; a small 'below-stairs' room, which had a lower ceiling and space for about thirty prints, and a larger room (holding between fifty and eighty prints) brought the total area to around 1,000 square metres (10,760 square feet). The premises were later extended to include more rooms on the same level, plus one on the ground floor. In the nine years of its occupancy, between 1984 and 1993,[8] the CNP usually held three simultaneous exhibitions per quarter, the largest of them in the great rotunda.[9] In all, 120 CNP exhibitions were mounted at the Palais de Tokyo.[10]

View of the Raymond Depardon exhibition *San Clemente*, 5 December 1984–25 January 1985, Paris. © CNP

The monumental layout was not in itself suited to displaying photographs, but when one arrived at floor level, in the dimmed light (better for preserving the prints), one could forget the vast scale of the place and simply concentrate on the pictures. Delpire's design consisted of modular display units that took the form of hollow blocks, 30 to 40 cm (11⅞ to 15¾ in.) deep and 2 m (6 ft 6 in.) wide, that could be moved anywhere but were heavy enough to remain stable, and that could be placed alongside one another to form a continuous display or combined with other stands. Electric cables for lighting ran inside the blocks and connected to sockets in the floor. The lighting system was designed on a scale that would suit the prints and provided a low level of light.[11]

The extremely innovative approach adopted by the CNP at the Palais de Tokyo was certainly facilitated by the flexibility of the rotunda's layout - used to its best advantage during major exhibitions - as well as by the spectacular setting. Each exhibition was designed like a stage set, taking into account not only the arrangement of the photographs, but also the way in which arriving visitors would perceive the exhibition within the space itself, particularly when viewed from the balcony. This particular spot provided a kind of introduction, allowing visitors to anticipate the tone and mood of the exhibition, its layout, the emphasis provided by the lighting, the colours of the display units and the graphics (the typography was always inventive). Another important element that helped guide visitors from the moment they arrived outside the building was the CNP's signage, designed by Delpire himself, and the CNP's logo. Every element of the graphic design (exhibition layout, catalogues, invitations) passed before Delpire's eyes.[12]

The main exhibition in the rotunda was arranged so as to allow for a clear line of sight from the balcony: the eye was directed towards a display featuring the subject of the exhibition, the name of the photographer and the theme, with a glimpse of a raised area beyond (which actually housed technical equipment, its rear serving as a projection screen). If we look back at photographs from this era, we can see how the mobility of the modular units allowed a degree of geometric flexibility, so that at floor level they could either function as freestanding blocks or form 'rooms' that were self-contained to varying degrees. The exhibition of Raymond Depardon's *San Clemente* (1984; p. 204), a series of photographs taken at a psychiatric hospital in Venice, was designed to create a sense of enclosure, including a 'dark room' (which served as a projection space) that stood within a larger white area with only one exit.

The images themselves were mostly large-format enlargements (with no mattes or frames), creating a striking impression when seen from the balcony, alongside recent prints in a 30 × 40 cm (11⅞ × 15¾ in.) or 40 × 50 cm (15¾ × 19⅝ in.) format, plus period and vintage prints for older work. The exhibitions *Julia Margaret Cameron* (1985) and *Alvin Langdon Coburn* (1985) featured only vintage prints; *Identités* (1985-86) combined period prints with enlargements; *Irving Penn* (1986) consisted only of original prints by the artist himself; and *Metropolis* (1985) and *Georges Méliès* (1986) were made up exclusively of enlargements of prints taken from original albums and archives.

View of the exhibition *William Klein: Le commun des mortels*, 18 December 1986–2 March 1987, Paris. © CNP

The exhibitions

Exhibitions at the Palais de Tokyo began on a somewhat paradoxical note, albeit deliberately so, with a show about contemporary art. *Contiguités: De la photographie à la peinture* (1984; p. 211) considered various fields of contemporary art, all connected by their use of photography. It was followed by *Regards sur l'art*, a series of photographs taken in museums, recording the reactions of visitors. Most of the CNP's exhibitions, however, were monographs. Some were retrospective, covering the greatest photographers in the history of the medium (René Burri, Bruce Davidson, Julia Margaret Cameron, Robert Frank, Robert Capa, Margaret Bourke-White, Garry Winogrand, Romualdo García, Werner Bischof, Marc Riboud); others were themed or selective (Cartier-Bresson in India, Sebastião Salgado in the Sahel, Keiichi Tahara and fin-de-siècle architecture, Josef Koudelka's *Exiles*). Dieter Appelt, Joel-Peter Witkin, Jan Dibbets, Robert Mapplethorpe and Pascal Kern provided atypical

incursions into the contemporary photographic art scene of the 1970s. One of the finest of the monograph exhibitions (and best attended) was *Irving Penn* (1986; p. 200), a show that came over from MoMA. The most extraordinary and most carefully devised, stemming from several decades of collaboration between William Klein and Robert Delpire, was Klein's *Le commun des mortels* (1986-87), in which massive enlargements of 35mm images - photographs of streets and demonstrations mounted as panoramas - formed a continuous sequence that wound around the rotunda (p. 207). The layout departed from that of standard photography exhibitions,[13] including those held at the CNP: the display was completely curved, and the pictures were shown without borders or frames, multiple images joined together to create a kind of panoramic and temporal continuity between individual shots. Visitors found themselves confronted by faces that were larger than life, inverting the usual relationship between the viewer and the photographic subject.

Aside from the biennial *Moins Trente*,[14] large-scale themed exhibitions were the main focus of the CNP. The themes would be discussed and defined beforehand, and it took several people many months to prepare all the necessary material, which would culminate in a catalogue-cum-book in which some of the works were reproduced. Perhaps the

View of the exhibition *Identités: De Disdéri au Photomaton*, 18 December 1985–24 February 1986, Paris. © CNP

most spectacular of these shows was *Identités: De Disdéri au Photomaton* (1985-86), which dealt with the crucial problem of identity in photography. In terms of historical variety and documentary breadth, it is worthy of attention.[15] The underlying idea was to examine the ramifications of the concept of identity (and identification) in photography as opposed to portraiture. The passport photo, which is the most common and yet the most personal and most symbolic image of individuality, lay at the heart of this theme, especially during the 1980s. Every possible form of enlargement, format and framing was utilized in this show. It began with Disdéri's visiting cards (*c.* 1860), which rapidly increased in popularity in the upper echelons of urban society, as an early example of individualization through images. Photography was also used by the nascent science of anthropology as a quasi-scientific aid to research. Its exploitation for purposes of repression during the Commune de Paris (1871) later led to Alphonse Bertillon's system of anthropometric photography for the Préfecture de Police during the 1890s; used to record details of suspects who had been interrogated, it consisted of full-face and profile photographs plus a table of descriptions and measure-ments. The exhibition included an original showcase of these early mugshot images, which was designed to illustrate Bertillon's method and the 'physiognomic features' (eyes, ears, nose, etc.) that could be used for identification, up to and including tattoos and other dis-tinctive marks. Nazi records of the Jewish prisoners in their concentration camps show the absurd lengths to which this system could be taken. The exhibition also highlighted the use of passport-style pictures on memorials and gravestones, as illustrated in the work of Ernst Haas, Gilles Peress, Josef Koudelka, Marc Riboud and André Martin, along with postcards, school photos and other contemporary documents. The Photofit image, made out of inter-changeable elements, reverses the idea of photographic identity by trying to reconstruct an unknown face. A key element in identity photos and image standardization is the photo booth, which had its beginnings in 1928; it was displayed here for the first time in its proper historical context, in the form of an original Photomaton booth from the 1950s.[16] Offering a greater degree of personal freedom, the photo booth opened up new possibilities of self-expression to its anonymous users, and thus to artists such as Susan Hiller, Gilles Blanchard and Carol Taback, who made use of its standardized images as a framework for freeform fantasies. The borderline between the identity photo and the portrait is indefinable, since both the concept and the practice overlap; the exhibition concluded by focusing on this in-between area, in which the application of strict rules of identification allows various forms of introspective portraiture (Pierre Radisic, Arnaud Maggs, Alex Kayser). *Portraits* (1985) by Patrick Tosani, which combined blurred head-and-shoulder shots with sequences of Braille lettering, was the final work in the show.

In the same spirit, *Le temps d'un movement* (1987) featured the chronophotographs of Étienne-Jules Marey - sequential frames of various subjects in movement. *L'oeil de la letter: La lettre dans la photographie* (1989) and *Photographie/Sculpture* (1991) intermingled photo-graphs from all periods; vintage prints were accompanied by enlargements specially made for this setting (a stylistic speciality of the CNP). *Botanica*, *Vanités*: *La photographie de mode*,

Panorama des panoramas and *Beyrouth, centre ville* were all collective exhibitions that included individual series. Among the CNP's specially designed one-off shows were *Metropolis* (film stills and set photography; 1985) and *Georges Méliès* (1986). The desire to encompass the entire field of photography – found photographs, documentary work, press photography, studio photography, advertising images – and to counter compartmentalization, ignorance and standardization influenced the way the works were shown. Display units and lighting were carefully employed to present each image as a separate work, establishing what is now a convention in contemporary photography.[17] In 1989, to mark the 150th anniversary of the invention of photography, Paris led the way in raising public awareness of the history of photography, staging *L'invention d'un regard* at the Musée d'Orsay and *L'invention d'un art* at the Centre Pompidou. The CNP itself mounted two exhibitions on this theme: *Histoire de voir*, a short history of photography, accompanied by three special-edition Photo Poche books; and *1839: La Photographie Révélée*, covering photography's early pioneers, which was held at the Archives Nationales.[18]

The Delpire spirit, having focused on publishing during the 1950s and exhibitions during the 1970s, found the Palais de Tokyo to be an ideal location for the Centre National de la Photographie and its avowed aim of bringing about a complete reassessment of photography as a whole.[19] The challenge posed by the Palais de Tokyo – its colossal scale – required a careful handling of space, an understanding of the drama of geometry and lighting, and a precise evaluation of the relationship between graphics and spatial proportions (sometimes worked out with the aid of maquettes). All of these factors allowed photography to achieve a status it had never before enjoyed on such a scale.[20]

Top: **The exhibition *Beyrouth, centre ville*, featuring the work of Raymond Depardon, Josef Koudelka, René Burri, Fouad Elkoury, Robert Frank and Gabriele Basilico, 3 February–12 April 1993, Paris.** © CNP

Above: **The exhibition *Hommage des amis d'Henri Cartier-Bresson*, 6 December 1988–16 January 1989.** © Bernard Baudin

DELPIRE AND THE EXHIBITIONS OF THE CENTRE NATIONAL DE LA PHOTOGRAPHIE

ALESSANDRA MAURO

Although inspired by the International Center of Photography in New York, the idea of creating a cultural nerve centre in France for the production, distribution and use of photography, first announced in 1975, stemmed from a specific political strategy. In 1978 the city of Paris set up an association called Paris Audiovisuel, which was responsible for organizing a festival, the Mois de la Photo ('Photo Month'), first staged in 1980. Paris Audiovisuel went on to collaborate with the Maison Européenne de la Photographie, the prestigious institution established in 1996 under the direction of Jean-Luc Monterosso.

When the Centre National de la Photographie opened in 1982, its new director, Robert Delpire, declared that he would focus on three different areas: the design and planning of major exhibitions; the provision of concrete support for creative photography; and the overseeing of publishing initiatives. The organization's primary aim was to seek widespread recognition for photography and to appeal to as many sectors of the public as possible through its exhibitions. Delpire insisted that he was a *monteur d'images* ('exhibitor of images'): 'That's exactly what I am. I choose the images, I format them and I exhibit them to a public I hope will be as wide as possible and to people who are likely to agree with the choice. I have no other aim in life.'[21]

The exhibition *Contiguïtés: De la photographie à la peinture*, 2 March–29 April 1984. This was the first exhibition held at the Palais de Tokyo.

EXHIBITIONS HELD AT THE CENTRE NATIONAL DE LA PHOTOGRAPHIE

Unless otherwise indicated, the venue for these shows was the Palais de Tokyo, Avenue du Président Wilson, Paris.

1983

- Moins Trente: Biennale de la jeune
  photographie en France
21 April to 28 May 1983
Société Française d'Architecture

- Photo Génie: Photographies de génie
  civil au XIXe siècle
14 September to 23 October 1983
École Nationale Supérieure des Beaux-Arts

- Georges Sirot: Une collection de
  photographies anciennes
15 September to 10 November 1983
Bibliothèque Nationale, Galerie Mansart

- Paris 1979–1982: Photographies
  de Jean Mounicq
15 November 1983 to 8 January 1984
Musée Carnavalet

1984

- Contiguïtés: De la photographie
  à la peinture
- Regards sur l'art
2 March to 29 April 1984

- René Burri: 30 ans de reportages
- Francesco Maselli: Quarante nuits
- Thierry Girard
25 April to 30 July 1984

- Claude Caroly
28 April to 30 July 1984

- Bruce Davidson: Rétrospective,
  et Le métro de New York,
  1980–1983
- Jeunes créateurs: J. E. Atwood,
  Q. Bertoux, M. A. Parkinson,
  A. de Roux et Didier Sorbé
25 September to 12 November 1984

- San Clemente: Photographies et
  un film de Raymond Depardon
- Martine Voyeux
- La chambre
5 December 1984 to 25 January 1985

1985

- British Eyes: Julia Margaret Cameron
- Alvin Langdon Coburn
- Quelques anglais pour voir…
8 February to 1 April 1985

- Naïves amériques: Collection Andreas
  Brown
- Barbara Norfleet
- Joe Steinmetz
11 April to 27 May 1985

- Moins Trente 1985: Biennale de
  la jeune photographie en France
- Prix Niépce 1985: Hervé Rabot
- Metropolis: Photographies d'un tournage
- Eugène Atget
19 June to 14 July and 1 August to 9
September 1985

- Henri Cartier-Bresson en Inde
- Images indiennes
- Autochromes
24 October 1985 to 13 January 1986

- Identités: De Disdéri au Photomaton
18 December 1985 to 24 February 1986

1986

- Robert Capa
6 February to 31 March 1986

- John B. Greene: Vues d'Égypte,
  1853–1854
- Bruno Requillart, 1972–1979
27 March to 9 June 1986

- Robert Frank: États d'urgence
- Harry Gruyaert: Lumières blanches
24 April to 9 June 1986

- Sebastião Salgado: Sahel, l'homme
  en détresse
22 May to 30 June 1986

- André François
12 June to 8 September 1986
Palais de Tokyo Annex

- Keiichi Tahara: Images de la fin du siècle
- Marc Trivier
- Georges Méliès
26 June to 26 September 1986

- Irving Penn
- Théâtre des réalités: 24 auteurs et
  plasticiens contemporains
9 October to 8 December 1986

- Prix Niépce 1986: Jean-Marc Zaorski
18 December 1986 to 26 January 1987

- William Klein: Le commun des mortels
- Donigan Cumming
18 December 1986 to 2 March 1987

1987

- Le temps d'un mouvement: Aventures
  et mésaventures de l'instant
  photographique
- Un si grand age
2 April to 8 June 1987

- Tierra y libertad: Mexique 1900–1935
7 Apri to 8 June 1987

- Charles Matton: Antipodes.
  Photos, peintures et reconstitutions
  de lieux
27 April to 6 July 1987

- Moins Trente 1987: Biennale de la jeune photographie en France
- Prix Kodak de la critique photographique 1986
- Prix Niépce 1987: Agnès Bonnot

16 June to 14 September 1987

- Procédés procédés
- De Niépce à Stieglitz: La photographie en taille-douce
- Martin Parr: Spending Time
- Romualdo García: Un photographe de studio au Mexique à la fin du siècle dernier

9 October to 30 November 1987

- Botanica: Photographies de végétaux aux XIXe et XXe siècles
- L'Arche de Noël: Une sélection de photos d'animaux de tout poil et de toute époque
- Mario Giacomelli
- Thierry Girard: Frontières, Le passage des Amériques, Marches en Charentes

10 December 1987 to 29 February 1988

1988
- Josef Koudelka: Exils
- Guy Peellaert

17 March to 30 April 1988

- Yousuf Karsh

19 May to 27 June 1988

- La photographie britannique: Collection de la Royal Photographic Society
- Lewis Carroll
- Prix Niépce 1988: Keiichi Tahara

23 June to 12 September 1988

- Elliott Erwitt
- Robert Mapplethorpe

23 September to 14 November 1988

- Regards d'acier: Photographies de Harry Gruyaert, Josef Koudelka et Sebastião Salgado

9 November to 30 November 1988

- Hommage des amis d'Henri Cartier-Bresson

6 December 1988 to 16 January 1989

1989
- L'oeil de la lettre: La lettre dans la photographie
- Martine Franck: De temps en temps
- Les acquisitions photographiques du Fonds National d'Art Contemporain

25 January to 27 March 1989

- Paralleles et contrastes: Photographies de la collection de Stephen White
- L'art de la photographie au National Geographic
- Dieter Appelt

19 April to 5 June 1989

- Les pictorialistes français: Collections de la S.F.P. (1896–1930)
- Margaret Bourke-White
- Chroniques siciliennes: Letizia Battaglia et Franco Zecchin
- Moins Trente: Biennale de la jeune photographie en France
- Prix Niépce 1989: Gladys et Patrick Zachmann

1 June to 4 September 1989

- Joel-Peter Witkin
- La Tour Eiffel
- Boris Zaborov

28 September to 7 November 1989

- 1839: La Photographie Révélée. 150ème anniversaire de la photographie

17 October to 17 December 1989
Archives Nationales, Paris

- Histoire de voir: L'aventure de la photographie de Nièpce à aujourd'hui

2 November 1989 to January 1990

- Le 40ème anniversaire de l'agence Magnum

2 November 1989 to 19 February 1990

- William Henry Fox Talbot

14 December 1989 to 19 February 1990

1990
- Singuliers-pluriels: Groupes 1900, anonymes français
- Neal Slavin: Photographies de groupes
- La collection Jean Henry
- Jean Mounicq: Les années 50
- Josep Renau: Photomontages

1 March to 14 May 1990

- Go West: Images de l'ouest américain
- E. G. Curtis
- Prix Niépce 1990: Hugues de Wurstemberger

23 May to 10 September 1990

- Naïves amériques

5 July to 4 August 1990
CCF Gobelins

- Chris Killip: Prix H.C.B. 1989
- Werner Bischof

3 October 1990 to 7 January 1991

1991
- Panorama des panoramas
- Jan Dibbets

16 January to 27 May 1991

- La photographie belge
- Prix Niépce 1991: Jean-Louis Courtinat

5 June to 16 September 1991

- Garry Winogrand
- Des vessies et des lanternes: Curiosités et mystifications photographiques
- Jean-Marc Tingaud: Intérieurs

25 September to 5 November 1991

- Photographie/Sculpture
- Pascal Kern

20 November 1991 to 23 March 1992

1992

- En préfiguration de Photofolie: Images à la carte
- 'Attention: le petit oiseau va sortir!' Une exposition préparée par les élèves de l'ENSCI à l'occasion de Photofolie.
- Louis Faurer
- Lee Friedlander: Autoportrait
8 May to 1 June 1992

- Annie Leibovitz
15 May to 27 July 1992

- Mary Ellen Mark
- La ménagerie du Palais
- Agustín Víctor Casasola
25 June to 25 October 1992

- Prix Niépce 1992: Luc Choquer
- Moins Trente: Biennale de la jeune photographie de France
17 September to 9 November 1992

- Digital Photography
22 October 1992 to 18 January 1993

- La photographie scientifique
- L'épreuve numérique
- La danse
6 November 1992 to 18 January 1993

1993

- Beyrouth, centre ville: Vu par 6 grands photographes: R. Depardon, J. Koudelka, R. Burri, F. Elkoury, R. Frank et G. Basilico
- Don McCullin: Rétrospective
- Martin Chambi
3 February to 12 April 1993

- Sebastião Salgado: La main de l'homme, 5 ans de reportages sur l'homme au travail
- Prix Niépce 1993: Jean-Claude Coutausse
- Milagros de la Torre: Photographe de studio péruvienne
30 April to 19 June 1993

The following exhibitions took place at the Hôtel Salomon de Rothschild, Rue Berryer, Paris:

1993

- Vanités: La photographie de mode au XIXe et XXe siècles
21 October 1993 to 7 February 1994

1994

- Brassaï: Du surréalisme à l'art informel
1 February to 9 May 1994

- Hommage à Robert Doisneau
1 May to 31 July 1994

- Felice Beato et l'École de Yokohama
1 June to 31 July 1994

- L'orient des photographes au XIXe siècle
7 June to 7 August 1994
Institut du Monde Arabe
A CNP/IMA co-production

- Les réfugiés: Photographies de John Vink (avec le concours de M.S.F.)
- Moins Trente: Biennale de la jeune photographie de France
- Prix Niépce 1994: Xavier Lambours
14 September to 17 October 1994

- Walker Evans et la ville
- John Gutmann: Talking Pictures
- George Segal: New York, New Jersey, 1990–1993
29 October to 5 December 1994

- Bill Brandt
- Le bestiaire d'Horvat: Frank Horvat
14 December 1994 to 27 February 1995

1995

- Sarah Moon: Vrais semblants
- Kasimir Zgorecki
15 March to 14 May 1995

- Alain Fleischer: La nuit lumière, oeuvres 1992–1995
3 May to 31 July 1995

- Martin Parr
- Prix Niépce 1995: Marie-Paule Nègre
- Samuel Fosso: Prix Afrique en créations 1995
13 September to 30 October 1995

- August Sander
- Henri Cartier-Bresson: Carnets mexicains (1934 et 1964)
8 November 1995 to 22 January 1996

NOTES

1   The originality of these exhibitions lay not only in their historical and scientific approach, which led to the reconsideration of forgotten practices and practitioners, but also in the fact that they displayed 'vintage' prints, especially from the 19th century. Living photographers did not exhibit old prints, preferring recent enlargements.

2   For more on his career, see *Delpire et Cie* (Paris: Delpire, 2009), which consists of three volumes: 1. 'Edition'; 2. 'Graphisme et publicité'; and 3. 'Expositions et films'.

3   For a history of his early work as a publisher and a list of publications, see Michel Frizot, 'Robert Frank and Robert Delpire', in *Looking In: Robert Frank's 'The Americans'*, ed. Sarah Greenough (exh. cat., National Gallery of Washington, 2009), pp. 190-98.

4   The Neuf series comprised eight titles; the Huit series, three titles in pocket format; and the Dix series, three in large format.

5   Delpire designed the layout of the Étienne-Jules Marey exhibition at the Centre Pompidou in 1977 on behalf of Kodak Pathé.

6   After September 1982, the CNP had three small offices on the premises of the Arts Plastiques, on the Avenue de l'Opéra. These were used by Delpire, Marie-Christine Wellhoff (the secretary general), myself (the project manager) and a secretary. In 1983 new and more spacious offices were allocated to a larger team in the Manufacture de Gobelins, on the Avenue des Gobelins. Those who worked there were: Catherine Sentis (the new secretary general), Marie-Pierre Magaud (assistant), Françoise Ducro (exhibitions), Françoise Bonnefoy and Benoît Rivero (publications), Maurice Lecomte (exhibition catalogues), Annik Duvillaret (touring exhibitions), Thierry Bouyer (technical team), and Laurence Brun and Olivier Cabon. The press officer was Catherine Philippot, who was succeeded by Elisabeth Pujol.

7   This was exclusively an exhibition hall, with an area for storage; the offices remained in the Avenue des Gobelins.

8   After this, the CNP moved to the Hôtel de Rothschild, still under the direction of Delpire, who retired in 1996.

9   Single exhibitions were rare, though an exception was *Identités*, in 1986. By extending the space, it was possible to mount up to five exhibitions at the same time.

10   Twenty-two exhibitions were held at the Hôtel de Rothschild until 1996; five were held elsewhere.

11   A semi-opaque cover could be placed over the narrow neon tubes to adjust their brightness.

12   A graphics studio was set up in the offices on the Avenue des Gobelins, run by Françoise Sadoux.

13   This exhibition reverted to some of the motifs of the 1930s and 1940s. These were rarely used in the 'museum-style' exhibitions of the 1970s, however, which generally favoured photographs without frames.

14   *Moins Trente* was held at the Palais de Tokyo in 1985, 1987, 1989 and 1992, and at the Hôtel de Rothschild in 1994.

15   The illustrated catalogue had the same title and was published as part of the Photocopies series produced by the CNP, with texts by Michel Frizot, Serge July, Christian Phéline and Jean Sagne.

16   To give an example of the state of historical research in the 1980s, Photomaton had never once been asked to lend documents concerning its past activities.

17   In 1977, the year of its opening, the Centre Pompidou held a major Kertész exhibition, which was confined to a narrow, barely adequate space behind the rooms used to show paintings. This demonstrated the status of photography in a national art museum, which as yet did not even have a photographic collection. The Étienne-Jules Marey exhibition was staged at the same time in the room reserved for graphic art; it was designed by Robert Delpire. Both projects were initiated by Pierre de Fenoÿl, who was then little known.

18   The commemorative exhibitions *The Art of Photography* and *Photography Until Now* were held respectively at the Royal Academy of Art, London, and MoMA, New York.

19   The CNP was thus the most important institution permanently devoted to photography.

20   As a participant in this adventure, I have first-hand knowledge of its history. I first became involved in the history of photography when I discovered the work of Marey in 1972. I met Robert Delpire in 1973, and worked closely with him, most notably on the catalogue for the Lartigue exhibition at the Musée des Arts Décoratifs in 1975, and on several other publishing projects. I was appointed to the CNP in October 1982 as the director's project manager.

21   Radio interview with Elisabeth Bouvet, 3 July 2009, for RFI; available at www1.rfi.fr/culturefr/articles/114/article_82203.asp (accessed 8 May 2014).

**The *Wolfgang Tillmans* exhibition
at Portikus, Frankfurt, 1995.**
© Katrin Schilling

The Installation as Work of Art:
From Conceptualism to Wolfgang Tillmans

Francesco Zanot

After the click: the conceptual revolution

On 2 September 1995 an untitled solo exhibition by the German photographer Wolfgang Tillmans opened in Frankfurt. It was held at Portikus, a prominent contemporary art centre that had opened in 1987 within the purposely refurbished Stadtbibliothek. Despite the artist's youth, his brief exhibition career (which had begun only in the late 1980s) and the limited size of the venue, this proved to be a decisive event. Tillmans not only designed the layout of the room where his photographs were presented, viewing it as an important factor in the way they would be perceived, but also conceived the whole as an installation environment in which images and space would evolve in tandem. In essence, his work no longer consisted of just the images he had taken through the camera lens, but also the venue that contained them, thus offering the spectator an experience of photography that was no longer merely front-on but essentially circular.

Tillmans's approach for the Frankfurt exhibition, repeated and reworked on numerous occasions thereafter as he gained in experience and had greater resources at his disposal, did not of course represent an entirely autonomous path, but was based on initiatives that many of his colleagues had adopted. For many years photographers involved in the art world had considered that their work culminated in the print-making process: being a photographer meant developing one's own personal imagery and working freely within it, pressing the shutter and then either carrying out or entrusting to others the steps necessary to produce the work. What happened after the image had been printed was largely of no interest to the authors, aside from their preference for neutral and standardized modes of presentation in exhibitions, ranging from the typical picture-gallery arrangements of the 19th century to the

combination of linear hanging, mounts and black frames familiar today. Historically, painters have long been able to influence the way their works are presented, albeit in a limited way, by choosing the size and shape of their support. Canvases, panels, works on paper and frescoes could measure a few centimetres square or cover several metres, radically altering the relationship between image and spectator. In certain other locations, such as public buildings and churches, it was possible to work on large cycles that took full advantage of complex spatial environments rich in symbolic potential.

In photography, this degree of flexibility occurred at a crucial moment in the medium's history. During the 1960s and 1970s, various photographers had begun to extend their interest beyond the realization and printing of images, at a time when the discipline was fully embraced by museums and curatorial practice. The Museum of Modern Art in New York had taken the lead two decades earlier,[1] and many American and European museums – including the Bibliothèque Nationale de France, the Art Institute of Chicago, the Museum of Fine Arts in Boston and the Victoria and Albert Museum, London – were now similarly endowed with departments devoted to the collection, study and display of photography. With the definitive acceptance of the photographic image within the art system, a significant

Joseph Kosuth, *One and Three Chairs*, **1965.**
© Museum of Modern Art, New York/J. Kosuth Studio/Scala

number of photographers finally began to extend their creative reach to include the dynamics of exhibition organization, adopting the museum as the preferred space for the fruition of a work. It was a logical step that well-established artists had already taken, many of whom considered photography as just another technique that would enable a more diverse style of production. Many of these figures belonged to a specific sphere of reference: conceptual art. Having originated in the United States, the movement was based on the ideas of Marcel Duchamp and Man Ray, and encouraged artists to sever the direct link to tradition in order to start afresh with issues of a linguistic and contextual nature.

Among the artists who first looked beyond the mere conception and realization of photographic images is the American Sol LeWitt who, before devoting himself to his celebrated 'wall drawings', carried out experiments with the medium in the mid-1960s. His works *Muybridge I* and *Muybridge II* are highly significant in this regard. Both consisted of wooden boxes about 250 cm (8 ft) long, divided into ten compartments, each containing a photograph that was illuminated by a light that flashed intermittently. The subject was a female nude, and the sequence of images was organized in such a way that, as they flashed on and off, the viewer felt that he or she was gradually moving closer to her navel. In the first instance (*Muybridge I*), the figure appears to move towards the spectator; in the second (*Muybridge II*), the image appears to recede. Leaving the theoretical implications of these works aside, it is evident that the photographs and the apparatus in which they are presented form a composite whole, the latter serving to reinforce their content. The box establishes the viewing sequence and, together with the flashing light, determines the way in which these images are experienced. The overriding impression is one of being inside the camera as it captures a moment of reality.

Among the best-known symbols of pure conceptualism, *One and Three Chairs* by Joseph Kosuth can also be included in this discussion, despite the fact that photography is only one of the techniques used to make it. Executed in 1965, it consists of three parts: a real chair, a definition of the word 'chair' taken from the dictionary, and, lastly, a photograph of the same object. The result is a complex reflection on the distinction between reality and imagination, referent and sign, signified and signifier, and on the possibility of achieving a sort of abstraction of a universal nature by combining various types of representation, concrete and mental. In 1969, in his essay *Art after Philosophy*, Kosuth wrote several statements that were perfectly applicable to his own work: 'Works of art are analytic propositions. That is, if viewed within their context - as art - they provide no information what-so-ever about any matter of fact. A work of art is a tautology in that it is a presentation of the artist's intention, that is, he is saying that that particular work of art *is* art, which means, is a *definition* of art. Thus, that it is art is true *a priori* (which is what Judd means when he states that "if someone calls it art, it's art").'[2] The way *One and Three Chairs* is displayed, in other words, assumes a crucial role in relation to the issues just mentioned, but it is also exploited by Kosuth in order to introduce two additional concepts: a disinterest in the aesthetic appearance of his own work, and the ambiguous role of curators and institutions in the art system.

Rather than being a finite and invariable piece, *One and Three Chairs* is installed according to a set of instructions that must be followed by anyone wishing to exhibit it. The essential steps consist of selecting a chair, placing it against a gallery wall, photographing it, making a print the same size as the original, hanging this on the wall to one side of the chair, and placing on the opposite side, at the same height, an enlargement of its written definition. Although he had removed himself from any practical intervention, Kosuth thus controlled the work's entire production process.

Unsettled Objects, realized in 1968-69 by Lothar Baumgarten, stands out from earlier examples for one fundamental reason. In this case, the possibility of conveying meaning through a display strategy also formed the work's subject. Baumgarten collected and ordered a series of images of the glass cases that hold the ethnographic collection at the Pitt Rivers Museum in Oxford, which has remained essentially intact since it opened in 1874. Simply by recording the way in which the material was classified, combined and displayed to the public, the artist enabled a series of Western prejudices to emerge. The artwork was presented in the form of a slideshow consisting of eighty slides, thus mimicking the same detached approach with which museums of history and science exhibit their own artefacts, prompting us to consider the social and political issues deeply rooted in our own culture.

Franco Vaccari, who was the subject of a solo exhibition at the 1972 Venice Biennale, is an artist who uses mainly photographic language. His *Exhibition in Real Time no. 4* is an

excellent example of an artist directing the presentation of his work in a gallery setting. As the subtitle suggests (*Leave a Photographic Trace of your Passing*), its success relied on the participation of the public. On this occasion, Vaccari simply placed an automatic photo booth in the gallery and set the participation process in motion by taking a self-portrait during the exhibition launch and hanging it on the wall. By the end of the show, there were over 6,000 strips, each containing four passport photos, arranged on the same wall. In the introduction to a book, published the following year, that summarized this experience, Renato Barilli wrote: 'The public, for the most part, has really shown that it has fantastical, inventive abilities. Inside the photo booth, intuitions, ideas, games, caprices, moods were born, sometimes simple and obvious, but more often than not innovative and sound. The performance devised by Vaccari therefore evolved into an effective means of aesthetic promotion, an invitation for all to see themselves "through different eyes", so that they might detach themselves, for a moment at least, from their established roles, with the complicity of the timer.'[3] As with Kosuth's *One and Three Chairs*, the artist did not work (or did so only to a minimal degree) on either the production or the exhibition of his work, but he planned the implementation of the second phase personally, following a concept that was finely balanced between organization and chance.

The photographers Bernd and Hilla Becher attributed significant semantic value to the format used to display their images. Devoted entirely to the representation of industrial buildings and structures, which were subdivided into uniform series according to typology and function, since 1967 they had exhibited their photographs in grids of six, nine or fifteen prints arranged in rectangles on the wall, always equidistant from each other (overleaf). The couple's photographs were so neutral and rigorously composed that they suggested a classificatory intent (the frontal viewpoint, distance from the subject and indirect lighting all remained unchanged in most cases), and the way in which they were exhibited had the same effect, prioritizing the whole and eliminating any hierarchy between the individual prints. Leaving aside the number of photographs they might contain, each of their series could be considered as a single work, majestic and compact. Their grid form recalled the simple modular structures that artists such as Carl Andre and Donald Judd were creating at the time. Even the industrial relics portrayed in the images had an involuntary sculptural quality; they were transformed into sober monuments of the modern era, to such an extent that Bernd and Hilla Becher were awarded the Golden Lion in the sculpture category at the 1990 Venice Biennale. Far from being seen merely as an image, in their hands the photograph was an object endowed with weight and volume.

Above and opposite: **Franco Vaccari, *Exhibition in Real Time no. 4: Leave a Photographic Trace of your Passing*, 1972.** Courtesy of Franco Vaccari

The large-format print: the Düsseldorf School and Jeff Wall

In 1976, Bernd Becher was appointed to the chair of photography at the Kunstakademie in Düsseldorf. Despite the fact that his wife, Hilla, was not officially permitted to teach in the same school, she did participate, and the course the Bechers devised together gave rise to a movement that was highly significant not only for photography, but for the contemporary art world in general. Laurenz Berges, Elger Esser, Andreas Gursky, Candida Höfer, Axel Hütte, Simone Nieweg, Thomas Ruff, Jörg Sasse, Thomas Struth and Petra Wunderlich are but some of the talents taught by the Bechers at Düsseldorf. (Some also studied under Gerhard Richter, who ran a painting course in the same school from 1971 until 1993.)

Although each photographer has followed an independent path, their work shares deeply rooted similarities, particularly in the three areas of theme, methodology and production. As far as the first is concerned, a recurrent theme in their photographs (though often relegated to the background while further investigations are carried out) is that of representation itself, complete with its complex philosophical, aesthetic, social and political

Bernd and Hilla Becher,
***Pitheads**, 1974.*
© Bernd & Hilla Becher/
Konrad Fischer Galerie

implications. Their method, on the other hand, is to adopt the strategy of 'critical mass', focusing on a specific subject by means of series and using repetition to reinforce their message. Furthermore, works produced by the Düsseldorf School are frequently recognizable by their large scale. They have adopted this approach for several reasons. First of all, by absenting themselves from the process of miniaturizing of the world typically associated with photography, the artists invite immediate comparison with painting and suggest that their works should be considered within the history of fine art. In addition, the size of the images establishes a clear separation between a viewer's experience of the original and of a reproduction in a book or catalogue. By choosing such a large format, the artists totally reject the intimacy normally associated with the act of taking a photograph and the traditional model of one spectator viewing one work at a time, in favour of a collective vision. The result has been defined by the critic Jean-François Chevrier as a 'confrontational experience',[4] and Michael Fried describes it as follows: 'A crucial aspect of the new relationship ... is an enforced distance between work and viewer, without which the mutual facing off of the two that underlies the notion of confrontation would not be possible.'[5] In sum, instead of having the impression of holding a fragment of reality in his or her hand, the viewer feels totally immersed in it. These works satisfy the illusionistic aspirations that have always animated the discipline.

The expressive value of the large format became evident during the first significant exhibition to bring together the central figures of the so-called Düsseldorf School, where it was revealed as a fundamental unifying element. Organized in 1991 by the curators Bernd Finkeldei and Maria Müller at the Kunstsammlung Nordrhein-Westfalen, Düsseldorf, *Aus der Distanz* ('From the Distance') presented a series of works of remarkable size. Although the Bechers never made gigantic prints, their grids of multiple images could be considered as single works, and their size would have provided a point of departure for the experimentation of their young students. Among this group the pioneer of gigantism was Thomas Ruff, who in 1986 had begun to enlarge portraits of contemporaries and acquaintances he had taken a year earlier, producing a new series of printed images that reached 210 × 165 cm (83 × 65 in.), as compared to the original size of 24 × 18 cm (9½ × 7 in.). In 1993, commenting on the reasons for this step, Ruff stated: 'Photographs aren't depictions, they're just images. With the portrait photographs, I worked on the basis that a photograph can't represent a person or a character, that a person has too many layers to be depicted in a photograph.'[6] The works included in the 1991 exhibition were part of another, more recent project that nonetheless played with the theme of scale. This was the series known as *Sterne*, or 'Stars', in which enormous prints measuring 260 × 188 cm (83 × 74 in.) reproduced details lifted from astronomic survey photos. In this vast programme designed to map the heavens, the stars are simply tiny dots on a dark background, whose intensity reveals nothing about their distance from the viewer and whose arrangement relies principally on the rules of perspective. Equally huge were the works by Gursky, Hütte and Struth, who were exhibiting some of the earliest key pieces in their artistic careers. These included the public spaces and workplaces explored from above by Gursky, who focused on the relationship between the immensity of space and the tiny actions of the people; Hütte's seemingly anonymous and linear constructions; and Struth's museums, in which the visitors converse with the great artworks of the past, transformed from observers into observed. Only the photographs by Candida Höfer and Petra Wunderlich were of modest proportions, but even they - Höfer in particular - would soon increase the surface area of their prints. The impact of *Aus der Distanz* as an exhibition was decisive. The 'distance' to which the title alluded did not refer exclusively to that between the photographers and their subject matter, but also implied the space that members of the public had to put between themselves and the works in order to view them in their entirety. Photographs, like the products of the other artistic disciplines, had also become monuments.

In considering the poetic, semantic and expressive functions of the large-format print, it would be impossible to ignore the figure of Jeff Wall. This Canadian artist began to increase the dimensions of his works in the latter half of the 1970s, choosing a path that, quite apart from any aesthetic considerations, served to alter the relationship between photograph and spectator. In an essay published in 2003 in *Artforum*, he stated: 'I extracted two things, primarily, from the Western pictorial tradition up through the nineteenth century: a love of pictures, which I believe is at the same time a love of nature and of existence itself, and an idea of the size and scale proper to pictorial art, and so proper to the ethical feeling for the world expressed in pictorial art. This is the scale of the body, the making of pictures in which the objects and figures are limned so that they appear to be on about the same scale as the people looking at the picture. I don't mean by this that there are no other valid or interesting approaches to the size of a picture; I mean that life scale is a central element in any judgment of an appropriate scale.'[7] The subjects of his earliest works created according to this logic, *The Destroyed Room* (1978; opposite) and *Picture for Women* (1979) - both of which were inspired by well-known paintings - assume proportions consistent with the milieu in which they are observed. The real world had hitherto been squeezed into the confines of the photo frame, but now the opposite occurred: the image invaded the space around it. Instead of constituting a small-scale duplicate of reality, these photographs in a sense replaced it. This was a momentous, revolutionary approach, as Wall himself has remarked: 'I realized that, in making photographs in or near life scale, photography could be practiced to a certain extent differently from the way it had been.'[8] Just as, when rock and roll arrived on the music scene in the post-war years, there was an increase in volume, here there was an increase in centimetres, so that the works were experienced almost bodily, with the whole physique. The body became like a sounding board that enriched the photographic experience.

Wall's works were distinguished by a further characteristic conferred on them after the shot was taken: in the majority of cases the images were mounted on a light box, evoking advertising posters found in bus shelters and film stills. In fact, 'cinematography' was the term that Wall often adopted to describe his photography, since it highlighted the very particular way in which he produced his images (they required a script, and the participation of

actors and a director) and the fact that they were the result of a performance. In short, their size and backlighting were enough to make his works completely novel in the photographic sphere. Referring to the slim catalogue that accompanied the one-man show organized at the Art Gallery of Greater Victoria in 1979,[9] David Campany wrote: 'With this publication, Wall was inaugurating a means of framing his practice that has since become the norm for him. While he did not pursue printed matter as a primary artistic form, it was clear the page would play an important role. His ideal viewer would be a gallery visitor attentive to the printed mediation and critical discussion of art. This was apparent even in the slightly recalcitrant title emblazoned on the catalogue's cover, the first word of which was "INSTALLATION", typeset in white on black and placed on the page as if scrolling upward like film credits. It served as a reminder that the images reproduced in the publication were not the artworks themselves, in the way art photography had traditionally inhabited the page. They were *representations* of works installed elsewhere.'[10]

Jeff Wall, *The Destroyed Room*, 1978, transparency in lightbox 159 × 229 cm (62⅝ × 90⅛ in.). Courtesy of the artist

Wolfgang Tillmans

'Installation' is one of the key words of contemporary art. By the time Jeff Wall adopted it, the term had already undergone a series of alterations and now referred to work that possessed a physicality that affected its interpretation. In its purest sense it indicates 'the type of art into which the viewer physically enters, and which is often described as "theatrical", "immersive" or "experiential"', according to Claire Bishop.[11] Coming from a more philosophical viewpoint, Juliane Rebentisch made the following observation: 'Installations are not only objects to be beheld but simultaneously also the site of reflection on the aesthetic practice of beholding. More than any other feature, what has often been called the "inclusion of the beholder" places installation art in direct relation to a central problem of modern philosophy: the problem of an ontology founded on the subject-object distinction.'[12] In other words, installations include all those works of art that, like buildings without façades, are observed from within and transform the spectator into one of their components. Two principal antecedents of installation art were Kurt Schwitters's *Merzbau* and the Exposition Internationale du Surréalisme.

The former was a work that the German artist constructed between 1923 and 1936 inside his home in Hanover: a series of objects and ephemera that related his life's story, that of his associates and the structure of his mind. The second, organized in 1938 at the Galerie des Beaux-Arts in Paris, was a large collective exhibition that brought together the works of more than sixty artists from all over the world. Apart from the exhibits themselves, some of which would be acknowledged as the cornerstones of the Surrealist movement, what really mattered on this occasion was the arrangement of the exhibition spaces, conceived by Marcel Duchamp (who also coordinated the contributions by Salvador Dalí, Georges Hugnet, Benjamin Peret and Man Ray) as a device to immerse visitors into a state halfway between dreaming and anxiety. The gallery's skylights were covered by approximately 1,200 coal sacks hung from the ceiling, dry leaves and other organic materials replaced the elegant red carpet, a loudspeaker transmitted the sounds of the German army, and several ornate beds made an appearance among the paintings and sculptures. Although the two examples were very different - a grandiose work by an individual artist on one hand, and an intervention of an essentially curatorial nature on the other - in both cases the result was similar: rather than being presented with a work face on, the visitor inhabited it.

The installation would become central to the activity of several art movements, including conceptual art, land art, Minimalism and Arte Povera, establishing itself as one of the most emblematic processes of artistic production during the 1960s and 1970s. Photography was also used, as we have seen above; alongside LeWitt, Kosuth, Baumgarten and Vaccari, we should add the names of Vito Acconci, Mel Bochner, Christian Boltanski, Victor Burgin, Jan Dibbets, Franco Guerzoni, Douglas Huebler, Richard Long, Gordon Matta-Clark, Bruce Nauman, Dennis Oppenheim and many others. However, the marriage between the photographic medium and the practice of installation reached its apogee several years later with Wolfgang Tillmans, who adapted the presentation of each of his works according to the space in which it was situated. The museum became an arena, the exhibition a laboratory testifying to the relationship between the artist and the exhibition space.

Born in 1968 in Remscheid, a small town in central Germany, Tillmans became interested in photography as a child, collecting pictures from newspapers and magazines and sticking them in notebooks. By the end of the 1980s, he was composing his first works with the same material, cutting it up and enlarging it with a photocopier. Despite these original beginnings, his reference point was in fact the avant-garde of the early 20th century, as he declared in an interview with *The Guardian* in 2010: 'When I was growing up … all the art that touched me was lens-generated, like Gerhard Richter, or Polke, Rauschenberg, Warhol. Those were the first artists I saw in the Museum Ludwig [in Cologne] and in Düsseldorf when I was 14, 15, 16. But it wasn't pop art that started this whole thing of taking photo-based images into art - there was, of course, Dada and Kurt Schwitters - he was a bit of a passion of mine. I was seeing art that touched me made out of cut-up newspapers.'[13] Schwitters, creator of the monumental *Merzbau*, lay at the root of Tillmans's artistic journey, in which an interest in installation was a logical consequence. In the meantime he developed an

imagery based on an amalgam of different photographic styles. His preferred subject matter came from his everyday world and included friends captured at a disco, at a party or at home in an intimate moment, naked; crowds of people demonstrating for peace or gay rights, streets, buildings, cities, flowers, clothes, even the contents of his fridge and enchanting natural landscapes. All of these subjects appeared in a 1995 exhibition at the Portikus gallery in Frankfurt, in which the layout served simultaneously as a display for individual photographs and a device that encouraged a fresh experience of that space. Having entered the exhibition, viewers found themselves not only in front of his works, but also within a larger work encompassing all of them.

The Portikus exhibition, which ran from 2 September to 15 October, was characterized above all by one feature: like the *Merzbau* - at least in its initial conception - it was a single room filled with many objects, each remarkably different from the next. Upon entering, visitors were immediately thrust into a complex and non-linear context; to interpret it, they were forced to construct a new frame of reference. Heterogeneity is a fundamental part of Tillmans's work: as well as styles and subjects, he also mixed different genres and ways of using this complex language. Despite bearing some resemblance to advertising and fashion photography, for example, his images are never the result of commercial assignments, yet they appear in the pages of niche magazines such as *i-D* and *Prinz* as well as gallery spaces and museums. His approach, which initially revealed a diary-like tendency in the wake of the intimate images of photographers such as Larry Clark and Nan Goldin, comprises the

democratic spirit of recent American tradition, according to which everything is worth photographing (William Eggleston), and the encyclopaedic rigour of the Germans (the Bechers and Gerhard Richter in particular). The result is a radical synthesis, and the conclusion is that photography must be considered in its entirety, free of compartmentalization based on form or content. This makes it possible to create unprecedented combinations of images (i.e. installations) that allow us to observe the complexity not only of the photographic medium, but also of contemporary existence.

In a conversation with the curator Hans Ulrich Obrist, Tillmans stated: 'My point of departure has always been the single image. Even though I continually challenge and test that "singularity", I do want each picture to be understood as its own self-sufficient entity. Each piece has to work on its own. If it's good enough to do that, it can be shown as part of a more complex installation. The non-hierarchical impression of my installations is intended to allow access to the images in ways that are not predetermined. As a visitor you have to attribute value to the things in your own way – not like, ah, single big-framed picture-important; small unframed picture unimportant.'[14] Hung on the back wall of the Frankfurt exhibition was an enormous print, much larger than all the others, which immediately captured the attention of anyone entering. It portrayed a black woman photographed before a classical-style landscape. This was Smokin' Jo, one of the most in-demand DJs on the techno music scene of the 1990s. The large scale – much greater than life size – had a dual effect. On one hand, the figure was transformed into a sort of goddess dominating the entire exhibition

Above and opposite: **The** ***Wolfgang Tillmans*** **exhibition at Portikus, Frankfurt, 1995.**
© Katrin Schilling

space, keeping every visitor under constant observation. She set the tone for the exhibition, which remained suspended midway between the frivolity of an evening at a discotheque and the spirituality of a temple visit. However, the visitor's failure to recognize the objective reasons for such a gigantic display caused a degree of disorientation, compounded by the fact that the only other image on the same wall, showing the face of a young man against a bright-red background, was decidedly smaller. It marked the triumph of deformity over the consistency that often characterizes the notion of the photographic series. The installation itself made this short circuit possible, through the careful curated management of a single physical space.

From a structural point of view, the exhibition could be considered as a whole made up of four parts. While the first consisted of the back wall described above, the second and third corresponded to the two lateral walls, each of which had a distinct character, one the opposite of the other. On one side twelve similar portraits were neatly arranged in two rows; on the other, twenty-six images of the most disparate objects were distributed from floor to ceiling in no schematic order, making viewing difficult. In the first case, photography was represented as an instrument of study and classification, while in the second its purely visual aspect and its role as an aid to personal memory prevailed. Essentially, the gallery display was inviting comparison with the artist's studio or the wall of a teenager's bedroom. Holding these images together and giving uniformity to the whole was the method of presentation. The images were displayed without frames or mounts, simply attached to the wall with pins or adhesive tape stuck to the blank margins. Not only did they acquire an extraordinary lightness that reminded one of the ephemeral nature of any photograph, but they became part of the architectural framework, transforming the Portikus's classic white cube into an enveloping kaleidoscope.

The fourth and final element consisted of a row of five display cases that crossed the room at intervals. Inside them were a collage of postcard-sized prints, photographs from the Chemistry Squares series, and most notably some copies of the September issue of *Spex* magazine, with a 32-page insert that exactly reproduced the plate section in the exhibition catalogue. It therefore acted as a reference to another context within which photography may be used - the editorial context - which is capable of radically reorientating its meaning, as well as introducing a strong element of spatial division into the exhibition. The portrait of Smokin' Jo appeared like an altarpiece against the back wall of the gallery, while these showcases resembled pews, keeping the audience in line and determining the sightlines of every viewer. As in a place of worship, Tillmans created this installation to encourage spectators to move around inside it rather than keep to the sidelines. Museums of contemporary art now adopt the same approach, acknowledging photography as a fundamental discipline worthy of inclusion in their own collections and of being exhibited in their own spaces.

NOTES

1   The Department of Photography of the Museum of Modern Art, New York, was established in 1940 under the directorship of the curator Beaumont Newhall.

2   Joseph Kosuth, *Art after Philosophy and After: Collected Writings, 1966-1990*, (Cambridge, Mass.: MIT Press, 1991).

3   Renato Barilli, introduction to *Esposizione in tempo reale* (Pollenza: La Nuova Foglio Editrice, 1973).

4   Jean-François Chevrier, 'The Adventures of the Picture Form in the History of Photography', in Douglas Fogle (ed.), *The Last Picture Show: Artists Using Photography, 1960-1982* (exh. cat., Walker Art Center, Minneapolis, 2003), p. 116.

5   Michael Fried, *Why Photography Matters as Art as Never Before* (New Haven: Yale University Press, 2008), p. 144.

6   'Reality So Real It's Unrecognizable', in *Flash Art International*, vol. 168 (January/February 1993).

7   Jeff Wall, 'Frames of Reference', in *Artforum*, vol. 42, no. 1 (September 2003), pp. 188-92.

8   Ibid.

9   Installation of *Faking Death* (1977), *The Destroyed Room* (1978), *Young Workers* (1979), *Picture for Women* (1979) at the Art Gallery of Greater Victoria, Ontario, 11 April-2 June 1979.

10 David Campany, *Picture for Women* (London: Afterall Books, 2011), pp. 17-18.

11 Claire Bishop, *Installation Art* (London: Tate Publishing, 2008), p. 6.

12 Juliane Rebentisch, *Aesthetics of Installation Art* (Berlin: Sternberg Press, 2012), p. 15.

13 Liz Jobey, 'Wolfgang Tillmans: The Lightness of Being', *The Guardian*, 26 June 2010.

14 Hans Ulrich Obrist, *The Conversations Series: Wolfgang Tillmans* (Cologne: Walther König, 2007), pp. 93-97.

The exhibition *Sebastião
Salgado: La main de l'homme,
5 ans de reportages sur l'homme
au travail*, at the Centre National
de la Photographie, Paris,
30 April–19 June 1993.

You Can't Look Away:
The Exhibition as Photojournalistic Essay

Alessandra Mauro and Alessia Tagliaventi

I went to an exhibition in Barcelona of African art. What I saw there were everyday things - cooking pots, household objects, things from everyday life. They were practical objects, but there, removed from their social contexts, they had become art objects. This is also what I do. I photograph everyday life. I am there, in the moment, my photographs show reality. But then the photographs can be seen as art, even though they are documents.
Sebastião Salgado[1]

On 18 April 1993 an exhibition entitled *Workers, An Archaeology of the Industrial Age: Photographs of Sebastião Salgado* opened at the Philadelphia Museum of Art. According to the programme, the exhibition was organized by Michael Hoffman, director of the Aperture publishing company and the show's principal architect. It was conceived as a travelling exhibition, and Philadelphia was therefore only the first in a long series of museums and exhibition spaces in which the same images, in the same order, recounted the epic story of human labour.

As the title stated, the show's aim was to narrate how the culture of work had evolved from the Industrial Revolution up to the present day, with the inevitable changes brought about by technological developments and the new economic order. The exhibition was conceived as a physical journey that - room by room, image by image - would lead the visitor from America to Asia, from Europe to Oceania. All the while it illustrated a theory expressed by the photographer and his wife, Lélia Wanick, the exhibition's curator: through photography it was possible to document not only human labour, but also (as the introduction to

the catalogue stated) our ability to 'create a new world, to reveal a new life, to remember that there exists a frontier for everything except dreams. In this way, [we] adapt, resist, and survive. In history there are no solitary dreams.'[2]

The exhibition comprised 250 photographs, the result of 42 separate reportages undertaken between 1987 and 1991. The images were presented in two different formats, 60 × 90 cm (23 ⅝ × 35 ⅜ in.) and 50 × 60 cm (19 ¾ × 23 ⅝ in.); both sizes had white mounts 10 cm (4 in.) wide and were framed in wood. Each photograph was identified by number, enabling the visitor to find his or her bearings and follow the correct exhibition route. The photos were accompanied by long and detailed captions that, in addition to indicating title and date, were designed to illustrate their meaning, reveal the story that often lay behind them and situate them within their proper context.

Each story had a symbolic and exemplary value. The first reportage was dedicated to basic crops, such as sugar processed in Brazil and Cuba, tea picked in Rwanda, the tobacco

Sebastião Salgado's *Workers* at the Philadelphia Museum of Art, 1993.

plantations and cigar factories of Cuba, cocoa farmed in Brazil and the extraction of essences used in perfumery on the island of Réunion. It continued with fishing in Galicia, traditional tuna fishing in Sicily and meat processing in the abattoirs of South Dakota. Next came the weaving of vegetable fibres into textiles (Bangladesh and Kazakhstan) and the transformation of metals into complex goods such as bicycles (China), scooters and motorbikes (India), and cars (Ukraine, Russia, India and China). This was followed by a journey through the shipyards of France and Poland, where cargo ships were built. The itinerary continued with a look at the process of ship demolition (Bangladesh) and the recycling of metals as raw material, ready to be used to make new goods. Next came the mining and processing of titanium, magnesium, lead (Kazakhstan), steel (France and Ukraine) and iron (Kazakhstan), and the construction of railways (France), before continuing with the mining of coal (India), sulphur (Indonesia) and gold (Brazil). A separate section was devoted to oil drilling (Azerbaijan) and the extinguishing of oil wells damaged in wartime (Kuwait). The final part of the exhibition itinerary focused on works successfully constructed by man from the same raw materials that he had mined and forged, as well as to collective ventures realized entirely by virtue of large workforces and multiple skills: the Eurotunnel connecting France and Great Britain, and the Sardar Sarovar Dam and the Narmada Canal in northern India.

Thus, in an approach permeated by Marxist thought, both book and exhibition celebrated the power and allure of labour, even lesser-known and seemingly negligible examples. But *Workers* itself was also the result of an impressive human endeavour. It reflected a far-sighted and unusual vision that was entirely novel in the context of photography exhibitions - one that testified to a search for a new type of meaning in photojournalism.

A year later, as *Workers* continued its triumphal journey around the world, a highly topical photography exhibition was staged in Switzerland and the United States almost simultaneously. This was *Farewell to Bosnia* by Gilles Peress, which opened on 2 February at the Fotomuseum in Winterthur, Switzerland, followed by an opening at the Corcoran Gallery in Washington, D.C., on 5 March. In both locations, visitors were confronted with between eighty and one hundred large-format images, the result of the three-and-a half months that the photographer had spent in Bosnia, documenting the civil war that had raged throughout the former Yugoslavia for over three years.

The initiative behind this project came from François Hers, then cultural director at the Fondation de France, who, familiar with Peress's long-term project *Hate Thy Brother*, which chronicled the re-emergence of hatred and racial discrimination in Europe, thought that his vision would be well suited to recounting current events. In the spring of 1993, Peress received a grant enabling him to travel to Bosnia, where he concentrated on the area surrounding Tuzla, and on Mostar and Sarajevo, cities once renowned for their multiculturalism. The aim was to produce a book and an exhibition that would travel to various cities in Europe and the United States, not only to denounce what was happening, but also to engage and appeal directly to public opinion. The show was organized by Philip Brookman, curator of photography at the Corcoran Gallery, and Urs Stahel, director of the Fotomuseum.[3]

With Peress's exhibition, photojournalism thus entered places of collective memory (the museums) with the intention of transforming them into active spaces. With a sense of the utmost urgency, visitors were presented with events that were still in progress and whose outcome was highly unpredictable. (The Dayton Agreement, which officially brought an end to the civil war in Yugoslavia, was not signed until November 1995.) Peress's exhibition was very different from Salgado's, but both had come about in the same way: in each case, the photographer-journalist used his work to make a precise statement, constructing a coherent, communicative project from the moment the reportage was conceived up to the actual shooting of the images, and completing his task by realizing a book and exhibition of which he was the curator or co-curator. These were certainly not isolated examples, but nevertheless represented significant steps in a process of transformation that photojournalism had undergone since the 1960s – in other words, since television images first began to challenge the role of the illustrated press directly.

Gilles Peress's *Farewell to Bosnia* at the Fotomuseum, Winterthur, 12 February–27 March 1994.
© Fotomuseum Winterthur

In an essay written in 2008, the historian Michel Poivert set out a brief but significant history of photography exhibitions - or, rather, exhibitions of photojournalism. Here he remarked on the ability of the Museum of Modern Art, New York, and of the photography curator John Szarkowski in particular, to recognize a type of photography created for the press, at the same time as identifying certain formalistic elements that proved its importance beyond a journalistic context and justified its display within a museum setting.[4] This acceptance of photojournalism, in Poivert's opinion, was exemplified by the 1973 exhibition *From the Picture Press* (see p. 197), in which the curator put together photographs showing the minutiae of everyday life - not formerly regarded as documents of great historical interest - to demonstrate how, time differences aside, there were recurring similarities in choice of subject matter and the way such images were used. Removed from their context, these photographs conceived for the press shared thematic and formalist affinities with photography as a whole. Once their original setting - the page of a newspaper - was gone, the transcendent aesthetic of the photographic document could be observed. As Poivert observed, 'This is in fact a central theme in John Szarkowski's approach: the media has not grasped that photography is, in essence, autonomous and incapable of producing a narrative. It is, on the contrary, defined as a fragment containing symbols, whose purpose is to assure the permanence of the image. In the end, John Szarkowski concludes his demonstration by characterizing press photographs as a series of variations on themes and motifs, comparing them to "a form of poetry rather than a form of narrative".'[5]

As current events - even the most ordinary and seemingly insignificant ones - began to enter the exhibition space, in 1977 a major exhibition in Paris entitled *Photojournalisme*, curated by Pierre de Fenoÿl, celebrated ten years of French photojournalism. The idea was not so much to evaluate the aesthetic components of photojournalism as to consider the way its images operated, their emotional value and their potential for increasing awareness. In 1984 the Musée d'Art Moderne de la Ville de Paris staged a further exhibition on photojournalism, entitled *60 photos qui racontent notre histoire* ('Sixty photographs that tell our story'), in which photographic imagery was singled out for the affective/effective contribution it made to our view of history.

Two exhibitions held at the Centre Pompidou (*Comment va la presse?* in 1982, and, to an even greater extent, *Le Forum du reportage*, on view between 1988 and 1989) would pave the way for a different treatment of photojournalism within museums. Here the major French photo agencies - Magnum and Vu to start with, followed by Gamma, Sipa and AFP - presented their own images and their own view of the contemporary world. History could be related through the imagery of sensitive and well-informed photojournalists. Poivert noted how 'staging photojournalism, and increasingly presenting objects such as magazine covers or reportage in the wings, enables photojournalism to be identified as a cog in the wheel of the information society. Its relationship to history could no longer be only that of a story in pictures, otherwise it would be necessary to reformulate the question of style, form and, in a word, art.'[6]

During the 1990s photojournalism reached its apogee of expression (or its crisis point, according to some) with the establishment of a global information economy and a standardized media culture in pursuit of exclusives. Since magazines and newspapers were no longer looking for complex images on either a compositional or narrative level, some photojournalists were forced to seek alternatives to the traditional way of working. Since newspapers and magazines were no longer the preferred means for presenting reportage to the public, photographers increasingly turned to books and exhibitions, and, more recently, the internet. The dialectic between the concepts of information, document and art has thus become more complex. Poivert remarked: 'Refusing to be considered as a mere operator, the photojournalist-author embodies a potential alliance between the journalist and the creator.'[7]

In *Regarding the Pain of Others*, Susan Sontag claimed that, for the very reason that images have entered museums and other places of collective memory, photography no longer has an informative function but represents an experience within the field of aesthetics and art.[8] Photojournalism found itself having to deal with the concept and function of testimony in a new way. It became permeated by individual experience, drew strength from its own subjectivity and, in narrating events, began to question history itself. The presence of the photographer was revealed within the facts that he was recording, affirming the subjectivity of his vision and his point of view. By freeing itself from the pressures of the information economy, his work in some way became a record of existential experiences. In this sense, the work of Salgado and Peress can be seen as pioneering. Both artists, although very different from each other, began a gradual process by which photographs came to be valued not only as evidence of the world around us, but also as analysis and interpretation: documents capable of arousing emotion, and perhaps of sparking debate and effecting change.

Salgado has explained his attitude to the world around him, writing that:

> I am often asked whether my training as an economist has influenced my work as a photographer. I think so, but it is more than that. In reality, I still bring all the baggage of past experience to what I photograph. The university studies, my work experience, everything has been important. But it is not just a question of education. Underlying my desires and my ability to work is a strong social motivation. I am from Brazil, a country of striking contrasts and struggles, especially social struggles. I have joined many organizations' battles, and been politically active in Brazil ... Everything in my background - my upbringing, my education, my focus on sociology, anthropology and geopolitics - has seeped into my photography.[9]

Workers by Sebastião Salgado

Salgado concentrates primarily on long-term projects that each last several years. With the help of his wife (his partner in both private and professional life), he organizes these multi-faceted projects into a series of different reportages, always managing to keep tight hold of the reins and ensuring that, once the project is complete, the images eventually support one

other in a great and often epic view of humankind and the world that surrounds us. This was true for *Workers*, and would also be the case for *Migrations*, dedicated to humankind's migratory movements, and for *Genesis*, an intense and vibrant visual exploration of the earth today, its uncontaminated regions and eco-sustainable balances. *Genesis* was designed as a warning and as an incentive to understand how vital it is to conserve and maintain the planet's ecosystem.

Salgado's projects have never aimed simply to illustrate a particular theme, but always to reveal truth and stir consciences. The realization of the projects themselves presents a challenge. While in some cases, such as *Other Americas* (1982), the exhibition is the result of a selection of works realized on a particular theme, for other projects the final outcome was planned and envisaged well ahead. For *Workers*, the exhibition itself became a raison d'être – the motivation for carrying out forty-two different reportages, one after the other, over a period of several years, and bringing them together in a rational whole. In other words, the exhibition and the accompanying book no longer constituted a retrospective selection but were the driving force behind the work: the visual story that the author wished to outline and the task that justified his own profession.

In the best of the tradition of 'concerned photography', *Workers* originated from its author's faith in the redeeming power of images and the need for all of us to comprehend through the act of seeing. We need to observe whatever might be happening in the world

The exhibition *Workers* at the Philadelphia Museum of Art, 1993.

and understand it. Salgado remarks: 'I believe there is no person in the world that must be protected from pictures. Everything that happens in the world must be shown and people around the world must have an idea of what's happening to the other people around the world. I believe this is the function of the vector that the documentary photographer must have, to show one person's existence to another.'[10]

Consistent with his interest in current events, Salgado is familiar with the wider world and understands it in depth. Such an undertaking as *Workers* needed a framework that had been worked out in advance, but it also had to be flexible, capable of assimilating changes dictated by constantly evolving circumstances and the demands of international politics. His working method resulted from the years he spent working with the press and was sustained by his training as an international economist:

> In my case, I prefer to work on very long-term stories. For all the stories I do, I write an outline. I create a framework where I concentrate my energies and ideas. Of course, in this framework there are plenty of doors and windows. I can come and go by any one. I can put things inside and take things out. Using this method, it is much easier for you to evolve and work with people. How are you to prepare the reportage? How are you to raise funds? What about the magazines that will use these pictures or the organization with which you will be working? Does the environment exist that will allow you to give to them and receive from them? I try to work in the most open way.[11]

A photographer's decision to restrict his images to only a few formats allows for the construction of an exhibition layout that is simple to follow. On the walls of an exhibition space,

The exhibition *Workers* at the International Center of Photography, New York, 1995.

the hanging sequence will create the story, modulating it in its various aspects and imposing a reading of the images that is reinforced by the accompanying captions. And while the skilful use of rich black-and-white tones and a dramatic emphasis on gesture, landscape and scenery might confirm an aesthetic interest and evoke a classical iconographic tradition, the images nevertheless fulfil their principal informative purpose.

In this sense, the textual content - the captions - play a fundamental role, anchoring every image, every face, every scene to a precise intent. While appealing to the emotions, at the same time the caption is also meant to inform. As the curator Dominique Versavel has remarked: 'The caption makes decoding possible, proposing a single reading of an image that might otherwise have many. In the logic of his photographic theses, Salgado channels the polysemy of his images by guiding their reception through a written accompaniment, admittedly deferred, but nevertheless present ... In an approach that is almost redolent of ethnology, the photographer links the text to the image, to bring to everyone's awareness that reality in which he has taken the time to immerse himself.'[12]

With Salgado, the emotions that the images arouse are channelled to sociological, even political, ends. To paraphrase Walker Evans, in Salgado's case the document becomes 'lyrical' so as to acquire a power of conviction and penetration it might not otherwise have. *Workers* - just like *Migrations*, *Terra* and, more recently, *Genesis* - established itself as a grandiose tool of communication that aimed to show and convince. Above all, it aimed to affirm the impact and power that photographs possess to an ever increasing extent.

Farewell to Bosnia by Gilles Peress

Farewell to Bosnia was the title Peress chose for his story: a valediction and a denouncement of what the photographer viewed as the unforgiveable abandonment of the country by the rest of Europe. During his journey in Bosnia, Peress encountered displacement, death, pain and great destruction; and he discovered what he felt to be the failure of European culture. In addition, his time in Bosnia also represented a constant questioning of his own photography and his role as photographer. In the accompanying book, published by Scalo, Peress wrote: 'Given the limited time to complete this project, I knew from the beginning I could not explain all that was happening in Bosnia - the historical intricacies, the weight of blood. I set out only to provide a visual continuum of experience, of existence. So this book is a raw take, a non-edit; the most un-photographic project I have done.'[13] It was certainly not the first war Peress had confronted: he had already undertaken an assignment on the events of the Iranian Revolution and produced a cult book entitled *Telex Iran: In the Name of Revolution*, and spent two decades recounting the conflict in Northern Ireland. Yet he felt that, in Bosnia, something shifted in his relationship towards photography and narration.

Both the exhibition layout and the book of *Farewell to Bosnia* aimed to preserve the story's character as a raw, open document. In all its urgency and ferocious complexity the historical present - current events, in other words - erupted out of the photographs and into

the museum's interior. Peress's photographs conveyed a powerful sense of chaos - an effect that the layout was designed to highlight. The visitor could no longer simply be guided, but in some way had to be assailed.

Urs Stahel, the Fotomuseum's director, recalled that the exhibition was rather claustrophobic in feel: the gallery, which measured 100 square metres (1,076 square feet), contained roughly one hundred photos printed on unframed canvas, each 1 metre long (3 ft 3 in.). They were nailed up in a double strip that ran round the gallery walls, and were also shown on a kind of display cabinet in the middle of the room. In the Corcoran Gallery, too, the images were hung in a space that was almost completely bare. Printed in large format right up to the edge of the canvas, the photos were unframed and dry-mounted onto polyester fabric. Arranged along the four walls of the gallery, they gave the impression - as some critics noted - of an exhibition staged in a hurried and rebellious manner.

The exhibition *Farewell to Bosnia*, at the Corcoran Gallery, Washington, D.C., 1994.

The photographs were organized into three sections: 'Road: Central Bosnia', with twenty-nine images; 'Home: Sarajevo', with forty-four; and 'Dismemberment: Sarajevo and Mostar', which contained twelve. Peress almost never covered the real centre of the action, unlike other great photojournalists working in Bosnia, such as Ron Haviv, James Nachtwey and Tom Stoddart. He showed no bombs exploding, no soldiers shooting, no children running to take cover from bullets. What could be seen, however, were the confused residue, the silence and the suffering left behind in places where events had occurred. He documented the signs of destruction and life's unsteady attempts to continue while in a state of shock, numbness and powerlessness. Here were fragments of experience, the ruins of homes and cities, bodies, corpses - the smouldering wounds of a civilization.

The exhibition layout presented the images packed closely together, one after the other, without captions and or frames to interrupt the narrative - like stills from an endless silent movie. Following the exhibition's preview at the Fotomuseum in February 1994, the journalist and critic Laurent Wolf commented in *Le Nouveau Quotidien*:

> The visit to the museum creates a strange impression. Giles Peress shares its spaces with a photographer who died in 1990: Ed van der Elsken, whose retrospective is interesting, but in reality a banal exhibition of first-rate photographs. That's what you feel after having been through the room devoted to Peress. There, no pretty framing, no rhythmic hanging alternating the white of the walls and the elegance of black-and-white exposures. The large-scale prints are lined up in tight rows, with no commentary, with no indications, with no aestheticization, with no pathos. You don't get a shock. You don't go from a feeling of calm to uncontrollable emotion. No. It is a wave that rises gently, an appalled astonishment you would like to hold at bay. You have to go to Winterthur to understand the extent to which our eyes are sullied and anaesthetized by the televised image.[14]

Philip Brookman, curator of the show at the Corcoran Gallery, tells of the impression it had on visitors: 'These are incredibly powerful pictures. I think the effect may have been summed up best by a young teenager who was here a few days ago. He said: "You can't look away." If you do, there's another image.'[15] In an article devoted to the same show, Chuck Myers remarked: 'Unless you close your eyes or turn away, the blunt power of the 80 full frame 30-by-40-inch black-and-white prints is inescapable. An examination of these images becomes an exhausting emotional experience not unlike viewing the horrific scenes of the Holocaust during World War II ... Due to the situation in Bosnia, there are no plans to take the show there. Instead, visitors are asked to leave their impressions of the exhibit on aerograms which will be delivered to the residents of Sarajevo.'[16]

In *Bosnia*, as in his other projects, Peress's intention was by no means simply to take and exhibit a series of outstanding individual photographs. What interested him was creating a continuum of images and experiences, without a true beginning or end: a means of communication that, like Salgado's (albeit in a completely different style), used photography to illustrate the photographer's point of view and his understanding of society - an interpretation of reality expressed through the images and the way in which they were displayed.

In an interview with Carole Kismaric conducted three years after the exhibition had closed, Peress confirmed: 'Although I take painstaking care to understand and to make good pictures, good frames, that's not ultimately what's important to me. I never was interested in making good pictures. That's a normative process that sooner or later sends you back to classicism and academic perfection. It's one of the least interesting concepts when it comes to what I call "the search." And, the search really has to do with connecting to reality and the process of living.'[17]

The subject of Peress's photography is always more complex than merely what is in front of his lens: in fact, it is the difficulty of finding, extracting and communicating meaning from reality. Yet his images remain open documents, a series of questions without answers:

> When I started to look at photographs, I was extremely disturbed by the univocalness of the transcription of reality, which seemed essentially to be reduced to one punctum, in the center of things. The job of the photographer was to eliminate any contradictory elements that could disrupt one meaning. When *I* looked at reality, *I* saw contradictions, confrontations between different meanings, different processes, different individual histories, all occurring at the same time. At a practical level, I have always tried to break the frame in little, physical ways, to reflect those contradictions. And, to go back to the notion of multiplicity of authorship, very early on I gave up the notion that a photograph represents *me* speaking to *you*. It is not for me a closed text in which I deliver you a message that can be inserted into a neat category. A photograph is an open text, in which half of the message, or half of the text, is in you and how you read it.[18]

The exhibition *Farewell to Bosnia*, at the Corcoran Gallery, Washington, D.C., 1994.

The images in *Farewell to Bosnia* do not show the action of warfare, but they have great symbolic potency: the power to suggest the invisible and to question the real. When they are presented to the public, the photographer, in his role as author and co-curator, can construct a suitable itinerary.

The cultural critic Susie Linfield observed in *The Cruel Radiance* that, whereas Salgado's images, with their compositional harmony and central gaze, suggest that the incomprehensible might perhaps be understood and even mastered (a process aided by an exhibition's precise, linear narrative), Peress challenges the spectator to discover his own path, become involved in the question and attempt to articulate an answer: 'For Peress, photography is a way to think about the world. His photographs seem to be arguments with and about what he is seeing rather than documentations of it.'[19] The story thus becomes a conversation in which the author is the most prominent voice, but not the only one; and the exhibition space is transformed into a place of dialogue in which to confront what Peress refers to as the 'curse of history'. In *Farewell to Bosnia*, this interactive approach was reinforced by the inclusion of a 'reaction room', in which visitors could record their private responses in front of a video camera and leave messages for the people of Bosnia.

In an extract from the Corcoran Gallery catalogue, Philip Brookman writes: 'With his camera, Peress addresses the impact of the current war on the Bosnian civilian population. His work bridges the gap between art and journalism, questioning many common ideas about aesthetics and quality in photography, and the relationship of art to the depiction of suffering. He presents his own impressions by creating a visual continuity from his perceptions, describing in almost cinematic terms the current experiences of Bosnian citizens. Numerous points of view are revealed in complex sequences. The psychological impact of the massacres, sieges, and ethnic cleansing is considered, creating a physical and emotional journey through this devastated land.' While, for Salgado, photography serves the purpose of salvation (through photography we save ourselves from the loss of meaning imposed on us by worldly chaos), for Peress it serves the purpose of memory: 'In the absence of justice, let there at least be a bit of memory.'[20] But that's not all. In his work on Bosnia and, to an even greater extent, Rwanda, Peress added to the realism of his images a moral message and a political stance in the face of violence and genocide.

The catalogue contains an extract from a letter addressed by Peress to Philip Brookman, in which he writes:

> I think I am unwell, and I don't know if I alone have caught the virus. I think I have a peculiar disease that has to do with time and history. I call it the curse of history, and it has to do with the fugitive absence/presence of personal and collective memory. The flashbacks started in a hospital room in Tuzla, filled with legless, armless men, all grimacing in pain. I remembered my father, his amputated arm and his pain, his descriptions of addiction to morphine, of World War II, the German occupation and the concentration camps. A flow of buried images started to come back to me. Pictures of destroyed villages like Oradour, executions of partisans, bodies, camps.

I began to think that I had come to Bosnia in part to see, almost to relive visions buried in my childhood memories. This flow started to submerge me and, like a tidal wave, it pushed through to my consciousness that the Yugoslavs (Croats, Serbs, Bosnians) must also be going through the same experience. Fathers telling horror stories from the war. Mental images so horrific that one is compelled to actually 'see' them to deal with them. And to see them, you have to act them out.

Here starts the curse of history, an illness that may not be so personal anymore. It may be a very European disease, after all, with a double-edged nature: you are damned if you remember - condemned to re-live, re-enact the images of your fathers; you are damned if you don't - condemned to repeat their hypocrisy.'[21]

In the relationship between text and images, Peress attempted to combine the various ethical, political and poetic dimensions in a narrative that was layered and non-linear. 'My photographs show a nation invaded, a nation at war. Refugees are on the road, drifting through the rain, moving through camps and hospitals, an endless cavalry of images flashing by in a blur: exhaustion, too many images, too much horror. The witness becomes indifferent. My point is that we, in the comfort of our lives, must question our role in the history of Bosnia, which is also our history.' At the end of the book, once more he states: 'It's Munich all over again. We, the Europeans, are floating in the vomit of our own past, refusing to confront our responsibility for non-intervention … There is a diabolical beast at work out there, re-emerging from the marshes of our history, looking over our landscape. We have blood on our souls. I feel sick, alone, scared.'[22]

Both Peress and Salgado tend to establish intense relationships with the historical events they are narrating, creating accounts that shift from the personal to the collective. Salgado's projects are all proudly rooted in the fabric of his personal experience. The author's vision is informed by his past as a Brazilian national, a former exile, a man from the southern hemisphere with an awareness of ecological issues: it is these facets that provide the driving force behind every photographic experience and the motivation for each project. Even his style conforms to personal experience: 'I believe that each photographer, each writer has a style, each person in your life has a different style, each marriage and behaviour inside the family has a different style. That is the fantastic characteristic of the human being. Photography can be no different. I have to show these things in my Brazilian way.'[23] It was precisely this highly personal 'Brazilian way' that Michel Guerrin, writing at the time that *Workers* was showing in Paris, justified an aesthetic that others had criticized harshly: 'Ingrid Sischy is forgetting one thing: the importance of the Latin-American imagination that fashions his photography. Salgado has no intention of changing the world, he just wants to remind us that it exists.'[24]

The dialectic between art and document is one of the most vibrant trends in contemporary photography, as a result of which the tradition of the 'concerned photographer' has been reconfigured and renewed. In this respect Gilles Peress and Sebastião Salgado have been perhaps the most skilful exponents of their generation. Susie Linfield has remarked: 'It is true that Salgado's photographs can veer into a kind of nostalgic romanticism that recalls the era of socialist-realism. His monumental scale can seem grandiose, and the chiaroscuro lighting he likes can appear arty. His self-consciously religious references can seem, well, self-conscious. But it is also true that Salgado has documented the workers of the world with more perception, care, and sheer interest than any other photographer I can think of: he has visualized the labour theory of value. And personalized it too: the unapologetic, forthright people in his portraits command our attention as equals, not "subalterns".'[25] As far as Peress is concerned, Linfield continues: 'His genius has been to accomplish just what the post-moderns couldn't: to incorporate a critique of photography's objectivity into that obstinate bit of bourgeois folklore formerly known as the truth. He embraces postmodern scepticism, but uses it to enlarge photographic possibilities rather than to discredit the medium. Peress has taken the alienated sensibility typical of, and prized by, modern photographers and fused it to passionate engagement with the world outside himself.'[26]

Farewell to Bosnia was only the beginning and would lead the photographer to experiment further, also where the aesthetic of the exhibition format was concerned. For *The Silence*, which focused on the genocide in Rwanda, Peress realized a book that contained 100 photographic testimonies, without captions, of the atrocities that had been committed there. It was subdivided into three parts, whose titles made reference to Christian terminology: 'The Sin', 'Purgatory' and 'The Judgement'. The book was accompanied by a pamphlet that included a chronology of Rwanda's history and an extract from the UN report in which genocide was mentioned. When Peress decided to exhibit his Rwandan images in a museum, he proposed a kind of installation that originated with the book itself. The exhibition in fact consisted of 104 copies of the book, arranged like a frieze; the images hid a reproduction of the UN text, denouncing the fact that it had been totally disregarded.

While the museum can operate as a new medium – a venue where messages find a new form of expression for committed photographers working in the narration and interpretation of reality – other possibilities have now been opened up by the internet, for both photographers and public. Peress himself had already started to experiment with the internet back in the mid-1990s with *Farewell to Bosnia*, overseeing the construction of a sort of online exhibition consisting of photos and textual extracts,[27] and continued to explore its opportunities with *Bosnia: Uncertain Paths to Peace*, a multimedia and interactive project created together with Fred Ritchin in 1996 for the *New York Times Online*. As was the case for other authors who alternated between testimony, visual document and the interpretation of reality, Peress found that the internet seemed an interesting place in which to try to construct an active space of dialogue between photographer and public – a space that, in his own words, would mean 'not just the democratic posting of images but the democratic *interpretation* of images'.[28] We must continue to ask ourselves a complex but fundamental question: 'How do you disentangle the surface of reality?'[29]

FOCUS

THE GENESIS OF *WORKERS*

LÉLIA WANICK SALGADO

I have worked on all of Sebastião's exhibitions, right from the start. The first major exhibition was on Latin America. It was not such an ambitious and complex project as *Workers*, but Sebastião often travelled in Latin America and, in the event, we created a book and an exhibition out of those images.

The case of *Workers* was different: it was the first true project, conceived, written and developed to be realized in this grandiose and far-reaching manner. We planned the work, asked for funding and - as often happens in these cases - had to sacrifice other things in order to complete it. It was a project originating from our work, but also from our everyday life and our ideology. Born and raised with the Marxist conception of working-class labour as the cornerstone of society, towards the end of the 20th century we started to see the world of labour as we had known it come to an end, almost crumble. Factories began to close, and the introduction of new, sophisticated machinery transformed the pace and meaning of manual work.

So we thought we would show work as it had been up to that point - still following the model of the Industrial Revolution in Great Britain - and how it was entering a period of serious crisis. First of all, we began to draw up an outline for the project and to research which jobs still existed within the old framework - tasks that would soon be swept away by technological innovations - and the cultures they sustained. We then began to seek the support of magazines and newspapers who might help by pledging to publish Sebastião's reportages periodically.

Each time he had returned from his various trips, he and I did the editing before passing our selection to Magnum (Sebastião was still working for the agency) to distribute the photos. The task of shooting the images lasted from 1987 until 1991, and once it was finished we considered how best to present them, choosing the format of book and exhibition.

In 1990, about eighteen months before the reportages were complete, I prepared a dossier to send to museums in which I explained the circumstances under which the photos had been taken. Things slowly began to develop and take shape; *Workers* has now been shown in seventy different museums across the world and still continues to travel.

The *Workers* exhibition consists of 250 images divided into sections that present stories from different parts of the world, so as to give the project some variety of rhythm. Yet everything is organized in one continuous flow, which connects the images from first to last. We didn't want to tell a story - there was no story to tell - but to develop a theme and, on the basis of this theme, assemble together various experiences. Of course, the theme was broad and inevitably affected the visitors: by including everything from unemployment to changes in production methods, everyone could feel involved and was able to identify with the images. In the end, the exhibition took on an educational aspect; in fact, we worked extensively on this side of things, including a series of didactic programmes.

Since this communication aspect is very important, it is vital that the theme under consideration should be organized according to a cast-iron logic, from the first image to the last.

The editing and the sequence are fundamental; the different parts of the exhibition cannot be mixed up, and the public must be prepared to enter a section only once they have understood the previous one. If, by some bizarre chance, the show had to be displayed on a single wall as long as a motorway, with each image occurring in proper sequence, it still would not work. Exhibitions - and this one in particular - require not only that the sequence be respected and that there should be enough space, but also that there should be intimate spaces within each section. In *Workers* we consider the theme of nutrition, showing the mussel-gatherers in Galicia, those who follow an ancient fishing tradition in the Mediterranean, and the culture that surrounds the production of sugar cane in Cuba and in Brazil. Visitors need to understand

Entrance to the exhibition
Workers, Philadelphia Museum
of Art, 1994.

these stories by encountering the protagonists and following their vicissitudes. For this reason the challenge within a museum context was to reconstruct a single narrative at the same time as preserving the sense of intimacy for each event depicted. For the first time, I realized that we needed to create an exhibition that could help people learn. This was the aim: to understand and to learn.

The informative aspect is important. The exhibition has introductory texts to explain the choice of overall theme, and to put each section and individual story into context. The images also have long and detailed captions, so that if visitors take the time to read everything in the end they will have learnt a huge amount about the economy and geography of the world.

I think that, to realize projects with as much impact as *Workers*, that are capable of reaching thousands of people, it is not absolutely essential to use photography. Other forms of expression could be used. The difference lies above all in your determination. In the end, our projects relate closely to our own life. Let's take the example of *Workers*: not only have we always worked but, with our background, we have always viewed manual work and workers as fundamental to society. As far as *Migrations* is concerned, we, too, were migrants: we had to leave our own country and live in exile for over ten years. Finally, *Genesis* - the last major project we realized - is part of our life. Everything started with the Instituto Terra, established over ten years ago in the Aimorés region in Brazil, which has enabled us to see the land flourish once again and to halt the process of environmental destruction. From this, we began to think about the land and the environment. Essentially, everything stemmed from our own lives. This is why I say that, if you have to do something big and powerful, you will succeed if you believe strongly enough in what you are doing - if it's not just a matter of work, but also of life.

NOTES

1   Cited in Parvati Nair, *A Different Light: The Photography of Sebastião Salgado* (Durham, NC and London: Duke University Press, 2011), p. 119.

2   The book *Workers* was published by Aperture in the US, La Martinière in France, Caminho in Portugal, Contrasto in Italy, Companhia das Letras in Brazil and Phaidon in the UK.

3   The exhibition was subsequently shown at the Museum of Contemporary Photography in Chicago, MoMA PS1 in New York, the Rhode Island College Art Center, New Langton Arts in San Francisco, the École des Beaux-Arts in Nîmes, the Dutch Institute of Photography in Rotterdam, and La Primavera in Barcelona. The majority of the funding for the exhibition was provided by the Glenn Eagles Foundation in Washington, D.C., and by the Soros Foundation/Open Society Fund - Bosnia and Herzegovina, an American non-profit association with offices worldwide.

4   Michel Poivert, 'De l'image imprimée à l'image exposée: la photographie de reportage et le "mythe de l'exposition"', in *Photojournalisme et Art contemporain. Les derniers tableaux* (Paris: Éditions des Archives Contemporaines, 2008).

5   Ibid., p. 91.

6   Ibid., p. 97.

7   Ibid., p. 102. In connection with this point, Poivert pointed out Salgado's paradoxical position: rather than vanishing behind the themes he examines on such a monumental scale, he remains central to their interpretation.

8   Susan Sontag, *Regarding the Pain of Others* (New York: Farrar, Straus and Giroux, 2003).

9   Quoted in *Grandi fotografi* (Rome: Contrasto, 2012), p. 407.

10 Ken Light, *Witness in our Time: Working Lives of Documentary Photographers* (Washington, D.C.: Smithsonian Institution Press, 2000), p. 111.

11 Ibid., p. 112.

12 Dominque Versavel, 'L'essai photographique selon Sebastião Salgado', in *Sebastião Salgado: Territoires et vies* (exh. cat., Paris: Bibliothèque Nationale de France, 2005), pp. 23-24.

13 Gilles Peress, *Farewell to Bosnia* (Zurich: Scalo Verlag, 1994).

14 Laurent Wolf, *Le Nouveau Quotidien*, 23 February 1994.

15 Philip Brookman, 'Photographer Captures The Horror of War in Bosnia', *Chicago Tribune*, 31 March 1994.

16 Chuck Myers, 'Photo exhibit at Washington, D.C., galleries chronicles horrors in Bosnia', *Knight-Ridder/Tribune News Service*, 9 March 1994.

17 Carole Kismaric, 'Interview with Gilles Peress', *BOMB*, no. 59 (spring 1997).

18 Ibid.

19 Susie Linfield, *The Cruel Radiance: Photography and Political Violence* (Chicago: University of Chicago Press, 2010), p. 246.

20 Gilles Peress in Édouard Launet, 'La guerre dans le viseur', *Libération*, 8 May 1999, p. 33.

21 Peress, *Farewell to Bosnia*, n.p.

22 Extract from a letter written by Peress to the publisher Walter Keller; see *Farewell to Bosnia*, n.p.

23 Quoted in Michael Hallett, 'Labour of Love. Sebastião Salgado's *Workers* is as much an expression of the photographer's own ideology as it is a study of human toil', *British Journal of Photography*, 30 November 1994.

24 Michel Guerrin, 'La sueur et l'odeur du sang', *Le Monde*, 29 April 1993.

25 Linfield, p. 57.

26 Linfield, p. 249.

27 See the *Picture Projects* website at http://www.picture-projects.com/bosnia.html (accessed 19 May 2014).

28 Linfield, p. 257.

29 Linfield, p. 258.

The exhibition *here is new york*,
Prince Street, New York, 2001.

11

'Anybody and Everybody': *here is new york*

Alessandra Mauro

Who can even begin to recount a tragedy as destabilizing as the one that befell New York on 11 September 2001? Who is best qualified to provide an accurate, sensitive first-hand account of an attack that erupted out of the blue into the city's rich, complex everyday life, turning the life of its inhabitants and visitors upside down, affecting the whole country - if the attacks in Pennsylvania and Washington, D.C., are taken into account - and, indeed, the entire Western world?

According to the curators of *here is new york*, the answer is: no one in particular, but everyone in equal measure. Anybody who recorded a personal view of the tragedy with a camera and kept this memento as a testimony of his or her individual experience was a trustworthy eyewitness to the events of that day and the days that immediately followed. And all these visual testimonies could be brought together on equal footing to form a collective exhibition.

The aim of the exhibition *here is new york: a democracy of photographs*, which opened in New York City on 25 September 2001, was to bear witness to and document the tragedy of those days, and also the possibility of a new sense of community that might rise from its ashes. As the show's subtitle and that of the accompanying book suggested, the great novelty of the *here is new york* project lay in its attempt to work with photography as a democratic and wide-reaching means of expression, as though it were a connecting tissue allowing a sense of collectiveness and identity.

It all began in a former women's clothing shop at 116 Prince Street in SoHo, about fifteen blocks north of Ground Zero, which had recently become vacant. The shop was next to the studio of Michael Shulan, an artist and art critic who, upon hearing of the attack, decided almost without thinking to stick a photograph of the Twin Towers, taken some time before, in the empty window.

It was an instinctive and emotional gesture that would give rise to the project itself, as Shulan recalled: 'A day or two later, Gilles Peress, who had been down at Ground Zero photographing for the *New Yorker*, called me on my cell phone and asked what I was doing. I replied that I was in the shop staring at a group of people staring at a photograph, and was thinking about putting up some more. "Do it," he said simply. We met the following evening with two other friends and colleagues, Alice Rose George and Charles Traub, and quickly devised a plan. In those turbulent days it seemed as if everyone in New York had a camera, and we decided that the exhibition should be as broad and inclusive as possible, open to "anybody and everybody": not just photojournalists and other professional photographers, but bankers, rescue workers, artists and children - amateurs of every stripe.'[1]

Everyone took part; everyone rapidly sent in photos. Within a short space of time 5,000 images had been collected, taken by 3,000 different people, some of them professionals, others amateurs. The idea was to scan all the images, turn them into digital files and to print them all in the same format before hanging them on wires, without frames or mounts, against the window of the SoHo shop and inside it. (Michael Shulan said the inspiration for this was a recent trip to Naples, where he had seen laundry hanging out to dry in the sun, suspended from wires above the narrow streets.) Once they had been recorded and displayed in this way, the images were available to buy at the easily accessible price of $25 each, the proceeds going to the Children's Aid Society.

With the help of a group of efficient volunteers, the show opened on 25 September and, owing to the initiative's incredible success, remained open for months, enjoying an unprecedented turnout, attracting queues in front of the shop and throughout the neighbourhood. There were excellent print sales, and a website was constructed that not only contained the photos in the exhibition, but also a series of touching interviews and video testimonies. Other satellite shows in the US and abroad replicated the vast selection of images that been acquired, echoing the project's collective and supportive spirit.

In short, *here is new york* (or *hiny*, as it was known) became a point of reference for the city, but also a symbolic and innovative way of creating, through photography, an event that was at once a documentary act of witness, a fundraising initiative and an exhibition of photos - something completely new and different. Everyone participated, both photographers and visitors (the distinction became increasingly blurred). Michael Shulan has described it thus: '*here is new york* is a very small part of the story of 9/11, but in its own way it became a microcosm of what took place in the disaster's aftermath at Ground Zero and elsewhere in the city. Not an art exhibition in the conventional sense - partly an impromptu memorial, partly a rescue effort, and partly a testimonial of support for those who were actually doing the rescuing - it became a rallying point for the neighbourhood and for the community at large.'[2]

Many remarked on how the tragedy of 9/11 seemed almost destined to be filmed and photographed. Fred Ritchin has spoken of screens being invaded, almost conquered, by the attackers,[3] and of how the image of the burning towers, transmitted non-stop by television channels and published in the press, became some kind of visual mantra. David Friend has also pinpointed the emerging role of digital photography in the 24-hour rolling news coverage that we now take for granted, and the existence of the internet – crucial factors that decreed the photographic and media significance of the attack on the Twin Towers in a decisive manner: 'At the start of the new millennium, news organizations phased in a pair of relatively new technologies that would prove transformative. These two advances, just coming of age in the 1990s, enabled the events of September 2001 to be the first such acts witnessed in "real time" in virtually identical fashion, by an overwhelming share of the world's inhabitants.'[4]

Thus the event was widely photographed and extensively shared. Everyone felt in some way involved: those who were on the city's streets that day, of course, but also those who saw what was happening live on television (thus becoming eye-witnesses). The general sensation of profound shock became a point of reference, an experiential watershed ('Where were you that day?'). For the first time, every citizen was witness to the story unfolding before his or her eyes and, on the basis of his or her own testimony, had the right to speak.

Years later, we can trace in those few days the genesis of a new, direct relationship with history, made and dismantled before our eyes and a myriad photographic lenses. This relationship fed on a sense of unity and identity; and photography was used to remember, testify, communicate and share individual experiences. It helped to relieve the pain. Photography became, so to speak, the event itself. David Levi Strauss has commented on how, in the face of the unspeakable horror that had occurred, the images, with their distance and sense of unreality, made the drama somehow much more acceptable than words could have done: 'In the hours and days following the events, words seemed inadequate and, curiously, too *real* to signify. Only photographs had just enough unreality and distance to "make it real" to us. Seeing is believing, but photographs are more accessible. We don't necessarily believe them, but we accept them. They have become our familiars, domesticated versions of our once wild sight.'[5]

Although photography played such a meaningful role in recording the facts and emotions aroused by the tragedy of 9/11, the experience of *here is new york* was larger than simple documentation. Both professional and amateur photographers were rapidly contacted

The exhibition *here is new york*, Prince Street, New York, 2001.

and asked to submit their contributions. With great speed, these images were scanned and immediately made available to view and acquire. The images were assembled indiscriminately: no photograph was given greater importance than the others or discarded as insignificant. Every witness had the right to tell his or her version of events and to include a photo in the show's memorializing family album.[6] Everyone was involved, immediately, because everyone remembered.

hiny's format was adaptable and soon evolved, finding new forms of visibility and participation. A year after the exhibition - which nevertheless remained the starting point, the moment the city's inhabitants came together - came the book, which out of necessity reproduced only a selection of the images that been amassed (though still contained over a thousand), followed by the website. In addition to constituting an incredible online archive, vast but clearly organized, the latter offered spoken and visual accounts: the 'voices' of 9/11.

The exhibition space - be it the venue on Prince Street or the virtual space that later appeared online - was a truly public sphere where a democracy of images was at work. It was open to all and encouraged active participation in the community's healing process; a kind of photographic ritual took place that allowed every individual to express his or her grief and transform it into a source of collective strength. A personal image, a fragment of everyday experience, became part of collective history. The rich and varied material that was assembled gradually adapted itself to new uses; as the cultural historian Miles Orvell has observed, this stream of images, all equally valid, suggested an new way of using photography and thinking of history: 'What we are presented with is, in fact, an alternative mode of photographic practice and history: not the great photographs of widely celebrated photographers, not the most "iconic" image, not a selection of "representative" images.'[7]

In Orvell's opinion, the project's momentum helped dismantle the established canons that, up to that point, had directed how photography should be displayed. *hiny* relied on the inclusivity of the curatorial effort rather than exclusivity (the organizers did not choose which images to exhibit, but simply selected all those relevant to the theme), thereby excluding the possibility of any hierarchy between the photographs. Any possible notion of visual economy - the principle that *less is more* - was swept aside. Moreover, these images did not repeat or reflect what had already been published in the newspapers (the press, it seemed, was no longer the main reference for news and current events) - if anything, they incorporated it into a much wider whole. In addition, the established journalistic market was totally undermined, given that all the images were obtainable for the same symbolic sum. Lastly, *hiny* completely overturned the value of aesthetic contemplation as the basis for visiting to a photographic exhibition. The spectator's experience was now entirely different: it demanded that he or she become involved in the project as though contributing to the realization of a collective work.

The interweaving of public and private in a dramatic visual experience, its fundamentally democratic set-up, the use of digital media, the deliberate lack of distinction between images that were meaningful and images that were redundant - all served in some sense

The exhibition *here is new york*,
Prince Street, New York, 2001.

to redefine the photographic medium. Orvell writes that: 'One wonders whether we might indeed be moving beyond the very notion of the definitive photograph or whether one will yet surface that seems to say it all; nevertheless, the very effort to move the record beyond the professional documentary or news photographer to this broad array of picture makers expresses not only the inescapable significance of the event but also the democratization of photography both as a medium of communication and as a means of coming together.'[8]

Now that the sharing of images has become commonplace, others have turned to the idea of using the internet to stream photographs that recount our daily lives. This accumulation of images constitutes a new kind of documentary account of our present, but has also redefined the way it is presented in exhibition form. The installation *24 Hrs in Photos*, presented by Erik Kessels in 2011 at Foam in Amsterdam, and in the summer of 2013 at the Rencontres d'Arles, for example, approached the internet and museum spaces as two possible poles of a relationship between the production of images and the location chosen for their display. In a single room, the curator physically assembled all the photographs posted on Flickr and Facebook on a single day. Rather than remaining within their virtual networks, the images now invaded physical space, occupying it like a river in full flow. Visitors were required to move between the photographs, select the ones they preferred, attempt to find their bearings in the visual stream at their feet, and construct their own, often difficult, path. Far from denying the importance of the container/museum room, this space thus presented an unrepeatable opportunity for unique experiences. Displayed in exhibition spaces, photographs can thus find a new purpose: once again they become objects to contemplate with a fresh gaze and a clear mind.

NOTES

1   Michael Shulan et al. (eds), *here is new york: a democracy of photographs* (Zurich, Berlin and New York: Scalo, 2012), p. 7.

2   Ibid., p. 8.

3   Fred Ritchin, *Bending the Frame: Photojournalism, Documentary, and the Citizen* (New York: Aperture, 2013), p. 97.

4   David Friend, *Watching the World Change: The Stories Behind the Images of 9/11* (New York: Picador, 2011, 2nd ed.), p. 15.

5   David Levi Strauss, *Between the Eyes: Essays on Photography and Politics* (New York: Aperture, 2003), p. 184.

6   Ritchin, p. 99.

7   Miles Orvell, 'After 9/11: Photography, the Destructive Sublime, and the Postmodern Archive', *Michigan Quarterly Review*, vol. 45, no. 2 (spring 2006).

8   Miles Orvell, *American Photography*, Oxford History of Art (Oxford University Press, 2003), p. 215.

Part of the exhibition *24 Hrs in Photos* by Erik Kessels, Foam, Amsterdam, 2011.

The exhibition *here is new york*,
Prince Street, New York, 2001.

***here is new york* and the 'Creative Interlocutor'**
Interview with Charles Traub, Chair, MFA Photography,
Video and Related Media, School of Visual Arts, New York

Alessandra Mauro

AM I will start with a very basic question. How did the *here is new york* exhibition begin?

CT The question 'What sparked the idea?' is frequently asked. It was simply the synergistic experience of a number of people coming together in a creative fashion to do something meaningful for the community. In 1998 I wrote a manifesto called 'The Creative Interlocutor'. It described the 'creative interlocutor' as someone who facilitates the exchange of ideas between one party in need and another, creating an energy that is both the product and the producer of enlightened engagement within the digital realm. These people serve as navigators, helmsmen, producers, directors and organizers of the infinite creative possibilities presented by the digital world. Moreover, they are editors, collectors and curators who make, weave, weld and build; in sum, they are distributors of inspiration. *here is new york* (*hiny*) is a perfect example of the results of creative interlocutorship.

Michael Shulan, one of the four principal organizers of *hiny*, and I had been talking for many years about computer interactivity: a new means of combining image, photography, and everything that could be reduced to zeros and ones. Michael had taught a kind of digital story-telling course in my department, SVA/MFA Photo, the first graduate programme to seriously explore digital photography and its use. As far back as 1988 SVA had digital printers. Michael lived on Prince Street in SoHo and was part owner of the building's storefront, which had been recently vacated. When the tragedy of 9/11 occurred, he reflexively put an amateur photo of the Twin Towers, bought in a flea market, in the storefront window as a kind of tribute.

Devastated by 9/11, my students at SVA (the School of Visual Arts) called a meeting to talk about their feelings. A number of us put our images of the World Trade Center on the walls of our exhibition space. I had made a documentary of the New York waterfront in 1988, and many of the stills included images of the Twin Towers. We put them up to say, 'Let's remember!' Meanwhile, journalists, artists, amateurs, everyone was photographing everything. It actually turned out to be the most photographed event in history.

The chronology of events is hard to remember now and of course has become distorted with time. History is like that! I do remember that Michael Shulan called me a week or so after 9/11 to say that people were gathering around the photograph in his storefront. 'Could we do some kind of exhibition down here?', he asked. I related what had happened at SVA and called another meeting with my students. Alice Rose George, an important photograph editor, and Gilles Peress, the noted Magnum photographer, both of whom had already been contacted by Michael, also attended the meeting.

We began brainstorming. That's where the synergy occurred; events began to gel. No single person could claim to be the originator of this remarkable exhibition. 'Well,' someone said, 'you know we could just call for photographs and let people come in with them.' Michael suggested that we string wires across the space like clothes lines and hang pictures from them. I reminded everyone of SVA's digital resources for printing. We decided to let everyone and anyone bring in their photos - a 'democracy of photographs', as someone said. Alice George agreed to call the professional communities she knew: journalists, editors and the Magnum photographers who happened to be holding their annual meeting in New York at the time of the 9/11 attack. It was decided that no distinction should be made between amateurs and professionals who offered their photographs to be displayed.

We agreed that everything would be printed the same size and displayed with no name that would distinguish one photographer from another. The idea was to give uniformity and sameness to all the photographs so that they would work together in their equal importance. A graduate student from Australia walked into the meeting and asked if anyone had read the 'Here Is New York' piece by E. B. White that the New Yorker had just reprinted. It was a celebratory article about New York, written right after World War II, that described the possibility of an airplane attack on our skyscrapers. Someone yelled, 'That should be the name of the show!' Gilles Peress suggested adding a dash and 'A Democracy of Photographs'. This was the spirit of the moment - we wanted to be positive, to create a community that held individuality at bay in order to share the bigger, collective idea of everyone expressing themselves freely. Inevitably, some egos raged and others acquiesced.

Students volunteered to man a number of printers that SVA gave to the project. Gilles designed the first window sign. We hung the wires and began a process of accepting photos, whether they were digital files, negatives, finished prints, prints made in a drug store or professionally done. One has to remember that the storefront was on a very busy and trendy street, in a popular area. In a matter of a few days, people from all walks of life were bringing images to this creative memorial. It could be a schoolgirl, a survivor, maybe a fireman, a newspaper photographer, whoever. We were jump-started by the participation of Magnum, the *New York Times* and Contact Press Photographers, which Alice had secured. Likewise, my call to the arts community generated even more participation.

AM Were professionals concerned about not being acknowledged?

CT Yes, some were. But when we explained that we were not going to showcase any individual above anyone else, we generally received their agreement. We told them, 'That's the way it is, and you don't have to participate if you don't want to share in this experience.' Of course, we are all human, and some were less happy than others. I remember one very well-known photographer complaining that his images were at the back of the room and saying that they should be moved up. One of the student volunteers told him that we were hanging the pictures as they came in, and rotating them as much as possible as we added wires to accommodate their increasing number. The photographer left sheepishly.

In the first few weeks, the idea of the show grew like wildfire. Photographers lined up to give us their images. Volunteers lined up to help us manage the work. Others queued round the block to bear witness to this makeshift memorial. Susan Sontag stood in line like everyone

The exhibition *here is new york*, Houston, 2002.

else to enter the small, crowded space. There were all kinds of celebrities - Denzel Washington, Susan Sarandon, Rosie O'Donnell, Spike Lee, Rosanne Cash and Wesley Snipes - as well as politicians, business moguls and everyday people who came together reverently and humbly to participate. Even Bill Clinton came!

AM How did you manage all of that? Did you have an overall plan?

CT It was all in the spirit of creative giving and the shared intention of a group of creative interlocutors. When visitors asked to buy some of the photographs, we agreed to print and sell them. Initially, people left with their images on the same day, but within a week such fulfilment was impossible. We set up more banks of printers, and new volunteers came in: some from foreign countries, some with specific expertise and some just to help. Brenda Manes, a new arrival from Texas, volunteered to help organize the print workflow. She stayed for two years and during that time supervised the production of over 40,000 prints. It appeared that we were going to make a profit, and someone suggested that we give the money to charity. Michael Shulan proposed the Children's Aid Society, which had already set up a fund for children of food service workers who were killed in the towers.

Since this was a 'democracy of photographs', everyone was allowed to donate their pictures. This created a greater workflow and a lot of redundancy. It took a significant amount of time to scan and input the images we were receiving. A number of professional picture editors volunteered to sit at tables day in, day out, to manage this process. By the time *hiny* closed, there were more than 7,000 pictures in the database. Orders for images swelled. A way to deliver them efficiently had to be found; we needed to organize packaging, postage, etc. Someone suggested that we hire a fulfilment agency, but one company I approached actually wanted a fee of $250,000. I said, 'You're crazy. This is a charity!' Someone then recommended that we buy mailing bags in bulk from a wholesale outlet and deliver our packages to the post office around the corner. A human assembly line sealed hundreds of freshly made digital prints, to be posted nightly.

We solved very complicated problems very quickly and on the fly. There were some organizers and leaders; Michael and I were there daily, and Alice and Gilles worked behind the scenes. As students went back to classes, new volunteers came in. There were lawyers, former firefighters, hairdressers, real-estate brokers, accountants, religious camp groups, a few homeless people and many others. Over the course of two years there were hundreds of volunteers. Alongside the community that unselfishly donated imagery, the big credit goes to the volunteers who became staff, and who took charge and used their own initiative to get things done.

A website was needed. My son gathered together a group of techies who were out of work, and they built an interactive, multimedia, pay-on-demand website in about two weeks. It would have cost thousands of dollars to do this work with outside contractors. We had no business plan for any of this, and what we originally thought would last a few weeks continued for over two years and travelled to more than forty countries in one form or another. It's estimated that 1.5 million people saw the show in New York City alone. There were well over a billion hits on the website.

We had very little outside financial support. SVA donated equipment; the Goldsmith Foundation gave us funds to pay our utilities through the first winter; Target sponsored shows in Minneapolis and Chicago; and a few private individuals donated paper and materials. The real fact is that the enterprise was produced and supported by the sweat equity of remarkable individuals working collectively, producing and selling thousands of prints for $25 a piece.

AM What do you think is the real significance of the exhibition?

CT As I've already outlined, a spontaneous, grassroots, collective energy created a place where anybody and everybody could come and metaphorically 'lay a stone at the grave'. It helped people come together, to share their experiences and to mourn. Perhaps the exhibition on Prince Street, and the community it created, helped people to access their feelings in order to cope better with this tragedy. Ultimately, it is a remarkable document of those terrible times. The accumulative meaning of those pictures is yet untold. Even within a single picture by an amateur photographer, something might be discovered years hence that will allow further understanding of the 9/11 tragedies. In the future, the entire collection of images will reveal itself to be a landmark, showing how anybody and everybody expressed themselves through photography.

Once the show got going, there was no stopping it. When the *New York Times* wrote an article about *hiny* a few weeks in, it became known worldwide and a destination for anyone in New York, locals and visitors alike. Furthermore, institutions around the globe sought to put on the exhibition in their cities. As a curatorial entity, it was distinct from any that had preceded it: as many as 1,000 images were clipped to wires that stretched across an inelegant space. It was crowded. You could go under the wires or around the wires. No one had to start here and end up there. Everyone became distracted in a good way, meandering wherever their emotions took them. People could move at their own pace, stare, look, talk to a stranger and make out associations between one picture and another, relying on their own interactive agenda. As the pictures were hung a little high, one often had to stretch to see the image, so no viewer remained passive. The show also served the wider community ... not just the elite, nor those who usually visited photographic exhibitions. Sometimes a fire truck would pull up after a wake or a funeral, and those mourning men would pour into the space for further solace. It was simply cathartic.

hiny wasn't only about the attack on the Twin Towers. It was about all tragedies and wanton destruction, man's inhumanity to man. It was apparent to all of us who worked on *hiny* that many devastating, catastrophic events were happening at the same time. In Africa, more than 3,000 people were dying each week from AIDS. All over the world, all kinds of civil wars and genocide were occurring; they were often forgotten or went virtually unnoticed. We thought that this exhibition would remind people of such horrors and of the fact that we really are all alike, thinking that maybe some spark of enlightenment could come out of it. We had even considered continuing the enterprise in order to mark other tragedies in the same way. That could never have come about, because we didn't have any infrastructure or real money, and the volunteers had to go back to day jobs. Yet in the back of the book that accompanied the exhibition there is an explanation of how to do just that.

I am careful about using the word 'art', but that's what it was: a collective piece of great meaning, creatively wrought out of tragedy. It will endure, since it is well preserved digitally, and duplicate sets of prints are in collections all over the world.

It is a great expression of humanism – a new way to tell a story about a terrible event, empowering everyone to add to the story. It is a great example of how we, as creative interlocutors, can create something of meaning for a massive audience.

AM What do you feel about subsequent events after 9/11?

CT Well, I'm a bit sad at this point. As you know, Iraq happened. And then Katrina happened in New Orleans a few years later. Our government failed us. Some 250,000 people never returned to New Orleans. It is estimated that there were 3,000 suicides in later years related to the trauma of the flood. Well-meaning nations got embroiled in cultural clashes throughout the world immediately following 9/11. Even years later, it is hard to estimate how all of that will finally unfold. There has certainly been a lot of unnecessary death and destruction. I think it's significant to note that it took only thirteen months, during the height of the Depression, to build the Empire State Building. Perhaps that was at a time when there really was a can-do spirit in the American

The exhibition *here is new york*,
San Diego, 2002.

The exhibition *here is new york*, Guardian Newsroom, London, 2002.

Overleaf: **The exhibition** *here is new york*, Dublin, 2002.

psyche. As of now, One World Trade Center is still incomplete, and the memorial to 9/11 that will sit at its base is still mired in bureaucratic chaos. In contrast, *hiny* was up and running in a matter of days, fulfilling the basic needs of a memorial in a remarkably simple way because people worked together democratically to serve each other creatively. Ironically, *hiny* may have changed how we view violence, but it probably had little effect on the propagation of it.

AM So the key words seem to be 'democracy' and 'rapidity'. Everything had the same value, printed using the same common denominator?

CT That's right!

AM I understand that the venue was crucial, but what happened when the exhibition travelled to a new site? Was *hiny* transformed into something different?

CT Well, that's an interesting question. The State Department approached us to do exhibitions in various embassies. We rejected the idea because we thought that the images would inevitably become politicized in that context, and some curators who requested the show even wanted to cherry-pick the images, to showcase the most sensational ones or those taken by the most famous photographers. We rejected all such requests. However, once we set guidelines as to how the show should be displayed (in the same way as on Prince Street: densely hung, on wires, with no names visible), most institutions complied. For example, in the Chicago Cultural Center, the Martin-Gropius-Bau in Berlin, the Corcoran Museum in Washington, D.C., the Louisville, Kentucky Public Library, and the Moscow Museum of Modern Art, more than 1,000 pictures were hung tightly in a manner very reminiscent of the New York show. Thousands of people visited these and other institutions to share their story and to witness others telling it. It's important to note that no institution charged admission. Furthermore, there was no pre-selection of images. And the photos we sent were put randomly in the packing boxes, so that they could not be hung in any prescribed order.

AM From a curatorial point of view, then, the exhibition was really very avant-garde. While you did some pre-selection, there was really no single curator. Visitors were allowed to select any picture they wanted to purchase. People had a lot of choice, didn't they?

CT That is correct. We did have to eliminate duplicate types of images, those that simply would not digitize properly and some that were out of context. But we did try to scan at least one image from everyone who offered.

AM For me, this was the first time I saw an exhibition that was randomly chosen, not based on a hierarchy of images or mounted in a thematic or chronological way. It was as if it deliberately avoided the 'right moment' or 'right author'. Photography was just photography ... something like Facebook is now. You just have streams of images. You just say whether you 'like' or 'don't like' a photograph. It generated all kinds of new possibilities in the medium for documenting everyday life. It was social media before we had social media. In Arles in 2011, the exhibition *From Here On*, conceived by a number of well-known curators, mimicked the same idea.

CT I think *hiny* was a precursor to many such assemblages. As I said earlier, it was the synergy in the totality of the images that told the story. Digital media – what I call 'the realm of the circuit' – are invigorating the very idea of storytelling, be it fictional, non-fictional, interactive, interdisciplinary or multimedia. Neither one image nor one photographer could possibly have captured the essence of 9/11. The big issue of creativity in the digital age is not the lionization of an individual photographer or the uniqueness of any one artist. It's the collective talents of many people that are significant. The people who facilitate these collective endeavours are the real creative artists. The genius lies in the collective organization of the enterprise. Again, I call these people creative interlocutors. They allow ideas to flow from many people to one person, from one person to many people, and back again.

This is why I am particularly proud of *hiny*. A group of energized people enabled the creation of something new, something useful, out of other people's need for expression; they allowed many people to have a voice and a democratically organized outlet. The internet is essentially about just that. That's why, today, social networks are so important. Facebook, Twitter and Instagram are some of the most valuable corporations in the world.

There was, and still is, a promise in what I call 'the realm of the circuit' for a type of democratic witness and free sharing of information. Oddly, although *hiny* was mostly experienced in the real world, it was the product of virtual processes.

AM Do you think that an event of a different nature from 9/11 could create a similar energy?

CT Well, of course we were in New York and millions of people saw the real event. And millions recorded it. Unfortunately, Ground Zero was a visible locus for the story. It was easy to get to Prince Street, and it was reasonably easy to disseminate our idea, because of the density and immediacy of the city. Nevertheless, now we are witnessing remarkable events through masses of imagery almost every day – the Arab Spring is perhaps the most obvious example to date.

The big problem in the digital world is not the making or finding of imagery but, rather, how that information should be organized and curated. Today more photographs are made in a single day than in the whole of the 19th century! How do you make sense of all that? How do you put it all together? Is there any truth in all that imagery? I often say there is no truth in one picture ... or even 1,000 words. But there is something of value in 1,000 pictures treating the same subject.

AM Someone has to collect the information, the pictures, the text, what have you. I guess this is where the creative interlocutor comes in.

CT I think that's right. A system or a collective must have some kind of filter, must select a portion of the whole for 'consumption' at a given point. However, the criteria for that selection must have a degree of accessibility and transparency for the potential audience that will inevitability reconfigure whatever is relayed. The real question is 'What is the story?' Throughout history, civilization is always re-creating narratives, both fiction and non-fiction. There is no real journalism anymore - but there is management of information. The pressing concerns are how this is done, who does it, and whom does it serve.

AM I understand how important it is to investigate the potential of recording everyday life. But I also sometimes find a kind of banality in exhibitions: people documenting the activities of their cat, or showing us what they have eaten for the last thirty days. It is narcissistic and meaningless.

CT Without context and without management, most of that imagery is boring. That's why we need creative intervention, to help us filter out that bombardment of banality. But the world-view is constantly changing. Since 9/11, technology has evolved radically. Images are delivered, almost in real time, to everybody and anybody. We can put a Go-Pro camera on a cat - on 1,000 cats - and get a whole new perspective on human behaviour. We are even observed from space. The camera lens is extending the power of the human eye, but are we actually learning more about human nature? Vision is only meaningful when it is interpreted, and allowing for interpretation is a creative act. Any interpretation is always subjective; it will change and be changed.

INDEX

Page numbers in *italics* refer to illustrations.